ENERGIES AND PATTERNS IN PSYCHOLOGICAL TYPE

This book encapsulates John Beebe's influential work on the analytical psychology of consciousness. Building on C. G. Jung's theory of psychological types and on subsequent clarifications by Marie-Louise von Franz and Isabel Briggs Myers, Beebe demonstrates the bond between the eight types of consciousness Jung named and the archetypal complexes that impart energy and purpose to our emotions, fantasies, and dreams. For this collection, Beebe has revised and updated his most influential and significant previously published papers and has introduced, in a brand new chapter, a surprising theory of type and culture.

Beebe's model enables readers to take what they already know about psychological types and apply it to depth psychology. The insights contained in the fifteen chapters of this book will be especially valuable for Jungian psychotherapists, post-Jungian academics and scholars, psychological type practitioners, and type enthusiasts.

John Beebe is a Jungian analyst in private practice in San Francisco. A former president of the C. G. Jung Institute of San Francisco, he is a prolific author and editor and has spoken on analytical psychology all over the world.

ENERGIES AND PATTERNS IN PSYCHOLOGICAL TYPE

The reservoir of consciousness

John Beebe

Routledge
Taylor & Francis Group

LONDON AND NEW YORK

First published 2017
by Routledge
2 Park Square, Milton Park, Abingdon, Oxon OX14 4RN

and by Routledge
711 Third Avenue, New York, NY 10017

Routledge is an imprint of the Taylor & Francis Group, an informa business

British Library Cataloguing in Publication Data
A catalogue record for this book is available from the British Library

Library of Congress Cataloging in Publication Data
Names: Beebe, John, author.
Title: Energies and patterns in psychological type : the reservoir of
    consciousness / John Beebe.
Description: Abingdon, Oxon ; New York, NY : Routledge, 2016. |
    Includes index.
Identifiers: LCCN 2015050382| ISBN 9781138918610 (hardback) |
    ISBN 9781138922280 (pbk.) | ISBN 9781315685946 (ebook)
Subjects: LCSH: Typology (Psychology) | Consciousness. | Psychoanalysis.
Classification: LCC BF698.3 .B435 2016 | DDC 155.2/644—dc23
LC record available at http://lccn.loc.gov/2015050382

ISBN: 978-1-138-91861-0 (hbk)
ISBN: 978-1-138-92228-0 (pbk)
ISBN: 978-1-315-68594-6 (ebk)

Typeset in Bembo
by Swales & Willis Ltd, Exeter, Devon, UK

For Adam Frey

CONTENTS

ILLUSTRATIONS

Figures

Tables

PREFACE

The psychologically minded analyst, therapist, or counselor soon discovers an interesting paradox: although people's unconscious habits are readily visible, the consciousness of others remains strangely opaque. As my colleague Donald Kalsched has observed in *The Inner World of Trauma*, "The self-same powers that seem so set on undermining our efforts … are the very reservoir from which new life, fuller integration, and true enlightenment derive" (p. 62). To believe that the psyche contains the seeds of its own healing is quintessentially Jungian.

This book brings together many strands of analytical, archetypal, and self psychology, including the complex theory over which Freud and Jung sparred; the archetypal psychology that James Hillman developed from Jung's later work; Kohut's image of a depth psychology centered in a 'little-s' self continually affected by the empathy, integrity, and the personal struggles of others; the defenses of the self as inspected by Michael Fordham; and the Jungian ego-Self axis as conceptualized by Neumann and Edinger. But it is the type theory that Jung brought to maturity in 1921 that I have drawn upon most to answer for myself which self-experiences these teachers are actually talking about.

What is new here is the degree to which our typology both creates and helps us to discover the self and its defenses in a personal way. It is thus a contribution to the understanding of the person in the psyche. That person is urged into being by archetypes, including the transpersonal Self that seems to drive human individuation; but the 'little-s' self we experience as persons has its own forms of consciousness, nested in the care of archetypes but capable of asserting and integrating themselves independently. I say this lest anyone reading what I have written about the archetypes in this book take the eight-function, eight-archetype model as an unaltering image of inevitable rigidity. Rather, it is the psyche's many dynamic parts that give it the flexibility, over time, to articulate the Self in a personal way that our adaptation to our typology makes us capable of displaying.

The reader is therefore advised to approach the book with this developmental perspective in mind. It may not be amiss, as I celebrate in these pages a full fifty years of reflecting on Jungian typology, to admit what by now must be obvious: that my own perspective on the subject is continuing to develop.

John Beebe
San Francisco, October 2015

ACKNOWLEDGMENTS

Most of the ideas presented in this book first found expression in my teaching and lectures. I'm grateful to all who have given me the opportunity to learn by inviting me to present. Particularly seminal opportunities to teach about type came from: the C. G. Jung Institute of San Francisco, especially through Barbara McClintock and Steve Zemmelman; Murray Stein and Nathan Schwartz-Salant, organizers of the Ghost Ranch Conferences; Lore Zeller for the Bruno Klopfer Workshop; Marla Herbig and David Hufford for the Seattle Jungians; the C. G. Jung Institute of Chicago; the Association for Psychological Type International and its chapters in Sacramento and the San Francisco Bay Area (especially through Richard Hendrickson) and Vermont (through Suzanne and Nord Brue); Bob McAlpine of Type Resources; Shen Heyong and Shen Gaolan in Macau and Guangzhou; and Beverley Zabriskie for the Jungian Psychoanalytic Association in New York.

I would like to acknowledge my early teachers in type, Jungian analysts Jo and Jane Wheelwright, John Perry, Elizabeth Osterman, Joseph Henderson, Donald Sandner, Wayne Detloff, and Mel Kettner, and friends who have encouraged my study of type in relation to analytical psychology, including Thomas Kirsch, Jess Groesbeck, David Rosen, Andrew Samuels, Hester Solomon, and Martin Stone. Murray Stein kept the spirit of this book alive through its very long germination; Jan Stein and Lynda Schmidt helped me to explore some of its psychology. I'm grateful for the support of Sonu Shamdasani, Ernst Falzeder, Meredith Sabini, Angelo Spoto, Katharine Myers, John Giannini, Dick Thompson, Vicky Jo Varner and Susan Nash. I'm also appreciative of the universities that have given me opportunities to teach about type, including Stanford, Sonoma State University, Pacifica Graduate Institute, Saybrook University, Fudan University, South China Normal University, and City University of Macau.

I owe a special debt to the people who have been most active in helping to disseminate my eight-function, eight-archetype model of type: Anne Singer

Harris, Linda Berens, Dario Nardi, Leona Haas, Mark Hunziker, Margaret and Gary Hartzler, Carol Shumate, Zhou Dangwei, Hanne Urhøj, Ann Casement, Shanping Wang, and (once again) Bob McAlpine.

Few of the chapters that follow would have made it into their present form without prodding, patience, and assistance from the editors who invited me to contribute to their books and journals: Murray Stein, Renos Papadopoulos, Thomas Singer, Linda Carter and Joe Cambray, Christopher Hauke, Luke Hockley, Leslie Gardner, Chris Blazina and David S. Shen-Miller, Hubert Hermans, Ernest Rossi, Dyane Sherwood, Katherine Olivetti, Kathryn Madden, and especially Gillian Clack.

For orchestrating the editing of this volume, I am grateful to Susannah Frearson of Routledge. I thank above all Adam Frey, who helped me bring the dream of this book to fruition and whose steadying hand can be felt in almost every chapter.

PERMISSIONS

Chapter 1, "The eight function-attitudes unpacked," was originally published in *TypeFace* 25(4), 10–12, 2014. Republished here with revisions by permission of the British Association of Psychological Type.

Chapter 2, "Once more with feeling," was originally published in *Jung Journal: Culture & Psyche* 3(4), 28–39, 2009. Republished here with revisions by permission of the C. G. Jung Institute of San Francisco (http://www.sfjung.org).

Chapter 3, "Understanding consciousness through the theory of psychological types," was originally published in *Analytical psychology: Contemporary perspectives in Jungian analysis*, edited by Joseph Cambray and Linda Carter, pp. 83–115, Brunner-Routledge, 2004. Republished here with revisions by permission of Taylor and Francis.

Chapter 4, "Archetypal aspects of masculine adaptation," was originally published in *An international psychology of men: Theoretical advances, case studies, and clinical innovations,* edited by Chris Blazina and David S. Shen-Miller, pp. 289–314, Routledge, 2011. Republished here with revisions by permission of Taylor and Francis.

Chapter 5, "*The Wizard of Oz*: A vision of development in the American political psyche," appeared previously in *Jung and Film II: The Return*, edited by Christopher Hauke and Luke Hockley, pp. 302–327, Routledge, 2011. Republished here with revisions by permission of Taylor and Francis.

Chapter 7, "Evolving the eight-function model," was originally published in the Association for Psychological Type International *Bulletin* Winter, 2005, pp. 34–39. Republished here with revisions by permission of the Association for Psychological Type International.

Chapter 8, "Type and archetype – Part I: The spine and its shadow," was originally published in *TypeFace* 18(2), 7–11, Summer 2007. Republished here with revisions by permission of the British Association of Psychological Type.

Chapter 9, "Type and archetype – Part II: The arms and their shadow," was originally published in *TypeFace* 18(3), 22–27, Autumn 2007. Republished here with revisions by permission of the British Association of Psychological Type.

Chapter 10, "Psychological types: An historical overview," was originally published in *The handbook of Jungian psychology: Theory, practice, and applications*, edited by Renos Papadopoulos, pp. 130–152, Routledge, 2006. Republished here with revisions by permission of Taylor and Francis.

Chapter 11, "The *Red Book* as a work of conscience," was originally published in *Quadrant* XXXX(2), 40–58, Summer 2010. Republished here with revisions by permission of *Quadrant*: the C. G. Jung Foundation for Analytical Psychology.

Chapter 12, "Psychological types in Freud and Jung," was originally published in *Jung Journal: Culture & Psyche* 6(3), 58–71, 2012. Republished here with revisions by permission of the C. G. Jung Institute of San Francisco (http://www.sfjung.org).

Use of material from Sigmund Freud's *The interpretation of dreams*, translated by Joyce Crick, originally published in 1999 by Oxford University Press, is included here by kind permission of Oxford University Press.

Chapter 13, "Difficulties in the recognition of psychological type," was originally published in *Jungian psychoanalysis: Working in the spirit of C. G. Jung*, edited by Murray Stein, pp. 71–80, Open Court, 2010. Republished here with revisions by permission of Creative Compliance c/o Cricket Media.

Chapter 14, "An archetypal model of the Self in dialogue," was originally published in *Theory & Psychology* 12(2), 267–280, 2002. Republished here with revisions by permission of Sage Publications.

Chapter 15, "Identifying the American shadow: Typological reflections on the 1992 Los Angeles riots," was originally published in *Psychological Perspectives* 27(1), 135–139, 1992. Republished here with revisions by permission of Taylor and Francis.

Use of material from C. G. Jung's Psychological types (*Collected works*, vol. 6), edited by H. Read, M. Fordham, & G. Adler, executive editor W. McGuire, translated by R. F. C. Hull & H. G. Baynes, originally published in 1971 by Princeton University Press and Routledge, is included here by permission of Princeton University Press and Taylor and Francis.

COLLECTED WORKS OF C. G. JUNG

Reference is made in this book to the following volumes of the *Collected Works of C. G. Jung* using the abbreviated form *Cw* followed by the volume number. The *Collected Works* is edited by H. Read, M. Fordham, and G. Adler. The series Executive Editor is W. McGuire. R. F. C. Hull is the translator for all cited material unless otherwise noted. The volumes consulted were published by Princeton University Press in Princeton, NJ unless otherwise noted.

Jung, C. G. (1973). Experimental researches (*Collected works*, vol. 2) L. Stein & D. Riviere (Trans.).

Jung, C. G. (1960). The psychogenesis of mental disease (*Collected works*, vol. 3).

Jung, C. G. (1967). Symbols of transformation, 2nd. ed. (*Collected works*, vol. 5).

Jung, C. G. (1971). Psychological types (*Collected works*, vol. 6).

Jung, C. G. (1960). The structure and dynamics of the psyche (*Collected works*, vol. 8). New York: Pantheon Books.

Jung, C. G. (1959). The archetypes and the collective unconscious (*Collected works*, vol. 9, i). New York: Pantheon Books.

Jung, C. G. (1968). Aion: Researches into the phenomenology of the self, 2nd ed. (*Collected works*, vol. 9, ii).

Jung, C. G. (1969). Psychology and religion: West and east, 2nd ed. (*Collected works*, vol. 11).

Jung, C. G. (1967). Alchemical studies (*Collected works*, vol. 13).

Jung, C. G. (1963). Mysterium coniunctionis: An inquiry into the separation and synthesis of psychic opposites in alchemy (*Collected works*, vol. 14). New York: Pantheon Books.

Jung, C. G. (1966). The practice of psychotherapy, 2nd ed. (*Collected works*, vol. 16). New York: Pantheon Books.

Jung, C. G. (1980). The symbolic life: Miscellaneous writings (*Collected works*, vol. 18).

Jung, C. G. (1983). The Zofingia lectures (*Collected works*, supplementary vol. A). J. van Heurck (Trans.).

PART I
Theoretical contributions

1

THE EIGHT FUNCTION-ATTITUDES UNPACKED

To help people apply their scores on the MBTI® to themselves, and to reap the deeper transformative benefits of Jungian type theory, we need to be able to recognize the different types of consciousness Jung originally described. Practically, that means we have to be prepared to recognize in someone's interactive or introspective personality style introverted feeling (Fi), introverted thinking (Ti), introverted intuition (Ni), introverted sensation (Si), extraverted feeling (Fe), extraverted thinking (Te), extraverted intuition (Ne), or extraverted sensation (Se), simply on the basis of what the person reveals in our presence. We also need to be able to assess how well the function-attitude displayed is actually working for the person who is showing it to us.

Consider the fresh daylight that an executive coach can potentially bring to a client when she says, "It sounds like you've done everything in your power to solve this problem using your preferred introverted intuition and extraverted thinking. I've also heard you express some introverted feeling evaluations of the situation. Have you considered calling out the reserves to see how some of the other types of consciousness might approach this quandary?" Then think how futile this intervention would be if the coach could not explain to the client what those other functions are like.

My own experience as a clinician who believes that type understanding is crucial to uncovering what limits people and what helps them to develop is that very few us, whether clients or type practitioners, can actually recognize the eight function-attitudes. To help us all meet this challenge, I will offer here some guidelines that I have developed to make the task of recognizing and identifying the different function-attitudes just a little easier when we are working with clients.

The first step I took toward this came about five years ago when a personal friend Diane Johnson, a successful novelist who had read some of my work on types, told me it would really help if I could find words in everyday language to correspond to the different processes that Jung, with his scientific background, felt he had to specify in psychological terms. The eight function-attitudes that he describes in *Psychological Types* (1921/1971, ¶¶556–671) were for him the 'psychological types.' This term meant something quite specific for him: the eight types of awareness capable of constituting a psychological individual's conscious psychology. They are mental processes that, even if still in the unconscious, are likely to press for integration into the psyche, where they can become, for the first time, consciousnesses. They hold the motivation to energize will and to develop over time—will and time being additional factors that can become linked to consciousness.

Working with the novelist's challenge, I came up with a set of eight keywords that I thought might get to the essence of the eight function-attitudes. I have been working on them ever since, testing and refining them at various conferences where I have been invited to share my latest thinking about types. Only recently have I been satisfied enough with what has emerged to commit it to publication. So here, beside each mental process whose functioning I have been trying to epitomize, I will offer the word in everyday language that I believe best gets at the heart of what that process is engaged in accomplishing.

Fi.	Introverted feeling	appraising
Ti.	Introverted thinking	defining
Ni.	Introverted intuition	knowing
Si.	Introverted sensation	verifying
Fe.	Extraverted feeling	affirming
Te.	Extraverted thinking	planning
Ne.	Extraverted intuition	envisioning
Se.	Extraverted sensation	experiencing

The reader may recall that each of these words is called in grammar a *gerund*, a verbal noun or process word. Each describes a procedure that a mind can follow over time, a procedure aimed at perceiving or judging reality as accurately as possible, which is the aim of any consciousness.

When I first tried to teach these words to people, however, as pathways into what the types 'are,' I realized that people could not always enter the phenomenon I was trying to get them to contemplate with just that single word on its door. And so, following a suggestion made by Dick Custer for introverted thinking, I decided to create a semantic field by offering two wing words for each word that I regarded as the heart of the process I was trying to convey. For introverted thinking, Dick had suggested other words I had mentioned in passing as synonyms for my keyword, 'defining.' These were 'naming' and 'understanding.' He drew a triangle, with 'defining' at the apex and 'naming' and 'understanding' at the lower corners.

After that, with other participants at the same Type Resources conference in Cleveland (2010) making suggestions, I established a similar semantic field for each of the types of consciousness that Jung had named. For ease in reading them here,

I will not present them as triangles, but as words across a page. The presentation on this page also reflects some adjustments in the order of words for each process, going across, that I have made in recent years:

Se.	engaging	experiencing	enjoying
Si.	implementing	verifying	accounting
Ne.	entertaining	envisioning	enabling
Ni.	imagining	knowing	divining
Te.	regulating	planning	enforcing
Ti.	naming	defining	understanding
Fe.	validating	affirming	relating
Fi.	judging	appraising	establishing the value

I found immediately that when I provided at least three words, listeners could begin to grasp what each of the mental processes was about, and could start to recognize it in themselves and others.

I realized later that what had unconsciously emerged in a particularly creative moment, involving at least as much my anima as my more preferred functions, was a deepening that each mental process follows as its potential is increasingly realized. The first of the three words (as we read across for each of the eight mental processes) can be thought of as what the process looks like on the surface, to another person seeing someone for the first time using that process—what we might call its *persona* level. The second, central, word captures the heart of the process—the one that is embraced by the *ego* as its chief concern. The third word embodies what the process becomes at its most evolved level when it is working in sympathetic harmony with what Jung calls the *Self*: one might call this the goal of the process. Thus, introverted feeling (Fi) can develop from an initial, near instinctual 'judging' into a mature, reflective 'appraising' before evolving to a more far-seeing 'establishing the value.' In this latter stage, which aspires to wisdom, the feeling reaction finds its ground in a more ideal, archetypal realm, which allows it to discriminate the value that has led to the earlier judgments and appraisals.[1]

Even as this sequence of three terms can describe a progressive maturation of the insight involved in making a particular feeling judgment into an appraisal and then a value, it also illustrates the fact that there is a temporal process within consciousness, which we can actually see unfolding in real time when we are privy to the operation of any type of consciousness. I can certainly say that, in my own case, my extraverted intuition (Ne) often begins its action as a mental process, with a stage of 'entertaining' that applies in two senses of the word: (1) interesting and amusing myself and others; and (2) beginning to consider or 'entertain' possibilities that I may want to go on to envision in greater detail. As soon as, through a process of 'envisioning,' I am firmly committed to advancing possibilities that I have formerly simply entertained myself with, I find that I become quite naturally interested in 'enabling' others to see and profit from these same possibilities. My extraverted intuition in this third stage is subtly informed by its communication with the inferior function of introverted sensation, lending my intuition a more grounded, effective quality. My whole career around the theory of psychological types, which I entertained in my mind as centrally important as early as 1968, and the possibilities of which I envisioned in a way that led to the model I produced based on a set of thought experiments that began in 1973, has led to my enabling audiences and readers to benefit from better understanding type.

The system of keywords and wing words has helped me to understand type better, especially in regard to the functions of consciousness that are normally in shadow for me and thus have been difficult for me to empathize with. One such type of consciousness is extraverted sensation (Se). Patients in my analytic practice for whom that function-attitude is dominant often cannot follow my rather abstract introverted thinking. It's just too disembodied to be tangible to them. The extraverted sensation type, I have realized, works quite differently, first by 'engaging,' then by 'experiencing' and finally (if it can get there) by 'enjoying' what it has engaged and experienced. Although the root word of function, as James Hillman (1971/1998, p. 91) noted, is the Sanskrit *bhunj*, which means to enjoy, I think it is fair to say that few truly enjoy the kind of understanding introverted thinking loves to savor. Rather, 'enjoying' is something people with developed extraverted sensation can only get to if they engage with something and experience it for themselves, having a sort of hands-on encounter with it that they will either enjoy or not. From both an intellectual–scientific and a spiritual–religious angle, enjoyment seems like a subjective, selfish goal, a form of entertainment that should not be confused with the responsibilities of consciousness. But, working with people whose dominant or auxiliary function is extraverted sensation, I have often noticed that, only if they have enjoyed something sufficiently, by bringing it near to themselves in an embodied way, and have found it, when truly touched, to be a source of concrete satisfaction, does it seem sufficiently real to them to say that they have become aware of what it consists of. This enjoyment has a hint of the spiritual to it, suggesting that the extraverted sensation function is in communion with its introverted intuitive opposite. As a consciousness, therefore, extraverted sensation in its stages of engaging, experiencing, and enjoying the reality of something is the difference between talking about it and getting to know it intimately. It involves touching and being touched by every part of it—a very different thing from a simply mental representation.

In this way, I have learned that the various types are exactly as Jung thought, psychological stances that permit consciousness of all the phenomena we describe as psychological. That our psychology, which inevitably has a goal, aims at all of these activities—establishing the value, understanding, divining, accounting, relating, enforcing, enabling, and enjoying—will perhaps be clearest to people who, through analytical psychotherapy, have been witness to the individuation process (Jung, 1959). A working analyst like myself sees that in psychotherapy our different consciousnesses do emerge and grow toward their particular goals. This is the deepest, Self-level of the drive to become conscious. But even a novice to psychology can quickly recognize that most people start by judging, naming, imagining, implementing (internal methods by which they have already learned to deal with what they encounter) and validating, regulating, entertaining, and engaging (methods by which they enact a genuine encounter with the Other).

I would advise people, whether veterans or novices at typology, who are still trying to learn what the types are actually doing, to focus on the central words in my horizontal sequences for the different functions of consciousness, using the wing words as the beginning and the end of the process whose functioning they are trying to become conscious of. Using this method of observation, it will become clearer the degree to which some people are centrally engaged in appraising, defining, knowing, or verifying as the internal process by which they hope to master the objects they encounter. Other people are more occupied with affirming, planning, envisioning, or experiencing as their way of expressing their willingness to subject themselves to the influence of the objects with which they are trying to connect. Seeing this fundamental difference between the introverted and extraverted functions, we can gradually come to understand not just the ways the functions differ in their introverted and extraverted aspects, but what the different purposes are that make them functions. At that point, we may be more able to understand what Jung, with his reliable introverted intuition, imagined, knew, and divined[2] that the recognition of the different types of consciousness could permit, provided we also join him in verifying the uncanny accuracy of his categories of consciousness as to how the individuating psyche actually functions on its trajectory toward consciousness.

Notes

1 I was sorry in Cleveland that I couldn't express this final stage of the introverted feeling process in a single word. For the group there, I tried 'valuating,' and, though it met with a certain approval from those practiced in introverted feeling, I realized it was not a word in common speech. The phrase, 'establishing the value' turned out to be clearer. This is the one place in the exercise where I had to use more than one word to convey my meaning, which I think says something quite fundamental about the difficulty of putting the introverted feeling process into words.
2 Like 'entertaining,' 'divining' has a double meaning in this scheme. It is not only seeing in what direction the future is bending. It is also descrying the divine purpose hidden in the developing situation. A recent article by Peter Struck (2016) makes explicit the historical link between divination and intuition.

References

Hillman, J. (1971/1998). The feeling function. In M.-L. von Franz & J. Hillman, *Lectures on Jung's typology* (pp. 89–179). Woodstock, CT: Spring Publications.
Jung, C. G. (1921/1971). Psychological types. In *Cw 6*.
Jung, C. G. (1959). Conscious, unconscious, and individuation. In *Cw 9, i* (pp. 275–289).
Struck, P. (2016). 2013 Arthur O. Lovejoy lecture: A cognitive history of divination in Ancient Greece. *Journal of the History of Ideas*, 77(1), 1–25.

2

ONCE MORE WITH FEELING

Reading the final lecture of Jung's closest analytic follower, Marie-Louise von Franz (2008), delivered in Küsnacht in 1986, one notices immediately how very loosely it is argued; how near it is, in fact, to a rant. As one who grew up on her cleanly delineated articulations of Jungian theory, I found this lecture something of a shock. At first I thought I was experiencing the overconfidence that can shadow an elder who has earned the right to say exactly what she or he thinks. Gradually, however, it dawned on me that, in writing this lecture, von Franz had performed the *sacrificium intellecti* that Jung describes at the beginning of *Psychological Types* (1921/1971, ¶¶15–20) in relation to the church father Tertullian, a scholarly theologian who burned his books so that his feeling relation to God could emerge. Von Franz must have deliberately short-circuited the formidable thinking that made her seminars so truly seminal for students of Jungian thought to get into the mindset of this last, great, and very different expression of her point of view. It is as if, realizing her subject is feeling, she has decided on this occasion to let feeling flow untrammeled by thinking considerations, to flood the reader as it were, with her own mercurial affectivity. We are closer here to how she feels about the contemporary situation than in any of her other works. She lets her evaluations of how dismally human beings interact with each other come to the fore at a pace few authors would dare to sustain. She is not afraid of the animus that is released in her by this effort to break from the tyranny of careful, cleanly discriminated Jungian thinking. She is in earnest where her own opinions are concerned, and she writes, for once, as if she trusts her own subjectivity to be objective enough for the task at hand. This is an individuated piece, in other words, in which the great Jungian author is transformed into a living philosopher's stone—what the black culture I encountered in America in my youth would have called 'a *stone* philosopher.' She no longer concerns herself with other analysts' thinking about feeling, emotion, and value. She doesn't make, in this lecture, any mention of a Jungian after Jung except Erich Neumann, and she brings him up mainly to mention the failure of his effort to establish a 'new ethic' (1949/1990) as a criterion for values that emerge for those who have tried to include the unconscious in their lives. She avoids all later refinements because her subject is *Jung's* rehabilitation of the feeling function in our civilization. That means she can ignore the finely drawn distinctions in Hillman's essay on the feeling function (1971/1998), her own careful work on the difference when feeling is extraverted or introverted and when it is a superior or an inferior function (1971/1998), Willeford's insistence on the primacy of feeling (1975, 1976, 1977, 1987), and even Jung's way of distinguishing between feeling and affect (1921/1971, ¶¶681–682, ¶¶723–730).[1] Such thinking discriminations don't serve her method here, which is to trust the *massa confusa* of her own emotions and let her own judgments about feeling emerge. If one has tried to think systematically about feeling and emotion, as I have spent most of my professional career learning to do, it is tempting to wonder if von Franz, at this culminating moment in her own public career, had simply lost the feeling for psychological ideas that earlier on had made her work so interesting; but such fears are put to rest when one realizes that she has chosen in this final lecture to stay true to the integrity of her subject and, as the alchemists rather strangely put it, wash her material "in its own water."

In alchemical texts of the sort that von Franz had helped Jung to translate when first exposed to analytical psychology as a young teacher of Latin, the idea of washing the material in its own water frequently appears. The 'water' of alchemy is the element mercury, a mysterious, fluid substance that chemically has a capacity to bond with gold and silver, but for the alchemists was also their original substance, a sort of mother to the metals, as much inherent in them (the way the unconscious is inherent in the conscious mind) as an agent to be applied to them. *Sol* and *Luna*, the traditional lights by which humankind has been able to see things, are fundaments of the mind, and the mercury released from them through the alchemical procedure was something in which they could be washed and born anew.[2] In this lecture, the fundament undergoing such baptism is neither Sol nor Luna but, so to speak, their *gravitas*, the affective matrix of mind itself, the tangle of valuations, emotion, and eros that forms the basis for human relatedness, out of which Jung's conscious 'feeling function' has differentiated itself.

The Jungian analyst Elizabeth Osterman, a great teacher, once told an analytic training seminar I was part of, "Watch what you hate—it's pure gold" (Osterman, 1973). If I hate anything in von Franz's lecture, it is probably its alchemical character. I have to admit, however, that, like an alchemical procedure, reading the lecture provokes a dissolving of fixed ideas about feeling and allows a different light on the subject to emerge—different, but not divorced from the shadows it is trying to illuminate. Alchemy may be about transformation of what is base and unredeemed, but it retains a relationship to its dark original materials throughout and so does this lecture. To read it is like being in a cave lit by torchlight. Remarkably, the lecture has set itself loose from the enlightened thinking language that psychology has devised to pretend that it knows enough about feeling, affect, eros, object relations, and emotion to distinguish cleanly among them. T. S. Eliot's remark that

Henry James "had a mind so fine that no idea could violate it" (1918, pp. 1–2) suggests one way for a psychological intelligence to transcend what it is supposed to know, but von Franz doesn't come from irony and rejects the fine mind, too, along with its ideas, to get what she achieves here. Whereas Henry James achieved his finest insights through his aesthetic anima, picking up relational vibrations that must never be exactly disclosed, von Franz has decided to unbridle the extraverted feeling somewhere in her psyche, letting it go on a brilliant run.

Her method is to let her extraverted feeling give us its reactions to the enormous deficits and limited prospects for rehabilitating human feeling in our time and show how Jung's psychology speaks to them. With all this attention to deficits and prospects, there is precious little room for the way most analysts think about feeling. I, for instance, have trained myself, when I lecture on the theory of psychological types, to teach the difference I see between feelings and feeling. *Feeling*, I tell my audiences, is the function that sorts out *feelings*. This is my way of differentiating feeling from emotion, the first step in that conceptual leap Jung made to describe feeling as a rational function, which Jo Wheelwright was fond of describing in his training seminars as "a landmark in the history of thought." My formula is also a user-friendly restatement of Willeford's understanding of feeling as the function that "discriminates affect" (1975). But here von Franz cuts through the conceptual flora as to what *feeling* really means (as if this would help us retrieve it for our world), simply by letting us know how she feels using her inferior feeling (see von Franz, 1971/1998, pp. 65–66, von Franz, 1974/1995, p. 5, and Sharp, 1987, p. 72). Sentence by sentence, paragraph by paragraph, that critical, angry, opinionated feeling holds this lecture together and gives it its remarkable inner light. Let us see how von Franz makes that happen.

She starts by quoting from a lecture Jung gave to his brother physicians-in-training in his medical school fraternity, which he introduces with a lofty passage from one of Kant's early lectures on Swedenborg: "God and the other world are the sole goal of all our philosophical investigations, and if the concepts of God and the other world had nothing to do with morality they would be worthless."[3] Can von Franz, the author of *Puer Aeternus* (1970/1981), see through the cloudiness in the airy dismissiveness of this assertion? Most probably, but she isn't disposed to say here. She knows Jung is going somewhere, and she lets him continue on to vent his skepticism, by contrast, of modern morality. She recognizes that, by stating so clearly what he finds unworthy, Jung the medical student can find the voice to say aloud what many medical students have felt but been less able to contend about the early phases of their education. "In institutions that offer training in physiology, the moral judgment of students is deliberately impaired by their involvement in disgraceful, barbarous experiments, by a cruel torture of animals which is a mockery of all human decency" (Jung, 1897/1983, ¶138). The emotional freedom to voice thinking many would find dubious has enabled Jung to achieve a breakthrough in feeling that allows him to deliver a judgment as brilliant as it is passionate: "I say we must teach that *no truth obtained by such means has the moral right to exist*" (¶45).[4] His philosophical argument anticipates Levinas—ethics as first philosophy, ahead of epistemology, logic, and the scientific method—thus changing the empirical mindset forever. The point of von Franz's demonstration of what Jung had already done before he was twenty-four years old is that, if you don't censor feeling because it is bad thinking, you can suddenly think in a very different—and much more exciting—way.

There is even more in her lecture to drive us out of our usual minds. Jung's strong polemic, she tells us, is mostly directed at "materialism." But what does Jung's own "belief in realities beyond the coarse material world" have to do with the refinement of his "moral attitude," which she equates with his "differentiated feeling" (2008, pp. 9–10)? If her passionately repeated assertions do not seem to help us absorb her point, it may be because, as she says, we have grown insensitive to what she means by "coarse materialism." She brings up the thousand-fold increase in the torture of animals since Jung's time and proceeds to quote diplomats who think that we can risk an atomic war because more millions will survive than will die and who actually give the numbers on which they base their optimism! You cannot read this lecture without counting carcasses and noting your own cold lack of caring. This hectoring line of argument culminates, in the lecture, with the terminal-care nurse who came to one of her lectures and learned that von Franz saw in dreams quite interesting evidence of survival after death. The nurse broke down because she had treated her patients callously, and now she knew they were still in a position, somewhere, to bear witness to her behavior (p. 12).

Yet von Franz is not trying to waken feeling where it will not go. "Who now remembers," she reminds us, "the name of that young German school-teacher who volunteered to enter the gas chambers in order to comfort his Jewish schoolchildren?" (2008, pp. 12–13). I am appalled that I have never heard of him, but her point is not to make me guilty. The feeling function itself is one of the carcasses, one of the casualties of having so much *virtual* exposure to unjust suffering that it is hard to keep track of what to care about. Von Franz has a nice definition of compassion. She calls it "feeling decency" and immediately reminds us that being decent works against any validation of the feeling involved, for "being decent is considered foolish, unwise, and naïve" (2008, p. 12). This suspicion has been constellated just about every time I acknowledge I care about something, and von Franz has obviously had that experience, too. She knows that, as a result, feeling goes into hiding, but hers is not an essay on traumatic and post-traumatic dissociation. The woman who lived on the moon[5] is nowhere here; rather von Franz is interested in how feeling lives on in the other world of the psyche—and gains status there. Among the dying patients who come, as on litters, to illuminate this lecture with the night-lights of their terminal experience is the one von Franz borrows from Liliane Frey, whose patient dreamed after a life "of constant failures" that a voice said, "Your work and suffering which you suffered consciously, have redeemed a hundred generations that came before you and will illuminate a hundred generations after you" (p. 13). It is as if the young German schoolteacher has suddenly been properly remembered, along with a number of my own patients, for whom the *opus* of our work has been simply to hold their suffering in consciousness, the first in their families to learn this experience. That's another of the meanings von Franz gives to feeling in this not-very-thinking paper: attending to suffering from another standpoint than is usually available in this world.

In this lecture, von Franz does not go into parapsychological experience; her argument is focused on empathy and sympathy and on distinguishing these, which she indiscriminately calls "feeling," from their shadow, sentimentality. Her method is to choose examples with a genuine pathos. There is even a sort of telepathy to her lecture, for it "feels at a distance" into many parts of the world's suffering, into many places and times of life, and especially into the many ways of being dead and dying in these various locations of the feeling-deprived psyche. For instance, when she brings up "the old ladies in our Christian world" who "knitted woolen garments for the poor little African children," while "the slave traders of that very same Christian civilization were destroying the lives of uncountable black people," the effect of the passage is to make the old ladies as pathetic as the children of the people who were being brutalized (2008, p. 16). The comparison works in part because she herself is brutalizing the Christian ladies with the thinking argument that surfaces at this point in the lecture, that their sentimentality "is a counterpart of brutality." The idea is from a letter Jung wrote in 1936 to Wilhelm Laiblin, a teacher (and later analytical psychologist) in Stuttgart, and his exact words were, "The counterpart of sentimentality is as we know brutality." Jung goes on to mention Wotan, whose "inner meaning," he instructs his schoolmaster pupil, "represented by his lost eye is Erda, the *magna mater*" (1973, 16 April 1936, p. 213). Germany comes up often through the cracks in this paper.

Here, the phrase "as we know" in the letter that von Franz refers us to says much about what Jung was feeling about what was going on in Germany in those early years when he was supposedly heedless. In an earlier letter to Laiblin, who had sent Jung copies of letters he had written to the bishop of the Evangelical Church, critical of church dogma, and which Laiblin had finally published in December 1933 as *Open Letters*, Jung had written, "I think I can understand why the bishop has not replied to your letters. Anyone who has to run a church under these circumstances cannot concern himself with problems that cast doubt on this same church." At the end of the letter, he adds, "I am naturally in complete agreement with the content of your letters. If one says it all, then one has to say it like that. I only ask myself whether it is the right time to say such things now" (1973, 19 March 1934, pp. 153–154). All this and more lies in the background of von Franz's reference to the correspondence with Laiblin. This letter from March 1934 was in reply to one from Laiblin that had included a dream giving the psyche's own take on what Jung called "times like these," the beginning of the Nazi era in Germany: "The sky changed, stars fell as in a cloudburst, and two, or even three moons disintegrated into small fragments which finally disappeared" (p. 153).

What is always interesting in anything von Franz says when she lectures is what you don't see, the thoughts in the background, and here they emerge like falling stars to illuminate the dark canvas with which she paints the feeling function.

Her lecture is a bit like a Gerhard Richter painting of the sort he was painting at the time she gave this address: vast, black, streaked with alchemical insight, a bit grim, and very moving.

As von Franz puts it, "We cannot return to the early Christians' ideal of love" (2008, p. 16). What's needed now, she feels, after a lifetime of confronting darkness (she gave this lecture when she was seventy-one years old) is a "much more differentiated" empathy. At this point in the lecture, her thinking kicks in: distinguishing the "driven love" of eros could "explain the cruelties of the Inquisition as being motivated by a zealous love for mankind, as an attempt to prevent people from falling into mortal errors from an Eros that is united with Logos, which brings a necessary distance to the way we relate to others" (p. 17). Her alchemical image of the tincture emanating from the Philosopher's Stone, "a rosy colored blood" that can heal all people, is both surreal and abstractly Christian, but her association of it with the *homo putissimus*, the "unalloyed man" who is "no other than just what he is" rings true (pp. 16–17). This is the feeling Jung wanted to give to his patients in treatment.

Elizabeth Osterman (1973) once described an encounter with Jung in which the *homo putissimus* was evident. Dr. Osterman was an extraverted thinking type who could sometimes deploy her extraverted feeling in a way that could be described as unmanning. In 1958, she had to do quite a lot of finagling to secure a meeting with Jung. She had allowed her friend Maud Oakes, who knew Jung, to pave the way, but when Elizabeth got to Küsnacht to have a rare hour with the eighty-three-year-old Jung, she still felt guilty about presuming on his time. Upon meeting the great man, she decided to use this feeling to make a gesture that would acknowledge his generosity. This is how she did it: "Time must be getting precious," she said. "You didn't need to do this . . ." No sooner had she opened with this sugary gambit than Jung looked back at her and said, "Ja. Now you can say that!" Elizabeth could see what she had done and that Jung had called her on it, and she acknowledged as much by a hearty laugh in which he quickly joined, making them friends. This was the unalloyed Jung, whom von Franz knew, who wasn't about to be preempted. In a published reminiscence, Osterman offers a more formal description of how Jung appeared to her on this occasion.

> The force that emanated from this man sitting beside me was amazing. He seemed at once powerful and simple; real, the way the sky and rocks and trees and water around him were real. He seemed to be all there in his own nature, but what made it so exciting was his *awareness* of it.
>
> *1963, p. 219*

Privately, she put it to me yet another way, "I felt he was with her—Sophia" (Osterman, 1973). Sophia, a figure who appears in Proverbs, is the personification of a feeling wisdom that can only come from experience. For the student of Jung, she is the final, fourth stage in the development of the anima who succeeds in tempering the force of *eros* with the wisdom of *logos*, an integrative stage beyond, but still including, lust (Eve), romantic love (Helen), and compassion (Mary). Jung conceived these stages of anima development in classically German, Goethe-influenced terms, and described them as "steps of culture of Eros."[6] This is what von Franz addresses in her discussion of the individuated emotional attitude of the *homo putissimus*, whose rosy-colored blood symbolizes the developed feeling function emanating from the man or woman who is able not only to be who he or she is but also to share what he or she has.

Such feeling is unalloyed by sentimentality (the sentimentality of piety, for instance) and uncorroded by cynicism (such as the cynicism that can infect secular modernity), and it is a feeling sponged in mortality. As an analyst, one feels it some-times in working with patients with whom one has suffered frustration, toward whom one has expressed anger, patients who have been wrong more than once and figured out that you have been wrong more than once as well. At that point in treatment, when insight has not brought cure, fellow-feeling is really all that is possible and all that will heal. We fear bringing this forward, sometimes, as analysts, because it is like the last antibiotic left, and if the patient develops resistance to it, too, there will be no way to prevent the infection of permanent psychological ill-ness. Yet, when a therapist's feeling for the patient as a fellow human being truly comes through in the treatment, no more potent healer exists.

To amplify in my own life the alchemical tincture, which von Franz identifies as the rosy-blood emanating from the philosopher's stone, my dreams presented me, near the end of my training to become an analyst, with an image of a pair of fine leather shoes that were still unstained. Their embarrassing milky whiteness in the dream was perhaps an image of the *albedo*, and the stain that I knew I needed to find to be able to wear them to my office was the *rubedo*, yet to come. I knew the dream was telling me of the testing that lay ahead, before I would "really" be an analyst, despite my imminent certification. But I did not understand how literally the psyche wanted me to take this image until one day when I was taking my actual office shoes to be shined by one of the two Italian men with shoeshine stands on Geary Boulevard, just off Union Square in San Francisco. They are both feeling types, one introverted and frequently angry at the beggars who try to work the theater district; the other, extraverted, and, nearer to the city's less elite downtown thoroughfare, Market Street, has a way with the street people. Once, as the kind one was shining my shoes on the little stand set up on the sidewalk, a street person came toward us shouting obscenities, raging in a disorganized way about cosmic figures fiddling with his fate. He was obviously psychotic, and I was afraid he might lose control and hit one of us, he was so mad. But my shoeshine man winked at me and, seeing that I was receptive enough to let him do what he could, called the other man over, a counterintuitive response that I found interesting enough that it calmed me a bit. "Hey Nick," he said, "C'mon over here." His evident interest in Nick had a strangely soothing effect on the psychotic man. Nick's ranting contin-ued, but in a few minutes it had become coherent. "The bastards . . . didn't mail my social security check . . ." Nick had been to the post office, and the money he depended on to live had not come in. The shoeshine man, with his tincture of appropriate extraverted feeling, had done what I, as a psychiatrist and now Jungian analyst, had still to learn how to do, just to be there for someone else and let that person's own psyche absorb the healing effect of the fellow-feeling.

When I had this experience, not long after the dream in which I found my unstained shoes, I didn't think to connect the shoeshine man with the tincture. Rather, the tincture of his feeling went into me while he was shining my shoes, and it became an image for me of being a different sort of analyst than I had trained to become. The analyst I wanted to be had read von Franz nonstop during his training and had learned from her to amplify almost any image and to make distinctions between psychological processes that were actually distinguishable in the psyche. That was the thinking von Franz, most evident in the way she cleanly distinguishes the eight types of inferior function in her part of *Lectures on Jung's Typology* (1971/1998). In his part of the book, James Hillman, on this occasion complementing von Franz's project, does the most advanced job anyone has done in discriminating the different clinical presentations of the feeling function, distinguishing superior feeling from inferior feeling; feeling from emotion, anima, mother complex; developed feeling from overly sincere *puer* or *puella aeterna* feeling; and (like von Franz) feeling from sentimentality. These distinctions have meant much to me in the daily work of trying to reach the emotions of patients with a feeling that does their affects justice. I wouldn't be useful if I couldn't help them sort through their feelings with my own, and it takes a lot of thought to do that well. But even better is what happens when we simply meet, at the end of, in the midst of, or sometimes before this 'work of analysis' is done, in the waiting room or on the street, as both of us are coming to the office. At such times, we are not simply greeting each other—because there is still a great distance between us, a sense that we really do live in different worlds.

Von Franz's citing of Jung's discussion, in another letter, of differentiated relationships requiring a certain "distance between people" reminds me of the other shoe repairman whom I used to frequent on Geary Boulevard, the one who screamed at the street people when they came too near and especially when they begged change from one of his customers. Jung's letter to Schmitz, which von Franz quotes, speaks to those moments:

> One of the most . . . difficult tasks in the individuation process is to bridge the distance between people. There is always a danger that the distance will be broken down by one party only, and this invariably gives rise to a feeling of violation followed by resentment. Every relationship has its optimal distance, which of course has to be found by trial and error.
>
> *1973, 20 September 1928, pp. 53–54*[7]

What the street people with their intrusive begging were interrupting was not just this shoeshine man's relationship with his customer; they were interrupting his vocation, his individuation. Of the two craftsmen, he was the greater artist, and, as with all true artists, his individuation was in his work. From him, I learned love of the work one does for a client, without which an analyst's feeling is fairly superficial. When he would finish his *opus* of getting layer upon layer of beautifully shined polish onto my shoes, which took him as much as half an hour to complete, he would look at me and say, "This is the best!" The rest of the time, he rarely talked, whether to me or anyone else. When it came time to pay, if I asked him how much, he would point to his sign. I always paid him double what he charged; his work was so good. After ten years, he told me, "You are a very nice man." The feeling I learned from him was also that of an unalloyed man, but it was an introverted feeling. It took the ten years I patronized him for me to realize that, when he yelled at a street person panhandling his customer, he was registering an abuse of power, to realize that his introverted feeling, in addition to pursuing its own idea of quality—the great, deeper shine he was able to give to my shoes in comparison with the easily worn off tincture applied by the other, kinder Italian shoeshine man—was ever tracking power. Even his customer was not immune from judgments about this, when I started to simply leave my shoes with him while I did some shopping because I didn't feel the patience to sit through one of his agonizingly careful shines. He did the work on the shoes I left just as carefully, and I continued to pay him just as much, but he knew I was getting ready to move on and thought it a pity. Only since I have left his care, and the other man's, for a shoe repair store nearer my office manned by a Lebanese-born man of Italian ancestry who shares my politics have I realized how hard the conscientious, irritable shoemaker from Calabria had tried to get me to slow down to experience the way he shined shoes—adding tincture whose luster would last.

There is a time dimension to feeling that von Franz does not directly touch in her lecture, but it comes through anyway in her discussion of the "religious world-embracing movement" that will rehabilitate the feeling our world will have to develop to survive. She knows that a deeper change than lessons in emotional intelligence is needed if we are to recapture what is exemplified by the two shoe-shine men I was lucky enough to train with in the hours I had between patients in my first years as an analyst, while trying to burnish my analytic persona, as if that could also make me competent. Only time can do that, and each year I have practiced I have said in the course of it once, "At last I know what analysis is." The development of the analytic attitude in the microcosm of an analyst's office is not unlike the development of the religious attitude that von Franz implies will take a very long time to restore in the outer world. What this analytic attitude finally might look like I have only had glimpses of, but it is definitely an eros tinged by logos that accepts the distances between people and yet enables sane-making greeting and meeting and that is filled not only with affection for the person I am working with, but also love for the work itself. At its best, it unites extraverted and introverted feeling into something akin to appreciation—appreciation of the shine that comes from someone else's shoes when you get very close to what it is like to be in them and have done what you can to make them nicer for the person who has to wear them.

Notes

1 See also "Empathy," ¶707, as well as ¶¶484–493.
2 See Edinger (1985, p. 48), where he quotes an alchemical recipe for reducing the substances to be transformed into *prima materia*:

> Dissolve then sol and luna in our dissolving water, which is familiar and friendly, and the next in nature unto them, and as it were a womb, a mother, an original, the beginning and the end of their life. And that is the very reason they are meliorated or amended in this water, because like nature rejoiceth in like nature.
>
> *Artephius, 2011, p. 39*

Finally, the water emerges from the substance being 'washed' alchemically (Jung, 1955, 1956/1963, ¶317). Edinger, echoing Jung, tells us that an old alchemist's recipe is, "If thou knowest how to moisten this dry earth with its own water, thou wilt loosen the pores of this earth" (1985, p. 80; Jung, 1955 and 1956/1963, ¶189). The text in which this recipe appears is attributed pseudonymously to 'Philalethes,' a name that might be translated 'lover of forgotten things,' and can be found in the *Musaeum Heremeticum* (Frankfurt, 1678), an alchemical miscellany edited and translated into English by Arthur Edward Waite (1893/2007).
3 Bishop (2000, p. 84 and p. 131n) locates the source of the quote in Kant (1997, p. 106).
4 The translation and emphasis is von Franz's (2008, p. 9), and she has also altered the published English translation, which has Jung saying, "We must teach that no truth obtained by unethical means has the moral right to exist."
5 Von Franz recounts a conversation with Jung about this patient, whom he saw shortly after going into private practice, in the film *Matter of Heart* (1985). This patient was a young woman with a dissociative psychosis who reported to Jung that she was living on the moon. The psychiatric history is detailed in Jung's lecture, "Schizophrenia," read at the Second International Congress for Psychiatry in 1957 (1958/1960, ¶¶571–572).
6 Jung, 1946/1975. I am using the translation of Gerhard Danielus, which appears under "Anima; Jung Quaternio and Stages of Anima" in his privately printed *A Concordance of Excerpts of the Works of C. G. Jung*. Within the published *Collected Works* (1946/1966), the passage about the four stages of the anima appears in *Cw* 16, ¶361, where the same phrase is translated by R. F. C. Hull as "four stages of the Eros cult," which doesn't convey the acculturation of feeling-relatedness that Jung (and Goethe before him) observed taking place with the maturation of the anima image in the course of anima development.
7 The part of the letter that is published begins, "I greatly appreciate your not having burst in on me unannounced in Bollingen with Frl. X. I do in fact dislike being disturbed, especially when working."

References

Artephius. (2011). *Secret book of Artephius*. Calgary: Theophania Publishing House.
Bishop, P. (2000). *Synchronicity and intellectual intuition in Kant, Swedenborg, and Jung*. Lewiston, NY: Edwin Mellen Press.
Edinger, E. (1985). *Anatomy of the psyche: Alchemical symbolism in psychotherapy*. La Salle, IN: Open Court.
Eliot, T. S. (1918). In memory of Henry James. *The Egoist* 5(1), 1–2.
Hillman, J. (1971/1998). The feeling function. In M.-L. von Franz & J. Hillman (Eds.), *Lectures on Jung's typology* (pp. 89–179). Woodstock, CT: Spring Publications.

Jung, C. G. (1897/1983). Some thoughts on psychology. In *Cw supplementary volume A*, (pp. 21–47).

Jung, C. G. (1921/1971). Psychological types. In *Cw 6*.

Jung, C. G. (1946/1966). The psychology of the transference. In *Cw 16*, 2nd ed. (pp. 163–201).

Jung, C. G. (1946/1975). Anima/eros quaternio and stages of anima. In Introduction to The psychology of the transference. In G. Danielus (Ed. and Trans.), *A concordance of excerpts of the works of Carl Gustav Jung*. Privately printed, courtesy of Nina C. Bushnell Foundation, Inc.

Jung, C. G. (1955, 1956/1963). Mysterium coniunctionis. In *Cw 14*.

Jung, C. G. (1958/1960). Schizophrenia. In *Cw 3* (pp. 256–272).

Jung, C. G. (1973). *Letters, vol. 1*. W. McGuire & A. Jaffe (Eds.) Princeton, NJ: Princeton University Press.

Kant, I. (1997). *Lectures on metaphysics*. K. Ameriks & S. Naragon (Trans.). Cambridge: Cambridge University Press.

Matter of Heart. (1985). M. Whitney (Dir.) King Lorber films. [Motion picture].

Neumann, E. (1949/1990). *Depth psychology and a new ethic*. E. Rolfe (Trans.). Boston, MA: Shambhala.

Osterman, E. (1963). C. G. Jung: A personal memoir. In M. Fordham (Ed.) *Contact with Jung* (pp. 218–220). London: Tavistock.

Sharp, D. (1987). *Personality types: Jung's model of typology*. Toronto: Inner City Books.

von Franz, M.-L. (1970/1981). *Puer aeternus*. Boston, MA: Sigo Press.

von Franz, M.-L. (1971/1998). The inferior function. In M.-L. von Franz & J. Hillman, *Lectures on Jung's typology* (pp. 3–88). Woodstock, CT: Spring Publications.

von Franz, M.-L. (1974/1995). *Shadow and evil in fairy tales*. Boston, MA: Shambhala.

von Franz, M.-L. (2008). C. G. Jung's rehabilitation of the feeling function in our civilization. Lecture, Küsnacht, Switzerland, November 25, 1986. *Jung Journal: Culture & Psyche* 2(2), 9–20.

Waite, A. E. (Ed. and Trans.) (1893/2007). *The hermetic museum, restored and enlarged*. Sioux Falls, SD: NuVision Publications.

Willeford, W. (1975). Toward a dynamic concept of feeling. *Journal of Analytical Psychology* 20(1), 18–40.

Willeford, W. (1976). The primacy of feeling (Part 1). *Journal of Analytical Psychology 21*(2), 115–133.

Willeford, W. (1977). The primacy of feeling (Part 2). *Journal of Analytical Psychology 22*(1), 1–16.

Willeford, W. (1987). *Feeling, imagination, and the self*. Evanston, IL: Northwestern University Press.

3

UNDERSTANDING CONSCIOUSNESS THROUGH THE THEORY OF PSYCHOLOGICAL TYPES

When Jung began to work on the psychological problem that he was attempting to solve with his theory of types, he had an international reputation as an investigator of the unconscious. Early on, he had allied himself with the burgeoning psychoanalytic movement, which had made the idea of the unconscious, already topical by the end of the nineteenth century, a world preoccupation. So in 1921, when his book *Psychological Types* appeared with its description of various attitudes of consciousness, it looked to some as if Jung had turned away from the concerns he had embraced so boldly in the first part of his career. He seemed a bit like that other prewar trailblazer Picasso, who elected in the 1920s to abandon his cubist explorations of painterly depth for a conservative, neoclassical style that emphasized contour drawing in a conventional rendering of the human figure. Freud, who had long accused Jung of being in flight from the real unconscious because he could not accept the sexual theory, was able to crow to Ernest Jones:

> A new production by Jung of enormous size, seven hundred pages thick, inscribed "Psychological Types," the work of a snob and a mystic, no new idea in it. He clings to that escape he detected in 1913, denying objective truths in psychology on account of personal differences in the observer's constitution. No great harm to be expected from this quarter.
>
> *Paskauskas, 1993, p. 424*[1]

Following Freud, most psychoanalysts assumed that Jung, in full retreat from the dynamic psychiatry the fathers of his early career had hoped he would help them build, had returned to the descriptive psychology that had informed Kraepelin. What he was no longer willing to deal with, it seemed to them, was the unconscious (Fenichel, 1945, p. 526; Glover, 1950, p. 102).

This perception, which I would call a prejudice, has affected the reception of the subject of psychological type among depth psychologists ever since, including the majority of analytical psychologists working today. I well recall a friend in analytical training asking me some years ago when I mentioned that I was hard at work on understanding the type theory and its application to clinical work, "Is that a valid method of analysis?" To him, Jung's typology seemed, at best, an approach to conscious psychology, not very interesting or important to the training of a depth psychologist. Today, however, when academic spokespeople from the fields of cognitive psychology and neuroscience such as Howard Gardner,[2] Daniel Dennett (1991), Antonio Damasio (2005),[3] and Nicholas Humphrey (1992) have renewed public and professional interest in the nature of "consciousness," depth psychologists have been inspired to take up anew the question of how patients in analysis become "conscious." A contemporary definition of consciousness is offered by Corsini:

> The distinguishing feature of mental life, variously characterized as the: (a) state of awareness as well as the content of the mind, that is, the ever-changing stream of immediate experience, comprising perceptions, feelings, sensations, images, and ideas; (b) central effect of neural reception; (c) capacity of having experience; (d) subjective aspect of brain activity; (e) relation of self to environment; and (f) totality of an individual's experience at any given moment.
>
> *2002, p. 209*

Jung's pioneering emphasis on the "attitudes and functions of consciousness" has finally begun to seem less like a digression from the cutting edge of psychological understanding than a prescient anticipation of a direction in which depth psychology has found that it needs to go.

In relation to the exploration of the unconscious, Jung's turn to the topic of types of consciousness was not so much a regression as a repositioning. It involved what he described elsewhere as *reculer pour mieux sauter*, stepping backward in order to take a greater leap. The type theory was a contribution to the problem of the standpoint from which the individual experiences the unconscious. That the conscious standpoint of the patient could hardly be ignored Jung had already learned from his practical experience as a psychiatrist attempting to understand dreams and symptoms, for the patient's conscious stance often turned out to be what the unconscious was actually responding to.

By taking up the way consciousness is structured, Jung was engaging with the problem that Friedrich Nietzsche and William James had recognized a generation before, that consciousness cannot be taken for granted. Nietzsche had seriously questioned consciousness's identity as a unity, arguing that when we orient ourselves to reality it is not through a fixed standpoint but through a series of perspectives. And William James, even more deconstructively, had written in 1904:

I believe that 'consciousness,' when once it has evaporated to this estate of pure diaphaneity, is on the point of disappearing altogether. It is the name of a nonentity, and has no right to a place among first principles. Those who still cling to it are clinging to a mere echo, the faint rumor left behind by the disappearing 'soul' upon the air of philosophy. During the past year, I have read a number of articles whose authors seemed just on the point of abandoning the notion of consciousness . . . and substituting for it that of an absolute experience not due to two factors [such as '[t]houghts' and 'things,' 'spirit and matter,' 'soul and body']. But they were not quite radical enough, not quite daring enough in their negations. For twenty years past I have mistrusted 'consciousness' as an entity; for seven or eight years past I have suggested its non-existence to my students, and tried to give them its pragmatic equivalent in realities of experience. It seems to me that the hour is ripe for it to be openly and universally discarded.

To deny plumply that 'consciousness' exists seems so absurd on the face of it—for undeniably 'thoughts' do exist—that I fear some readers will follow me no farther. Let me then immediately explain that I mean only to deny that the word stands for an entity, but to insist most emphatically that it does stand for a function. There is, I mean, no aboriginal stuff or quality of being, contrasted with that of which material objects are made, out of which our thoughts of them are made; but there is a function in experience which thoughts perform, and for the performance of which this quality of being is invoked. That function is knowing. 'Consciousness' is supposed necessary to explain the fact that things not only are, but get reported, are known. Whoever blots out the notion of consciousness from his list of first principles must still provide in some way for that function's being carried on.

James, 1904, p. 477

By developing a theory that situates knowing within different types of psychological orientation, Jung found a way to incorporate both Nietzsche's emphasis on perspectives and James's insistence that consciousness can only be approached practically, through careful study of the way we actually 'know' things. When in *Psychological Types* Jung sets out the case for basic "attitudes" of consciousness, we can feel the influence of Nietzsche's perspectivism, and when he writes of "functions of consciousness" we encounter language that reflects James's pragmatism.

But something else had been added, out of Jung's own experience, first, with the different understandings of the unconscious between Freud, Adler, and himself that had split up the early psychoanalytic movement into 'schools,' and, second, through direct active imaginative encounters with the unconscious (Jung, 1963, pp. 179–199, 2009) that drove home to him the reality of the psyche and the importance of the standpoint taken toward it. Jung told the students in his 1925 English seminar that:

Through the fact that I worried about my difficulty with Freud, I came to study Adler carefully in order to see what was his case against Freud. I was struck at once by the difference in type. Both were treating neurosis and hysteria, and yet to the one man it looked so, and to the other it was something quite different. I could find no solution. Then it dawned on me that possibly I was dealing with two different types, who were fated to approach the same set of facts from widely differing aspects. I began to see among my patients some who fit Adler's theories, and others who fit Freud's, and thus I came to formulate the theory of extraversion and introversion.

Jung, 1926/1989, p. 31

These terms for the basic attitudes of consciousness were apparently derived from words, *externospection* and *introspection*, that Binet had come up with to describe the different types of intelligence displayed by his own two infant daughters (Binet, 1903, cited by Oliver Brachfeld, 1954 in Ellenberger, 1970, pp. 702–703). Jung's insistence on this differentiation would have been impossible had he not also come to the conviction, arrived at independently of any of his teachers and colleagues, that there was a reality that psychological consciousness was expected to construe whenever the unconscious was confronted. On the basis of his experience with the psyche, which Jung also shared with the members of his English seminar (Aniela Jaffe included this material in *Memories, Dreams, Reflections*), Jung had grasped that psychological consciousness was not just a knowing about, or a construction or reconstruction of, but (as the etymology of the word 'consciousness' suggests) 'a knowing with' unconscious reality. Edinger has noted that this etymology points to the "unconscious side of the term consciousness":

Conscious derives from *con* or *cum*, meaning 'with' or 'together,' and *scire*, 'to know' or 'to see.' It has the same derivation as *conscience*. Thus the root meaning of both consciousness and conscience is 'knowing with' or 'seeing with' an 'other.' In contrast, the word science, which also derives from *scire*, means simple knowing, i.e., knowing without 'withness.' So etymology indicates that the phenomena of consciousness and conscience are somehow related and that the experience of consciousness is made up of two factors— 'knowing' and 'withness.' In other words, consciousness is the experience of *knowing together with an other*, that is, in a setting of twoness.

Edinger, 1984, p. 36

Something like what Jung means by consciousness is conveyed by Heinz Kohut's much later assertion that "introspection and empathy are essential ingredients of psychoanalytical observation and that the limits of psychoanalysis are defined by those of introspection and empathy" (Kohut, 1959/1978). By the time Jung set out to write *Psychological Types*, consciousness had come to mean for him the way the reality of the psyche is both accessed and assessed, or what he sometimes called "understanding" (Jung, 1914/1972), which he made the basis of his entire approach to psychology. Consciousness, in this sense, was the indispensable investigative tool for all further work on the unconscious.

How this consciousness is achieved is the problem that Jung seeks to address in his book. As he put it, much later, "I considered it my scientific duty to examine first the condition of the human consciousness" (Jung, 1957/1977, p. 341).

The individuation of consciousness

What is not immediately apparent to those who try to approach Jung's psychology as if it were another science, albeit a science of the unconscious, is that consciousness, for Jung the tool with which the unconscious must be investigated, is an emergent property of the unconscious itself (Cambray, 2006). Only secondarily does consciousness collect in the center he calls the ego and even then it is not entirely located there. Jung does not make this as explicit in *Psychological Types* as he might have. There he defines consciousness in terms of its relation to the ego:

> By consciousness I understand the relatedness of psychic contents to the ego . . . in so far as they are sensed as such by the ego. In so far as relations are not sensed as such by the ego, they are unconscious. Consciousness is the function or activity which maintains the relation of psychic contents with the ego. Consciousness is not identical with *psyche*, since, in my view, psyche represents the totality of all the psychic contents, and these are not necessarily all bound up directly with the ego, i.e. related to it in such a way that they take on the quality of consciousness. There exist a great many psychic complexes and these are not all, necessarily, connected with the ego.
>
> *Jung, 1921/1923, pp. 535–536*

This unfortunate passage, all too self-evidently trying to meet the logical requirements for distinguishing consciousness from the unconscious, has led too many students of Jung's psychology to look for a structure called 'ego' and a process of 'ego development,' neither of which is exactly supported by phenomenological observation of the growth of an individual's consciousness even though some Jungians have made heroic efforts to demonstrate that they are (Neumann, 1954; Edinger, 1973).

Perhaps the most interesting of these attempts is Erich Neumann's landmark book, *The Origins and History of Consciousness*, which offers a model for the development of consciousness out of the unconscious that draws upon quite specific imagery from world mythology. Neumann uses myths, particularly myths of the hero in the process of surviving various monsters that can be equated with aspects of the unconscious, to find evidence of the ego's emergence, survival, and progressive strengthening, thus organizing the myths along a continuum of the hero's progress to generate a stage-by-stage model of ego development. The archetypal "stages" of ego-consciousness he educes have generated a clinical mythology among Jungians (e.g. "The patient's ego is contained in the maternal uroborus").[4] This has been the model of the development of consciousness that many Jungian analysts have drawn upon to gauge where their patients are in the individuation of consciousness. This model has been criticized as identified with "the hero's Apollonic definition of consciousness" (Hillman, 1972, p. 289) and thus with the nineteenth-century notion of progress that influenced the development of 'medical' psychology by both Freud and Jung (see also Giegerich, 1975).

Jung's own way of speaking about the growth of consciousness in human beings tended to be simpler, and, from a contemporary standpoint, more soulful. For instance, while giving a seminar, he was once asked, "Is not individuation, in our sense of the word here, rather living life consciously? A plant individuates but it lives unconsciously." Jung's answer was:

> That is *our* form of individuation. A plant that is meant to produce a flower is not individuated if it does not produce a flower, it must fulfill the cycle; and the man who does not develop consciousness is not individuated, because consciousness is his flower; it is his life, it belongs to our process of individuation that we shall become conscious.
>
> *Jung, 1934/1997, pp. 758–759*

In allowing the subtitle of the first English translation of *Psychological Types* to be "The Psychology of Individuation," Jung implied that the flowering of consciousness has something to do with the progressive emergence of the psychological types, and it's this idea I prefer to the idea of a monadic 'ego' developing over time. Sticking to Jung's metaphor of flowering, I find it best to say that if a person individuates, that is, goes on to flower, then the various functions of consciousness that Jung describes in *Psychological Types* will be the petals of his or her flower. This notion does not assume that consciousness originates in the ego, even though when consciousness emerges it is associated with an ongoing narrative of self, that is, as part of what a person can refer to as 'mine.' If anything, consciousness would seem to arise out of what Jung described in a talk with students as "the peculiar intelligence of the background" (Jung, 1958/1970, p. 178).

The idea that consciousness already resides in some form in the unconscious gives another meaning to the idea of 'knowing together with an other.' The idea of a teamwork between ego-consciousness and a consciousness that already resides in the unconscious is particularly appropriate to the understanding of the psychological functions Jung has called 'thinking,' 'feeling,' 'sensation,' and 'intuition.' In *Psychological Types*, he conceives these as two pairs of opposites: thinking and feeling (evaluative functions) defining one axis of consciousness, sensation and intuition (perceptive functions) the other. Asked for definitions of these four functions of consciousness, Jung told an interviewer:

> there is quite a simple explanation of those terms, and it shows at the same time how I arrived at such a typology. Sensation tells you that there *is* something. Thinking, roughly speaking, tells you *what* it is. Feeling tells you

whether it is agreeable or not, to be accepted or rejected. And intuition— now there is a difficulty. You don't know, ordinarily, how intuition works. When a man has a hunch, you can't tell exactly how he got at that hunch, or where that hunch comes from. There is something funny about intuition. [Jung gives an example.] So my definition is that intuition is a perception via the unconscious.

Jung, 1957/1977, p. 306

So far, this seems like a reasonable enough orientation to reality from the standpoint of an ego trying to cope with it. But in discussing intuition, the 'difficult' function to explain, Jung tells us:

It is a very important function, because when you live under primitive conditions a lot of unpredictable things are likely to happen. Then you need your intuition because you cannot possibly tell by your sense perceptions what is going to happen. For instance, you are traveling in a primeval forest. You can only see a few steps ahead. You go by the compass, perhaps, but you don't know what there is ahead. It is uncharted country. If you use your intuition you have hunches, and when you live under primitive conditions you are instantly aware of hunches. There are places that are favorable, there are places that are not favorable. You can't tell for your life what it is, but you'd better follow those hunches because anything can happen, quite unforeseen things . . . You can also have intuitions—and this constantly happens—in our jungle called a city. You can have a hunch that something is going wrong, particularly when you are driving an automobile. For instance it is the day when nurses appear in the street . . . And then you get a peculiar feeling, and really, at the next corner there is a second nurse that runs in front of the automobile.

Jung, 1957/1977, pp. 307–308

I like to read that amplification of the intuitive function as a gloss on the purpose that *all* the functions of consciousness—thinking, feeling, and sensation too— serve. All of them are required because life itself presents problems that are already differentiated in such a way that only a particular function of consciousness can solve them. In that case, we would be justified to speak of a problem presented by a patient as a thinking problem, a feeling problem, an intuitive problem, or a sensation problem. Similarly, a dream, which reveals to us "the actual situation in the unconscious" (Jung, 1948/1960, ¶505) of a client, lays out the situation for us in such a way that we can 'type' it, if we wish, as a thinking situation, a feeling situation, an intuitive situation, or a sensation situation. The problem is then coming up with the function of consciousness appropriate to the situation, or, in other words, meeting the situation's own peculiar consciousness as to what it is with a consciousness that matches it. From this perspective, the development of consciousness involves the ability to summon the various functions at appropriate times in appropriate ways.

Unfortunately, we are not always so adaptable. In the book *Lectures on Jung's Typology*, Marie-Louise von Franz and James Hillman (1971/1998) each address the problem of bringing an appropriate function of consciousness to a situation that calls for it. Von Franz's theme is the unevenness in type development that leads one of Jung's four functions to remain "low" in its degree of differentiation. This Jung had called the "inferior function," and I have found the designation accurate, phenomenologically, because each of us usually has an inferiority complex around that particular area of our conscious functioning. Von Franz points out that the inferior function tends to behave like Dummling (the 'simpleton' youngest son) in a Grimms' fairy-tale and yet, like that son, serves as the bridge to the unconscious that the more differentiated functions (symbolized by the arrogant elder brothers in the typical tale) cannot provide, bringing some kind of renewal to the kingdom, i.e. the sphere of consciousness. This function is the area of our consciousness that is least under the control of our good intentions, slowest to take training despite our best efforts, and most tied up with the unconscious. Hillman's description of the inferior feeling function well conveys the problem that arises on the basis of this association with what is ordinarily repressed:

> Inferior feeling, to sum it up, may be characterized by contamination with the repressed which tends to manifest, as the Scholastic would have said, in *ira* and *cupiditas* [anger and desire]. Inferior feeling is loaded with anger and rage and ambition and aggression as well as with greed and desire. Here we find ourselves with huge claims for love, with massive needs for recognition, and discover our feeling connection to life to be one vast expectation composed of thousands of tiny, angry resentments. This expectation has been called an omnipotence fantasy, the expression of the abandoned child with his leftover feelings that nobody wants to take care of—but is this enough? Omnipotence is more than a content; rather it expresses, as does the child, an impoverished functioning that insists upon more sway and exercise. Without this exercise, feeling turns upon itself, morbidly; we are envious, jealous, depressed, feeding our needs and their immediate gratification, then rushing out intermittently to meet someone to help or for help. The cat neglected becomes the unconscious tiger.
>
> *Hillman in von Franz & Hillman, 1971/1998, p. 135*

It should be pointed out that this description of the emotional attitude of a function of consciousness in the inferior position is strikingly similar to Adler's description of the inferiority complex (Ellenberger, 1970, pp. 612–613).

Hillman's description of the complex that feeling can display when it is an inferior function helps us to recognize that the behavior of a function of consciousness is affected by its position within the total hierarchy of functions.

For his seminars, Jung liked to diagram this hierarchy in various ways according to a fourfold model, specifying a superior function, an auxiliary function, a tertiary function, and an inferior function. I have standardized Jung's diagram as follows for my own classes on psychological types:

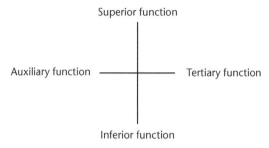

FIGURE 3.1 Jung's hierarchy of the types of consciousness in an individual

This diagram can be read as a stick-figure representation of a right-handed person, who might be imagined standing erect with feet together and back placed flush against a blackboard with his or her arms spread-eagled, for the purpose of revealing the relations of his or her functions of consciousness. Each of the qualifying adjectives for the four functions shown in the diagram—superior, auxiliary, tertiary, and inferior—describes the 'position' of one of the person's four functions of consciousness in relation to the others. What is suggested is a hierarchy of the functions that, though it begins according to their degree of differentiation, ends up being as qualitative as it is quantitative. That is to say, the way the function is experienced, both by the person who possesses it and by the others he or she deals with, is as much a result of its position in the total hierarchy of functions as of its actual degree of differentiation. The positions themselves convey certain qualities to the functions that occupy them, as von Franz and Hillman demonstrated for the 'inferior' function and I have proceeded to do for the other three positions.

Further, these named positions, as Figure 3.1 shows, define a pair of axes, a vertical axis (between the superior function and inferior function), which I think of as the 'spine' of consciousness defining the person's conscious standpoint, and a horizontal axis (between the auxiliary and tertiary functions), which for me are the 'arms' of consciousness, since it is the task of these functions to handle the relation to the world once the individual standpoint of the person is established.

Type as a method of analysis

As I have given much attention to the behavior of the functions in each of these positions in the course of my own development of consciousness, I will now offer a series of vignettes from my personal analytic process. What follows may be considered an autobiographical case report of a typological analysis.

My discovery of my superior function, intuition, came in the first year of my analysis. I had come into therapy at the age of 26, a few months after graduating from medical school, complaining of 'depression,' by which I think I meant a general malaise and feeling of blocked libido, the manifest symptom being the inability to finish any professional book I started to read. In the third or fourth session, while I was in the midst of reiterating these complaints, my analyst asked, "Do you ever dream when you're depressed?"

It was as if a light had been turned on in a dark room. Of course I dreamed; I had always dreamt, and in fact that's where my mind was when people complained I wasn't paying attention. I was dreaming! No wonder I couldn't keep track of practical things. In a flash I knew that what I was superior at—dreaming—was the cause of what I was inferior at—paying attention—something that in turn my mother, my father, my teachers, and my peers had all tried, with little success, to shame me into being more responsible about. A few months later, I had the Jungian words for those processes that had defined my gift and its accompanying limitation: I was an intuitive type, with inferior sensation. But immediately upon realizing that what I was best at and what I was worst at were two aspects or "ends" of the same thing, I had a dream that I was an obstetrician delivering a baby from myself. In experiencing my superior function and my inferior function as belonging to the same reality, I had discovered the reality of my own vertical axis, and it became a channel for experiencing a new identity.

Realizing that I was an intuitive type gave me a lot of energy. The dreams I was now recording daily and bringing to my analyst twice a week gave me plenty to read, and I found I could also read Jungian books that taught me more about the inner life I was discovering. In my relief at finding something I really liked to study, I discovered my true auxiliary function, introverted thinking. My father, a military man who had commanded a battalion in Korea, was an extraverted thinking type, and he had bought heavily into the American cultural belief that knowledge is power. When I would interrupt the nightly radio news broadcast to offer opinions of my own about what the developments might signify, my father would say, "Shut up, son. You don't learn from people who know nothing." My analyst, also a man, never interrupted, or almost never. He let me think out loud about my dreams and my reading to my heart's content. Even though this meant that I was rethinking much of Jungian psychology and making it my own so that I could take it in (and this meant that I was not simply accepting Jung's way of formulating the big ideas, in which my analyst had been trained), he let my thinking go its own introverted, subjective way. I would only accept something if it was true to my experience, which of course was very Jungian in one way, but would not allow me, in another, to accept the dogma that Jungian psychology had already started to become. I will always be grateful to my first analyst for (1) allowing me to think in his presence without complaining, as many another therapist might have, that I was intellectualizing and avoiding the feelings that were the "real" stuff of depth work and (2) tolerating, without retaliation, a rethinking of the very psychology in which he was so heavily invested. In this way, he let my auxiliary function express itself, which it had never been able to do before, inhibited as it was by the extraverted thinking of my father and other authorities, including the psychiatry professors whose books I could no longer read. As a psychoanalyst might have said at the time, I was fortunate in having a transference situation that would enable me to solve my Oedipal problem in this way.

From a cultural angle, I realize that I was also availing myself of a form of empowerment that was much more open to men than to women in 1966 and 1967, when these events were occurring. I was a doctor, and so was my analyst. There was in medicine a long tradition of learning how to think and function medically, codified in the aphorism we all often heard about learning new medical procedures, "See one, do one, teach one." This was a totemic, patriarchal tradition, for the most part: in some parts of the United States, women were still not even admitted to medical school. I am aware that having my superior function mirrored and my auxiliary function given space would have been far less likely to occur with the very same analyst had I been a woman. Though differently problematic from that of my father, this analyst's anima[5] would, I believe, have been far more likely to insist upon feeling expressions from a woman of my psychological type, in accord with the then prevalent Jungian notion that feeling was more feminine than thinking.

No such impediment to empowering my thinking came up in my analyst's initial overt countertransference, and so I experienced the ideal conditions for a therapy described by Carl Rogers and his colleagues: genuineness, unconditional positive regard, and accurate empathic understanding (Rogers & Truax, 1967). For this reason, I became precociously clear about the nature of my own typology as part of my self-experience. I believe that only some such direct experience of the types as one's own, and the permission to consider them in one's own way, can enable a patient to avail himself or herself of the individuation potential of the type theory. Otherwise, type becomes another way to learn from others what one is, and a new set of tasks to be learned in the effort to adapt more effectively to the environment. There can be value in type still in discovering new energy for adaptation, but this is not the same as individuation.

As my dream of delivering a baby from myself perhaps conveys, I came into possession quite early in my analysis of a sense of personal selfhood as my typology unfolded in a way that felt authentic to me in the facilitating environment of the therapy. As I have indicated in other writings (Beebe, 1988, 1992), I believe that it is only through experiencing one's personal, 'little-s' self in a way that has 'integrity in depth' that the 'big-S' Self of Jungian psychology, the instinctive knowledge of how to live, can be authentically accessed.

The opening up of my typology led to a great deal of energy pouring into my psyche from the Self. My new problem, replacing the depression I had come to therapy with, was a tendency to get too excited. I sometimes imagined my superior intuition was like the head of a rocket ship, ready to take off. I needed desperately to hold myself to the earth, to stay with the tasks associated with medical training. At that early stage, my inferior function, sensation, simply did not have the necessary weight, the specific gravity, to anchor me. But I noticed that my auxiliary and tertiary functions could be enlisted to keep me connected to the demands of the world. Thinking, after intuition my strongest function, and therefore my auxiliary, helped me to define my situation and identify the issues I needed to work on. And my feeling, less confident and more vulnerable, kept me guessing what my impact was on other people and working to discover what my actual relationships with them were. The combined effect of using these two processes, thinking and feeling, was to slow me down and keep me out of the most irrational flights of my intuition. I first became aware in an inner way that my thinking and feeling form an axis, just as my superior intuition and inferior sensation do, when I had the following dream: A father (a man who was maybe in his fifties) was chasing his son (a young man in his twenties) around a dining room table, waving a butcher knife.

Working on this dream in my analysis, I was able to associate to the image of the young man. Although the echoes of my feeling reactions to a critical father were clear, the young man in my dream, in his fearfulness, was not anything like my waking personality. At that time, if anything, I had not learned to fear.

The son in the dream reminded me of a young man I knew at the time, whose feeling function was well developed and who thought very slowly. The butcher knife, with its capacity to cleave and dissect, seemed to me the image of a thinking function that makes separating distinctions between things. That an older man wielded it in a terrorizing way toward a younger suggested to me, when I thought about it intrapsychically, that a more developed function was somehow bullying a less developed one. The dream may, of course, have been a commentary on the way I used thinking around my feeling-type friend, but at the time I also needed to focus on how I was relating to myself. I decided that the father symbolized my auxiliary thinking and the son my tertiary feeling. They are related to each other—in the same family—but in my situation at that time the relationship appeared to be a sadomasochistic one.

It did not satisfy me to see the dream merely as a reenactment of the humiliations I had received from my father in childhood, such as when I had tried, rather rudely, to express the thoughts that occurred to me at the dinner table while his 'news briefing' was on the radio. Yes, my father had bullied my introverted thinking with his extraverted thinking, but what I was doing to myself now, as reflected in the dream, was allowing my relatively strong thinking function to browbeat my much less developed feeling function.

Chastened by the dream, I gradually became less aggressive about applying overriding thinking formulations to the understanding and dismissal of my feeling when it was upset. In time, my thinking became less tyrannical and began to take a more protective attitude toward my shakier, immature feeling. My relation to feeling-type patients and friends also got kinder.

Up to this time, my use of the type theory to make sense of myself had pretty much concentrated on which functions were strong, and which at risk. I was not particularly focused on whether the functions that I was discovering and analyzing were introverted or extraverted, and indeed I could not make up my mind whether I myself should be described as an introvert or an extravert. My first analyst had said it was a 'continuum' and, while half of my friends saw me as more extraverted, others who knew me just as well said I was the only true introvert they knew! As I had now entered analytic training, it was an embarrassment to me that I did not know. Around this time, I learned from a member of the training committee at my Institute, Wayne Detloff, to whom I confided my confusion, that there was a point of view not often expressed in the circles frequented by Jungian analysts and candidates, that if the superior function is extraverted, the auxiliary function is introverted and vice versa. Although I had actually taken the Myers–Briggs Type Indicator, as part of a research study in which all the first year residents in my psychiatric residency were asked to participate in 1968, and its finding that I was an ENTP seemed to confirm the 'intuitive thinking' diagnosis I had given myself on the basis of my analytic discoveries of my typology, Dr. Detloff's explanation was my first introduction to the theoretical ideas of Isabel Briggs Myers about type development, which at that time went largely untaught in my Institute.[6]

The received version of type there was that of Jo Wheelwright (1982), who, with his wife Jane and Horace Gray, had created their own diagnostic instrument, the Gray-Wheelwrights Jungian Type Survey. On it, as on the Myers–Briggs, I came out extraverted and an intuitive thinking type. And in my Institute that meant that *both* my leading functions were extraverted. What introversion I had was supposed to come from my inferior function, sensation. But in truth, although von Franz and Hillman's *Lectures on Jung's Typology* had now been published and I could follow this argument, as far as it went, I still saw my inferior function in a less differentiated way, as just 'inferior sensation,' and, as I have indicated, I was really not all that sure about the extraverted diagnosis for my superior function.

Dr. Detloff, however, was quite clear that introverted sensation and extraverted sensation were so different that he wondered why they were even both called 'sensation.' Later I came to see that introverted sensation concerns itself primarily with finding order, organizing experience, and monitoring the comfort of the body on the inside, whereas extraverted sensation involves compelling, often shared, experiences of the textures, smells, sights, sounds, and tastes of the world—a direct relationship with reality. Similarly, I decided that introverted feeling is mainly concerned with the values that matter most to oneself, while extraverted feeling seeks to connect with the feelings of others. Extraverted intuition, as friends often verified after some of my uncannily telepathic moments in their presence, seemed rather easily to pick up on what was going on in other people's minds, and it was certainly seeing possibilities in what was more consciously shared with me that others might never have imagined; whereas introverted intuition, I noticed (for instance, in Jung) looked at the big picture in the unconscious, where the gestalts that moved nations, religions, and epochs lay, even in the midst of apparently 'individual' experience. And the two kinds of thinking, though both concerned with defining things, also did so in very different ways: extraverted thinking such as my father's was interested in definitions that would hold true for everyone, according to ideas everyone might agree with, whereas introverted thinking such as mine had to reflect on whether a particular construction really accorded with the conviction of inner truth, regardless of what the received opinion might be.

These distinctions were a helpful orientation to other people's psychology, but they were not of the greatest personal interest at this stage of my development, for I had more urgent issues in my analysis to deal with, or so I believed. My core depression was still untouched, and still further years into the analysis I was often beset with migraine headaches and accompanying states of severe exhaustion. In my dreams, I saw stretches of scant and barren vegetation. My analyst (by this time I had switched to a woman) interpreted this as a picture of my vegetative nervous system, as it looked during these periods of burnout.

Then I dreamed of a woman sitting alone in a room. She was Chinese and had a glum look on her face. The room she was in was bare, without other furniture than the chair she was sitting in. This was so because her husband spent all his money doping and gambling and so had nothing to bring home. My analyst was very insistent about the importance of this dream. "She doesn't have anything," she pointed out.

I associated to the woman. I knew her in life: she was the laundress at the Chinese launderette to which I entrusted my washables at that time. A practical, unadorned woman, she worked very efficiently. She was clearly no extravert, but she was quite concerned with sensation matters in her introverted way. I decided she was an introverted sensation type. I had recently read von Franz's essay on the inferior function and also Gareth Hill's essay on "Men, the anima and the feminine" (1998), which at that time was unpublished, but described eight types of anima, using both the four function types (feeling, thinking, intuition, and sensation) and the two attitude types (introverted and extraverted) to arrive at his eight possibilities for the type of the anima, just as von Franz had done in establishing eight types of inferior function in her essay.

The husband in the dream who was given to gambling seemed to me to represent a less flattering side of my superior function, extraverted intuition. That seemed to fit the image of the husband as a gambler, someone who pursues possibilities and takes his energy into the world, leaving his introverted wife at home alone, not giving her much. But what did this have to do with me? I did not drink and gamble, but I was drawn to chase after possibilities to extend my life, even after it was time to go home and rest. The newest movie, the latest book, even the next dream one of my patients would bring to me, were causing me to transgress the limits of my personal comfort. For the first time, the importance of the extravert/introvert distinction really was brought home to me. If the husband represented my unbalanced extraversion, the clear message of the dream was that I was neglecting the introverted side of myself, represented by the forlorn and unfurnished anima figure, the Chinese laundress. The dream was saying, very specifically, that my introverted sensation was not getting anything from me. When I conveyed this conclusion to my analyst, she said, "I couldn't agree more."

I thought long and hard about how to rectify that state of affairs. Introverted sensation, I knew by this time, lives on the inside of the body, and seeks to keep it from getting overstimulated, overheated, too tired, too hungry, or too filled with the wrong foods, etc. I looked at what was happening with my patients in my developing psychotherapy practice. I was very excited to hear everything they were telling me, so much so that I was listening with bated breath, neglecting even to breathe properly. No wonder I came home to migraine headaches: I was retaining carbon dioxide. I made up my mind that I would have to attend to my breathing while listening to patients. This opened a series of spaces that allowed me to be aware of my body as I practiced therapy. I then noticed that in my body, as I attended to it, were clues to what was going on in my patient beyond anything dream interpretation could have revealed. If my stomach or chest felt tense, that was a signal that my patient was feeling 'uptight.' I found if I attended to these sensations, and eventually took up with the patient the feelings I was introjectively identifying, relevant material would emerge which would move the therapy forward. When I succeeded in getting the patient to express the feelings that my body had picked up, I wouldn't leave the session with a headache, and I would end the day of doing psychotherapy energized, not depleted. Apparently this method was a tonic for my inner life. A subsequent dream about the Chinese laundress found her happier: her husband had been taking her out for ice cream!

There is a tradition in Jungian analysis that the type problem becomes especially important when the inferior function starts to 'come up' as a topic in analysis, and that then one needs to pay very close attention to the type. Certainly that turned out to be true in my case. Once I knew that my anima was an introverted sensation type, and that I tended not just to be woefully inefficient in this area (as I had recognized as soon as I realized I was an intuitive) but also destructively neglectful (which I had not realized until I dreamed of the Chinese laundress whose husband was not providing for her), I became much more interested in the exact situation of all my functions, and gave a lot of thought to what in me was extraverted and what introverted.

It made sense that my intuition was extraverted and my thinking introverted. I was pretty sure, also, that my feeling, to the degree that it was differentiated at all, was extraverted. Since my sensation had turned out to be introverted, on the evidence of the Chinese laundress anima, I decided that the types alternated through the hierarchy of functions in their extraversion or introversion like a system of checks and balances. In my case, the typology looked like this:

Here at last, in a convincing way, were the four functions that Jung had indicated represented an oriented ego, the fourness suggesting an aspect of selfhood,

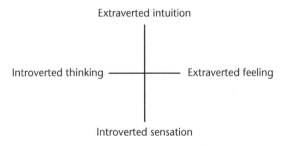

FIGURE 3.2 My mostly conscious orientation

which I eventually came to call, refusing the heavy Kantian implications of Jung's and Neumann's emphasis on 'ego,' the 'little-s' self. This was the typology of my everyday self-experience, the basis of my ongoing consciousness as a person having his own standpoint with its inevitable strengths and weaknesses.

There is something seductive about the sense of wholeness that comes with the number four, which Jung considers the archetypal number designating the 'big-S' Self. I was at least seven years into my analysis before the four functions that make up my typology were clear to me, and it was hard not to believe that I had somehow 'arrived,' from the standpoint of individuation, even though I was only thirty-four years old. Today this seems to me a bit like the naïvety of a relatively young person, but the inflation of self-discovery can threaten at any age. To assume that type development ends with the discovery of the inferior function, at which point the Self is constellated and from then on one is engaged in relating to the unconscious in its deeper aspect, can actually interfere with the development of consciousness. In reality, type remains an issue throughout the individuation process, although analysts do not always recognize this.

Type development

Not long after I had recognized the differentiation of my first four functions, including their alternation of extraversion and introversion, I came across Isabel Briggs Myers's book, *Gifts Differing* (1980), which contained five chapters on the dynamics of type development. I was particularly struck by the chapter "Good type development," which confirmed many of my own discoveries about my type development in therapy, which had indeed felt "good" to me. Elizabeth Murphy also takes up this theme in her book *The Developing Child* (1992, pp. 12–13), in which she points out that the superior and auxiliary functions may develop naturally in childhood, but that the tertiary and inferior functions normally do not appear until adulthood. I believe that my first analysis unblocked this normal developmental process in me. One of Myers's most important ideas, which she and her mother had culled from Jung, was that "For all the types appearing in practice, the principle holds good that besides the conscious main function there is also a relatively unconscious, auxiliary function which is in every respect different from the nature of the main function" (Jung, 1921/1923, p. 515, quoted in Myers, 1980, p. 19).

As Myers insisted:

> The operative words are "in every respect." If the auxiliary process differs from the dominant process in every respect, it *cannot* be introverted where the dominant process is introverted. It has to be extraverted if the dominant process is introverted, and introverted if the dominant process is extraverted.
>
> *Myers, 1980, p. 19*

Myers quotes two other passages from Jung that she feels support this interpretation. The first concerns the attitude type of the inferior, auxiliary, and tertiary functions in someone whose superior function is introverted thinking: "The relatively unconscious functions of feeling, intuition, and sensation, which counterbalance introverted thinking, are inferior in quality and have a primitive, extraverted character" (Jung, 1921/1923, p. 489, quoted in Myers, 1980, p. 20).

The second concerns the attitude of the other functions in someone whose superior function is extraverted: "when the mechanism of extraversion predominates . . . the most highly differentiated function has a constantly extraverted application, while the inferior functions are found in the service of introversion" (Jung, 1921/1923, p. 426, quoted in Myers, 1980, p. 20).

What I find most striking in these passages is Jung's assumption that only one function, the superior, is likely to be particularly differentiated. Therefore, the other functions all take on the unconscious character of the inferior function, and operate in a crudely compensatory way. That actually describes the undifferentiated way my unconscious compensated me before I went into analysis, but it was not particularly helpful to understanding the ways my function types sorted themselves out, as to attitude, once they started to become differentiated in analysis.

One way I was experiencing this differentiation was that I was becoming more particular, and not less, when I practiced psychotherapy, so that I often suffered if a person in my practice had introverted feeling that I could not take care of with my extraverted feeling. I devoted a lot of attention to this problem, and was particularly helped by a passage in von Franz's essay on the inferior function in *Lectures on Jung's Typology*. She had been asked the question, "Does an introverted feeling type experience introverted thinking, or is it always extraverted thinking?" She replied:

> If you are an introverted feeling type, you *can* also think introvertedly. You can naturally have all the functions all ways, but it won't be such a great problem, and there will not be much intensity of life in it. Jung has said that the hardest thing to understand is not your *opposite* type—if you have introverted feeling it *is* very difficult to understand an extraverted thinking type—but the same functional type with the other attitude! It would be most difficult for an introverted feeling type to understand an extraverted feeling type. There one feels that one does not know how the wheels go round in that person's head; one cannot feel one's way into it. Such people remain to a great extent a puzzle and are very difficult to understand spontaneously. Here the theory of types is tremendously important practically, for it is the only thing which can prevent one from completely misunderstanding certain people.
>
> *von Franz & Hillman, 1971/1998, p. 64*

I addressed the subject of type incompatibility in my first full-length essay on the role types play in transference, countertransference, and the therapeutic interaction (Beebe, 1984). In that publication, I recommended that analysts try to determine for each of a client's four functions whether that function is being used in an introverted or an extraverted way. I also suggested that the analyst should make an effort to figure out if he or she is deploying that function with the same, or with an opposite, attitude with respect to introversion and extraversion. It is on this basis, rather than whether one person in the therapeutic dyad has feeling as the superior function and the other thinking, or has an extraverted superior function when the other has an introverted superior function, that I established type compatibility, meaning whether there would be easy empathic understanding between the partners or whether there would be frequent clashes.

In that same essay, I looked at the other potential basis of incompatibility Jung discusses, and that Isabel Briggs Myers explores at great length in her book. That, for Jung, is whether the person's superior function is rational (his term for the evaluative functions, thinking and feeling) or irrational (his term for the perceptive functions, sensation and intuition). Because she was working out a type assessment instrument that focused on easily identifiable behaviors in the outer world, Myers felt that she had to get at the difference between rational and irrational modes of consciousness by looking at the individual's leading *extraverted* function, whether superior or auxiliary. On the Myers–Briggs Type Indicator (MBTI), this extraverted function is therefore given a letter code, J or P, to indicate whether it is a judging function (her way of referring to Jung's rational functions) or a perceiving function (her way of identifying Jung's irrational functions).

For me, Jung's approach is the more psychological. When assessing type compatibility between people, I prefer to look at each individual's vertical axis, or spine of consciousness, which connects the superior and inferior function, rather than privileging extraversion. Thus, I noted early on my incompatibility with an introverted feeling type companion (we were both 'P's according to the MBTI system, since his leading extraverted function was his auxiliary extraverted sensation). I found that our spines tended to cross: he often heard my perceptions for judgments, just as I mistook his judgments for perceptions, a source of many misunderstandings.

As the types became more real to me, I became ever more aware of the roles they were playing within my psyche. Following Jung (1926/1989, pp. 56–57; 1963, p. 179ff. and 173ff.), I associated the strong, effective superior function with the archetype of the hero. Tipped off by my dream about the father and son, I added the innovation that the auxiliary behaves like a parent, whether helpful or critical, the tertiary like a child, either divine or wounded, and thus in the language of Jungian psychology a *puer aeternus* or *puella aeterna*.

Puer aeternus means 'eternal boy,' or, as one of my patients called it, 'endless boy.' The term was taken by Jung from Ovid's knowing salutation to the child god Iacchus, who with his 'unconsumed youth,' figured in the Eleusinian mysteries of renewal: *tibi enim inconsumpta iuventa est, tu puer aeternus, tu formosissimus alto conspiceris caelo; tibi, cum sine cornibus adstas* (Metamorphoses, Book IV, lines 18–29 as found at http://www.sacred-texts.com/cla/ovid/meta/meta103.htm), the last part of which has been rendered by Rolfe Humphries (Ovid, 1955) as "Behold *puer aeternus* with his angel seeming face, But oh, those invisible horns!" This archetypal description of a personality style has been applied to a problem in adult development, that of the charming, promising, but ultimately unreliable character of certain eternally youthful and often very seductive men and women. Von Franz (1970) and Henderson

(1967), focusing on its role in masculine development, relate the excessive reliance on this archetype in daily interactions with others to the narcissistic mother complex of the immature man. But Hillman believes that the concept most generally "refers to that archetypal dominant which personifies or is in special relation with the transcendent spiritual powers of the collective unconscious" and is thus an aspect of the creativity in all of us (1989, p. 227). I am using this term, in tandem with *puella aeterna*, Latin for 'eternal girl,' to refer to the eternal youth in all of us, the brilliant but volatile side of ourselves that is by turns the seemingly immortal Prince or Princess and the helplessly vulnerable, wounded boy or girl.

There was also an analytical tradition, passed onto me by William Alex, who had been in the first training class at the C.G. Jung Institute in Zurich, that the anima or animus "carries the inferior function." In her writings, von Franz has associated the inferior function with the anima/animus, but somewhat less specifically than I would assert. She states:

> The inferior function is the door through which all the figures of the unconscious come into consciousness. Our conscious realm is like a room with four doors, and it is the fourth door by which the shadow, the animus or the anima, and the personification of the Self come in.

She later adds that "when one has become somewhat conscious of the shadow, the inferior function will give the animus or the anima figure a special quality" so that, if personified by a human being, the anima or animus will "very often appear as a person of the opposite function" (von Franz & Hillman, 1971/1998, pp. 67–68).

In my own work on myself and with patients, I most often found the inferior function, with its uncanny emotionality, to have the character of the anima or animus,[7] the 'other' within us, which becomes profoundly upset when its ideals are not met and nearly ecstatic when they are. It had been symbolized that way by my dreams of the Chinese laundress. I could then diagram my four functions again, showing the archetypes associated with them as I had encountered them.

My shift into Latin in naming the archetypes associated with the tertiary and inferior functions is deliberate. These functions, though still part of one's complement of ego-syntonic consciousnesses, are more archaic than the superior and auxiliary and present themselves in more classically 'archetypal' ways, having a god-like entitled quality to them, whereas the superior and auxiliary functions are more adapted to this time and place and more considerate of the perspectives of one's contemporaries.

This archetypal analysis of the first four functions provided the basis for the model of type I was able to present at the Chiron Conference for Jungian psychotherapists held at Ghost Ranch in Abiquiu, New Mexico in 1983, and to write up in my 1984 essay, "Psychological Types in Transference, Countertransference, and the Therapeutic Interaction." It has proved very helpful both to me and to

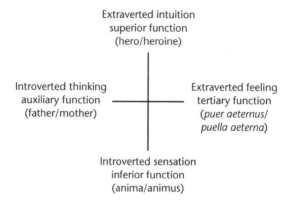

FIGURE 3.3 My orientation with archetypal complexes

others in clarifying how a well-differentiated consciousness might arrange itself in the course of individuation. We might note several features of this model.

1. The model asserts, with Jung and subsequent Jungians, that if the superior function is irrational the auxiliary will be rational, and vice versa.
2. It agrees with Myers and the MBTI counselors that if the superior function is introverted the auxiliary will be extraverted and vice versa.
3. The model specifies the tertiary function as opposite in attitude to the auxiliary just as the inferior is opposite in attitude to the superior.
4. Following the Jungian tradition, the model maintains that if the superior function is rational, the inferior will likewise be rational; if the superior function is irrational, the inferior function will also be irrational.
5. The tertiary function is represented as matching the auxiliary with respect to rationality or irrationality.
6. The model therefore defines two axes of consciousness, one between the superior and inferior functions (spine), the other between the auxiliary and tertiary functions (arms). If the spine is rational, the arms will be irrational and vice versa (see Figure 3.4).

I believe that this model makes sense of the way the types differentiate in some-one who is showing what Myers calls "good type development" and Jung would call individuating according to the law of his or her own being. It does not account for the many falsifications of type (Benziger, 1995) that involve substituting other functions out of a need to satisfy or defend against the type demands of an environment that is not facilitative of individuation.

Types of the shadow

At the 1983 conference were two analysts-in-training—Paul Watsky and Laura McGrew—whose comments proved very helpful to the growth of my understanding of type over the next decade. Watsky pointed out that Jung lists eight functions

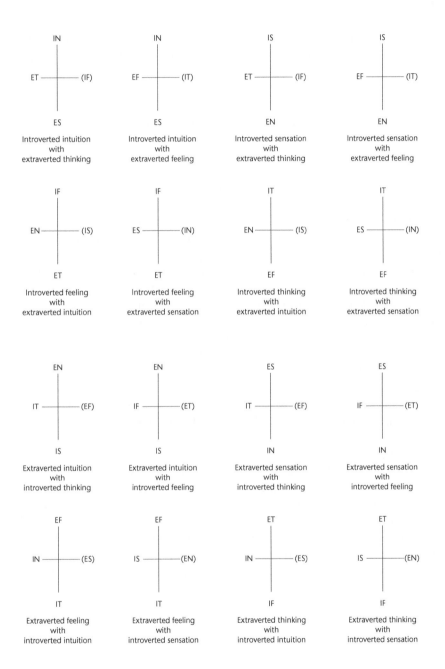

FIGURE 3.4 Configurations of consciousness corresponding to the 16 MBTI types (Code: E = extraverted; I = introverted; N = intuition; S = sensation; T = thinking; F = feeling. Tertiary functions are shown in parentheses. By convention, the four letter MBTI codes list the irrational function before the rational one, regardless of which is the superior and which the auxiliary; the P and J refer to whether the leading extraverted function is irrational (perceiving) or rational (judging)). See also Table 7.1.

of consciousness in *Psychological Types*. If someone succeeds in differentiating four of those functions to achieve the good type development of which Isabel Briggs Myers had spoken, Watsky said, it's as if the north 40 acres of their psychological field has been hoed; the person still needs to cultivate the other four functions: the south 40. These four were presumably in shadow. Laura McGrew came back to Ghost Ranch the next year with a sketch of a diagram indicating what the archetypes associated with the four functions in shadow might be. For the shadow of the mother, she had put "witch."

'Witch' is a deeply problematic term, which, as early as L. Frank Baum's *The Wonderful Wizard of Oz* (1900), was deconstructed for the better as referring to a woman in command of magic that was as potentially good as it was bad, and for a long time I preferred to use the term 'negative mother' to convey the quality of the shaming, blaming, limit-setting female parent. But I have decided that 'witch' with its freight of negative connotations gets at the specific characteristic of this position of shadow in women (and some men). Like all the shadow archetypes, the witch 'fights dirty' to defend the personality. She uses her capacity to cast spells that immobilize in an underhanded way, but this is a survival consciousness that resides in the shadow that can be used to stop others in their tracks when they are threatening the personality or its values. In terms of gender politics, the witch uses her feminine authority in a way that can be extremely paralyzing to the anima of a man. In a man's psyche, the shadow side of the good father would be the *senex*, which exerts the same sinister limit-setting control when he 'pulls rank,' and which can similarly paralyze a woman's animus. I have since learned that the negative 'witch' and the *senex* can appear in both genders as a kind of "withering authority" (Frey, 2011) that can be both dogmatic and mean. And I have often come to see the wisdom in the limit-setting of these archetypes, despite their initially sinister presentations.

As I recall, Laura McGrew and I agreed that the shadow of the *puer aeternus* carrying the tertiary function had to be the trickster. Neither she nor I was satisfied with designations for the shadow side of the hero and the shadow side of the anima/animus. It was clear that the shadow archetype carries the same function of consciousness as its ego-syntonic counterpart, but with the opposite attitude with respect to extraversion and introversion.

Here, then, was my shadow, in terms of the types of consciousness involved:

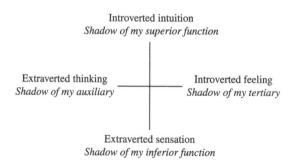

Introverted intuition
Shadow of my superior function

Extraverted thinking   Introverted feeling
Shadow of my auxiliary   *Shadow of my tertiary*

Extraverted sensation
Shadow of my inferior function

FIGURE 3.5 Orientation of my shadow

I set it as my task to learn how this shadow was actually expressed in my dreams and my outer behavior and, in this way, I was able to do some of the internal work Paul Watsky suggested still needed to be done by someone who laid a claim to "good type development." I then began to look closely at others as well as myself, and I found I was able to answer Laura McGrew's question empirically, by noting the characteristics of dream figures who seemed to display the negative of our preferred typologies. This work of observation of self and others occupied me for another seven years, so that it was not until 1990 that I had finally come up with the following model to describe my shadow in terms of a complement of consciousnesses that were more negative and destructive in their archetypal functioning than the consciousnesses I had identified as mine thus far in the course of my analysis:

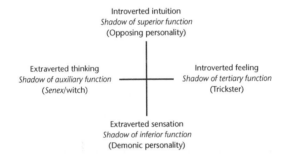

FIGURE 3.6 Orientation of my shadow with archetypal complexes

There is much in the Jungian literature already about *senex*[8] and witch and trickster, just as there is much about father and mother and *puer aeternus*. I introduced the archetypal roles I describe here as 'opposing personality' and 'demonic personality,' and this introduction can be found in the second revised edition of Murray Stein's *Jungian Analysis*, in the chapter I wrote with Donald Sandner, "Psychopathology and analysis," in a section entitled "The role of psychological type in possession" (Sandner & Beebe, 1995).

The most unexpected discovery was the archetype I call the opposing personality, which is characterized by behaviors that may be described in the language of character pathology: oppositional, paranoid, passive-aggressive, and avoidant. This is a shadow that is very hard to see in oneself (it seems to fall in the blind spot of the superior function) and very easy to project onto another person, especially a person of the opposite sex. The archetype of the opposing personality often appears in dreams as a contrasexual figure, but, unlike the anima, the opposing personality is antagonistic to the ego rather than helpful in connecting it to the needs of the Self. Classical Jungians have sometimes identified this figure that opposes, criticizes, and seduces the ego as the 'negative' animus or anima, but this intuitive shorthand ignores the real type difference between the opposing personality and the anima or animus. In adopting the rather clinical sounding term, 'opposing personality,' rather than a name such as 'the Adversary' or 'the Antagonist' that has a more dignified and archetypal connotation, I have tried to convey the unconscious and undeclared quality with which this archetype usually operates. It is often more like a symptom than like a dashing enemy on a black horse.

In associating to a dream figure, it is important to try to establish the figure's psychological type, which is often surprisingly easy to determine. At the Ghost Ranch conference, I called attention to Jung's foreword to the Argentine edition of *Psychological Types* (1936/1971, p. xiv) in which he had emphasized that the theory of psychological types should be used not as a way of classifying people but for "sorting out the empirical material" that comes up in the course of a therapeutic analysis. The method of analysis that results has the advantage of enabling a patient to see where a particular complex lives in the psyche.

The opposing personality lived in me as a tendency to become detached and avoidant in a schizoid way in relation to certain kinds of situations that I didn't immediately know how to handle. This came up in my practice as a tendency to 'tune out' in the face of affects I didn't know how to deal with. It was as if my introverted intuition was working in this shadowy way to find some kind of image that would make sense of the emotion for me, but mostly my patients experienced me at such moments as leaving them. As I meditated on that behavior, I realized it was a defense of the self I had often used in my life—to the extent that some of my friends in college had complained, after a summer of putting up with my withdrawn inattentiveness, that I had become more 'John-ish' than ever. Until I decided, however, to look hard at the shadow side of my superior function, an extraverted intuition that many had experienced as extraordinarily 'present' to them, I never took such complaints seriously. Instead, as is so often the case with a shadow function, I tended to project the difficulty within me onto other people whose avoidant traits were particularly pronounced. In my practice, I seemed to keep encountering a certain kind of introverted intuitive woman who I felt would not 'come clean' with her intuitions, so that I would experience her as being stubbornly resistant to the therapy. Only gradually did I come to recognize that the oppositional woman was even more characteristic of a side of myself, and that to some extent I had been projectively identifying her onto introverted intuitive clients who might have certain "hooks" to catch the projection.

The trickster was the one aspect of my shadow that I had worked on fairly early on in my analysis. However, I had not thought of my trickster as having a type. It had, however, often been projected onto difficult male or female analysands whose intense subjectivity seemed constantly to undercut my efforts to help them with psychological understanding. These were analysands who might have fit the diagnostic criteria for borderline personality disorder, which I have elsewhere discussed as a "primary ambivalence toward the Self" (Beebe, 1988), but the issue that kept coming up for me was the degree to which my feeling was no match for the patient's. In the service of being a good doctor, I was trying to use extraverted feeling in a sincere, compassionate way that begged the hostility the patients were directing toward me. As one man put it to me, "Western medicine, Eastern too if you consider Buddhism, is based on compassion. When people are compassionate toward me, I become this bitch."

It was in this feeling context that I came more personally to understand the difference between extraversion and introversion. I had concentrated on developing my extraverted feeling, since I recognized that as a relatively weak function in myself, and since this consciousness was carried in me by the archetype of the *puer aeternus*, I could leap to unusual heights of empathic compassion, privileging the other person's feeling above my own. I would, however, plunge to the depths of despair when the person I was dealing with abandoned my feeling for their own and did not show any gratitude for the compassion I was dispensing. Gradually, I learned that this was a normal difference between extraversion and introversion. In meeting a situation that involves another person, extraversion moves to create a shared experience, by reaching out to 'merge' in some way with the other person (Shapiro & Alexander, 1975), whereas introversion steps back from the experience to see if it 'matches' an archetype within that carries an a priori understanding of what an experience like this is supposed to consist of. As I learned to honor my introverted feeling, which in the manner of a trickster did not feel bound by medical and Christian cultural expectations, I learned to make statements such as "I'm not sure I can work with you if it's going to be this negative." I had realized that the bullying I had been receiving from my 'borderline' patients did not accord with my introverted feeling sense of what a mutually respectful medical treatment ought to be like, and, once I had grasped the validity of this perspective, I was able to assert it in a way which, though it was a manipulation of the transference, enabled my difficult patients and me to work together in an atmosphere of more regard, if not for each other, which would be extraverted feeling, at least for the value of what we were trying to accomplish. I found my patients could accept this, even though they still had much ambivalence, envy, and negativity to work through in their actual experience of me as a person.

The *senex* extraverted thinking was particularly hard to see as a part of myself. I had thoroughly projected this onto my father, who did affect a stentorian, nineteenth-century personality that was aloof and, to my ear, somewhat pompous. I always imagined myself to be more laid-back. But there was a side of me, too, that could be quite arrogant and dogmatic in the way it delivered its opinions and interpretations. This was my *senex* extraverted thinking.

In coming to terms with my demonic extraverted sensation, I felt that I was encountering the problem of evil in myself. My colleague Herbert Wiesenfeld, an introverted feeling type whose anima grappled with ideas, finally decided that 'evil' in Jungian psychology refers to the quality of being undermined. The demonic personality, then, is that part of ourselves that operates in the shadow to undermine others and ourselves. Certainly in my own case that is extraverted sensation. My body language is often the opposite of what I mean to convey. My relation to physical geography is such that, when trying to find my way along an unfamiliar route, the opposite of where I think I should be going is almost always the correct way. But most importantly, I sometimes misjudge in therapy the relative distance from consciousness of an unconscious complex and assume, with my optimistic extraverted intuition, that the client is ready to benefit from openly discussing something that the client is, in fact, not ready to look at yet. This miscalculation of psychological reality can lead to interventions that shock the client and, for a time, undermine the therapy. Occasionally, such interventions can also enliven a therapy that has become too polite, reminding us that, just as Lucifer is the light-bringer, the demon is sometimes a daimon.

As I surveyed my shadow, I could see that it too carried 'consciousness,' but consciousness used in antagonistic, paradoxical, depreciating, and destructive ways. The archetypal complexes of the shadow could sometimes move a stuck situation, but they could also be quite hurtful to others and myself. Specifying these defensive consciousnesses was, however, helpful in getting a handle on them and developing a measure of choice in how I deployed them.

By this point, I was convinced I had been able to locate all eight functions of consciousness in myself and to see how the archetypes that were carrying them operated to structure my dealings with others. (See Figure 3.7. MBTI users may want to see also Table 7.1 (pp. 123–124), which shows how the types of consciousness are distributed archetypally for each of the 16 MBTI types.)

Conscious		
Hero/heroine	*area of strength and pride*	Organizes adaptation, initiates individuation
Father/mother	*area of fostering and protecting*	Nurtures and protects others
Puer/puella	*area of immaturity and play*	Endearing, vulnerable child who copes by improvising
Anima/animus	*area of embarrassment and idealization*	Gateway to the unconscious
Unconscious		
Opposing personality	*area of frustration and challenge*	Defends by offending, seducing, avoiding; self-critic
Senex/**witch**	*area of limit-setting and control*	Defends by refusing, belittling, inactivating; sets limits
Trickster	*area of manipulation and paradox*	Mischievous, creates double binds, circumvents obstacles
Demonic/daimonic	*area of undermining and redemption*	Undermines self and others; creates opportunities to develop integrity

FIGURE 3.7   Archetypes and the areas of personality they pattern

What I then realized would be necessary was a validation of this eight-function, eight-archetype model as generally applicable. Although I experimented with it often in clinical situations, seeing the figures in my patient's dreams as so many personifications of typological part-personalities, which could not only be typed but matched to an archetype within the scheme I had developed, I realized I would need a more generally available arena where the types and archetypes could be readily visualized by others. This came through movies, at least those that could be recognized as personal expressions of an auteur director putting out his or her own complexes for an audience to see. I found that my model worked particularly well as a way to analyze films (by then already a topic of intense cultural scrutiny) and I have recorded the results of this kind of analysis in numerous lectures and in two essays that analyze *The Wizard of Oz* (revised as Chapter 5 in this volume) and Woody Allen's *Husbands and Wives* (reproduced as Chapter 14).

The eight-function model I have developed (see Figure 3.8), as an "addition and extension" to Jung's analytical psychology (Henderson, 1991), asks that we re-examine some of the earlier findings that our field made about type using a four-function model. For instance, Hillman's description of "inferior feeling," cited earlier in this chapter, might better be understood as a description of demonic introverted feeling in an introverted thinking type. My dream about the 'father' brandishing a butcher knife chasing his 'son' around the dining room table, though it opened me up to the idea of the 'father' and *puer* as referring to the more and less developed types on the axis of my auxiliary and tertiary functions, is actually such a shadowy situation, with an obvious reference to Saturn's sickle, that it is more likely a depiction of *senex* vs trickster. (At the time of the dream, I had not developed my introverted feeling enough to notice that the young man my unconscious selected to serve as the 'son' was actually a very provocative person, who used his

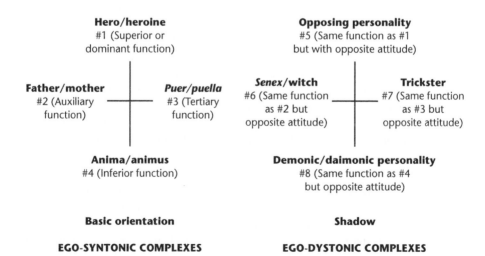

FIGURE 3.8 Archetypal complexes carrying the eight functions

introverted feeling in a manipulative way, thus occasioning the *senex* response in the unconscious.) I now see my early, somewhat faulty, interpretation of the dream as a 'creative misreading'—one of those helpful misunderstandings which not infrequently serve to advance our thinking (Bloom, 1985).

Let us close with a look back at the inferior function and, implicitly, its demonic shadow, in the following passage from von Franz:

> The little open door of each individual's inferior function is what contributes to the sum of collective evil in the world. You could observe that very easily in Germany when the devil slowly took over the situation in the Nazi movement. Every German I knew at that time who fell for Nazism did so on account of his inferior function. The feeling type got caught by the stupid arguments of the party doctrine; the intuitive type got caught by his dependence on money. He could not give up his job and did not see how he could deal with the money problem, so he had to stay in it despite the fact that he did not agree, and so on. The inferior function was in each personal realm the door where some of this collective evil could accumulate. Or, you could say that each one who had not worked on his inferior function contributed to this general disaster—in a small way—but the sum of millions of inferior functions constitutes an enormous devil! Propaganda against the Jews was very cleverly made up in that respect. For example, the Jews were insulted as being destructive intellectuals, which completely convinced all the feeling types—a projection of inferior thinking. Or they were accused of being reckless moneymakers; that completely convinced the intuitive, for they were his inferior sensation, and now one knew where the devil was. The propaganda used the ordinary suspicions that people had against others on account of their inferior function. So you can say that behind each individual the fourth function is not just a little kind of deficiency: the sum of these is really responsible for a tremendous amount of trouble.
>
> *von Franz in von Franz & Hillman, 1971/1998, p. 82*

What she is describing here is a relation between the inferior function and a demonic function that tests the integrity of the inferior function. To the degree that the inferior function has not been taken up as a problem by the individual in the course of the development of his consciousness, it is no match for the demonic aspect of the unconscious, rather like the Chinese laundress in my dream who has no power to stop her husband from spending all his money drinking and gambling. At the time I had that dream, I felt the husband represented my own superior function of extraverted intuition; now I would say he represents a much more shadowy aspect of me, my extraverted sensation (which, like the husband in the dream, is usually not even seen). At the time I had the dream, I felt it was necessary for him to take better care of her, i.e. that I should take better care of my anima. But a healthier anima would also have the integrity to stand up to him, bringing her integrity to bear upon his problem of character (Beebe, 1998).

As the notion of good type development moves, both in MBTI counseling and in Jungian analysis, toward a 'whole type' eight-function model,[9] in which each of Jung's eight types of consciousness is represented within a picture of the person's consciousness that includes both ego-syntonic functions and functions in shadow, the ethical aspects of this development will become ever more evident. Gradually, perhaps, consciousness will realize its potential to become conscience.

Notes

1 This passage from *The Correspondence of Sigmund Freud and Ernest Jones 1908–1939* (ed. Paskauskas) is cited by Jung's faultfinding biographer Frank McLynn (1996, p. 267), who devotes much of his chapter on "Psychological Types" to the objections that have been raised to Jung's contribution within depth psychology.

2 For a comparison of Gardner's multiple intelligences and Jung's functions of consciousness, see Kirk Thompson's (1985) review of Howard Gardner's *Frames of Mind: The Theory of Multiple Intelligences* (1983). Thompson found strong analogies between Gardner's seven "intelligences" and seven of Jung's eight "function types of consciousness" (the Jungian function for which he could not find an analogue in Gardner's system was introverted intuition). This article is cited in Gardner (1999).

3 For a discussion of Damasio's work in relation to analytical psychology, see Tresan (1996).

4 In his teaching at the C. G. Jung Institute of San Francisco, John Perry often criticized this type of Jungian dogma (personal communication, 1970).

5 Anima is the Latin word for soul, which is defined by Jung in *Psychological Types* as referring to "a definitely demarcated function-complex that is best characterized as a 'personality'" (1921/1923, p. 588). For Jung, anima as a feminine noun refers to the contrasexual character of the inner, subjective attitude in a man, which is often symbolized in dreams by a feminine figure and in the man's outer behavior by the kind of soulful opinionatedness about woman's obligations to men that we now recognize as sexist. My own experience of anima has been that she personifies moods, is concerned with integrity, and is passionate about causes, which she takes personally. For many years, the jazz singer Billie Holiday was an anima figure for me.

6 I have addressed the development of thinking about type in both the Jungian and the MBTI movements in Chapter 10.

7 Animus, which is Latin for mind or spirit, is often used differently in Jungian psychology from its standard English dictionary meaning of 'hostile opinion,' to represent the spirit of a woman that helps her to focus her self-experience and express it in the world. Despite excellent discussions of the animus and its development by Emma Jung (1957/1985) and Ann Ulanov (1971), there is still a tendency even among analytical psychologists to depreciate the woman's sometimes-severe spirit as a form of competitiveness and spite, confounding it with the 'opposing personality' that I will discuss later in this chapter.

8 "*Senex* is the Latin word for 'old man.' We find it still contained within our words *senescence, senile,* and *senator* . . . As natural, cultural and psychic processes mature, gain order, consolidate and wither, we witness the specific formative effects of the *senex* . . . Longings for superior knowledge, imperturbability, magnanimity express *senex* feelings as does intolerance for that which crosses one's systems and habits . . . The temperament of the *senex* is cold, which can also be expressed as distance" (Hillman, 1989, p. 208).

9 For the definition and development of Jung's original eight function-attitude model within the wider type community represented by the Association for Psychological Type International, see Thompson (1996), Geldart (1998) Myers and Kirby (2000), Clark (2000), Haas, McAlpine and Hartzler (2001), and Chapter 10 in this book.

References

Baum, L. F. (1900). *The wonderful wizard of Oz*. Chicago, IL: George M. Hill Co.

Beebe, J. (1984). Psychological types in transference, countertransference, and the therapeutic interaction. In N. Schwartz-Salant & M. Stein, *Transference/countertransference* (pp. 147–161). Wilmette, IL: Chiron Publications.

Beebe, J. (1988). Primary ambivalence toward the Self. In N. Schwartz-Salant & M. Stein (Eds.), *The borderline personality in analysis* (pp. 97–127). Wilmette, IL: Chiron Publications.

Beebe, J. (1992). *Integrity in depth*. College Station, TX: Texas A&M University Press.

Beebe, J. (1998). Toward a Jungian analysis of character. In A. Casement (Ed.), *The post-Jungians today: Key papers in contemporary analytical psychschology* (pp. 53–66). London: Routledge.

Benziger, K. (1995). *Falsification of type*. Dillon, CO: KBA.

Binet, A. (1903). *L'Etude expérimental de l'intelligence*. Paris: Schleicher.

Bloom, H. (1985). *A map of misreading*. New York: Oxford University Press.

Brachfeld, O. (1954). Gelenkte Tagträume als Hilfsmittel der Psychotherapie, *Zeitschrift für Psychotherapie, IV*, 79–93.

Cambray, J. (2006). Towards the feeling of emergence. *Journal of Analytical Psychology, 51*(1), 1–20.

Clark, P. (2000). Work and the 8-function model. *Bulletin of Psychological Type, 23*(7).

Corsini, R. J. (2002). *The dictionary of psychology*. Hove, England: Brunner-Routledge.

Damasio, A. (2005). *Descartes' error: Emotion, reason and the human brain*. New York: Penguin Books.

Dennett, D. C. (1991). *Consciousness explained*. New York: Little Brown & Company.

Edinger, E. F. (1973). *Ego and archetype*. New York: Penguin Books.

Edinger, E. F. (1984). *The creation of consciousness*. Toronto: Inner City.

Ellenberger, H. (1970). *The discovery of the unconscious*. New York: Basic Books.

Fenichel, O. (1945). *The psychoanalytic theory of neurosis*. New York: W. W. Norton & Co.

Frey, A. (2011). Beebe's contributions to type: The basics. Presentation to the Bay Area Association for Psychological Type, Millbrae, CA., September 10, 2011.

Gardner, H. (1983). *Frames of mind: The theory of multiple intelligences*. New York: Basic Books.

Gardner, H. (1999) *Intelligence reframed: Multiple intelligences for the 21st Century*. New York: Basic Books.

Geldart, W. (1998). Katharine Downing Myers and whole MBTI type: An interview. *The Enneagram and the MBTI: An electronic journal*, http://tap3x.net/EMBTI/j4kmyers.html, (February 1998).

Giegerich, W. (1975). Ontogeny = phylogeny? A fundamental critique of Erich Neumann's analytical psychology. *Spring* 1975, 110–129.

Glover, E. (1950). *Freud or Jung*. Evanston, IL: Northwestern University Press.

Haas, L., McAlpine, R., & Hartzler, M. (2001). *Journey of understanding: MBTI® interpretation using the eight Jungian functions*. Palo Alto, CA: Consulting Psychologists Press.

Henderson, J. (1967). *Thresholds of initiation*. Middletown, CT: Wesleyan University Press.

Henderson, J. (1991). C. G. Jung's psychology: Additions and extensions. *Journal of Analytical Psychology*, *36*(4), 429–442.

Hill, G. (1998). Men, the anima, and the feminine. *San Francisco Jung Institute Library Journal*, *17*(3), 49–61.

Hillman, J. (1972). *The myth of analysis: Three essays in archetypal psychology*. Evanston, IL: Northwestern University Press.

Hillman, J. (1989). *A blue fire*. T. Moore (Ed.). New York: Harper Perennial.

Humphrey, N. (1992). *A history of the mind: Evolution and the birth of consciousness*. New York: Simon and Schuster.

James, W. (1904). Does "consciousness" exist? *Journal of Philosophy, Psychology, and Scientific Methods*, *1*, 477–491.

Jung, C. G. (1914/1972). On psychological understanding. In *Cw 3* (pp. 179–193).

Jung, C. G. (1921/1923). *Psychological types*. (H. G. Baynes, Trans.). New York: Harcourt & Brace.

Jung, C. G. (1926/1989). *Analytical psychology: Notes of the seminar given in 1925*, W. McGuire (Ed.). Princeton, NJ: Princeton University Press.

Jung, C. G. (1934/1997). *The visions seminars*. C. Douglas (Ed.). Princeton, NJ: Princeton University Press.

Jung, C. G. (1936/1971). Foreword to the Argentine edition of Psychological Types. In *Cw 6* (pp. xiv–xv).

Jung, C. G. (1948/1960). General aspects of dream psychology. In *Cw 8* (pp. 237–280).

Jung, C. G. (1957/1977). The Houston films. In W. McGuire & R. F. C. Hull (Eds.) *C. G. Jung speaking* (pp. 276–352). Princeton, NJ: Princeton University Press.

Jung, C. G. (1958/1970). Fragments from a talk with students (recorded by Marian Bayes). *Spring* 1970, 177–181.

Jung, C. G. (1963). *Memories, dreams, reflections*. New York: Pantheon.

Jung, C. G. (2009). *The red book: Liber novus*. S. Shamdasani (Ed.), M. Kyburz, J. Peck, & S. Shamdasani (Trans.). New York: W. W. Norton.

Jung, E. (1957/1985). *Animus and anima*. (H. Nagel & C. F. Baynes, Trans.) Thompson, CT: Spring Publications.

Kohut, H. (1959/1978). Introspection, empathy, and psychoanalysis: An examination of the relationship between mode of observation and theory. In P. H. Ornstein (Ed.), *The search for the Self*, vol. 1 (pp. 205–232). New York: International Universities Press.

McLynn, F. (1996). *Carl Gustav Jung: A biography*. New York: St. Martins.

Murphy, E. (1992). *The developing child*. Palo Alto, CA: Davies Black Publishing Co.

Myers, I. B. (with Myers, P. B.) (1980). *Gifts differing: Understanding personality type*. Palo Alto, CA: Consulting Psychologists Press.

Myers, K. & Kirby, L. (2000). *Introduction to type dynamics and development*. Palo Alto, CA: Consulting Psychologists Press.

Neumann, E. (1954). *The origins and history of consciousness*. Princeton, NJ: Princeton University Press.

Ovid. (1955). *Metamorphoses*. (R. Humphries, Trans.). Bloomington, IN: Indiana University Press.

Paskauskas, A. (Ed.). (1993). *The correspondence of Sigmund Freud and Ernest Jones 1908–1939*. Cambridge, MA: Harvard University Press.

Rogers, C. & Truax, C. B. (1967). The therapeutic condition's antecedent to change: A theoretical view. In C. Rogers (Ed.), *The therapeutic relationship and its impact* (pp. 97–108). Madison, WI: University of Wisconsin Press.

Sandner, D. & Beebe, J. (1995). Psychopathology and analysis. In M. Stein (Ed.) *Jungian analysis* (pp. 294–334). LaSalle, IL: Open Court.

Shapiro, K. J. & Alexander, I. E. (1975). *The experience of introversion: An integration of phenomenological, empirical, and Jungian approaches.* Durham, NC: Duke University Press.

Thompson, H. L. (1996). *Jung's function-attitudes explained.* Watkinsville, GA: Wormhole Publishing.

Thompson, K. (1985). Cognitive and analytical psychology. *The San Francisco Jung Institute Library Journal, 5*(4), 40–64.

Tresan, D. (1996). Jungian metapsychology and neurobiological theory. *Journal of Analytical Psychology, 41*(3), 399–436.

Ulanov, A. B. (1971). *The feminine in Jungian psychology and in Christian theology.* Evanston, IL: Northwestern University Press.

von Franz, M. L. (1970). *Puer aeternus.* New York: Spring Publications.

von Franz, M. L. & Hillman, J. (1971/1998). *Lectures on Jung's typology.* Woodstock, CT: Spring Publications.

Wheelwright, J. (1982). Psychological types. In *Saint George and the dandelion* (pp. 53–77). San Francisco, CA: C. G. Jung Institute of San Francisco.

4

ARCHETYPAL ASPECTS OF MASCULINE ADAPTATION

Prologue: masculine psychology

In his book *Proust Was a Neuroscientist*, which links the recent findings of brain researchers to the way artists in the nineteenth and early twentieth century recorded the phenomena of consciousness, the journalist Jonah Lehrer (2008) quotes the early stream of consciousness novelist Virginia Woolf's description of her own mind. It was, she said, "very erratic, very undependable—now to be found in a dusty road, now in a scrap of newspaper in the street, now in a daffodil in the sun." Lehrer adds that "At any given moment she seemed to be scattered in a million little pieces" (p. 169) and tells us that:

> Woolf's art searched for whatever held us together. What she found was the self, "the essential thing." Although the brain is just a loom of electric neurons, Woolf realized that the self makes us whole. It is the fragile source of our identity, the author of our consciousness. If the self didn't exist, then we wouldn't exist. "One must have a whole in one's mind," Woolf said, "fragments are unendurable."
>
> *Woolf, 1989, p. 110, cited in Lehrer, 2008, p. 169*

It would be hard for me to imagine a man describing his mind this way, and if he did, I would assume he was not describing his experience of his *masculine* mind.

The masculine mind, as I have encountered it in men who have submitted their mental processes to me for therapeutic analysis, organizes itself according to separate modules of identity, each for a time lived as if it were his only self—that is, identified with, defended, and reified into a role by which the man who latches onto it tries to live—unless of course the man is preferring to dissolve his mind in a Dionysian way with the aid of alcohol, drugs, music, a sex partner, or even a mood, in which case his femininity emerges to release the disorganized flow that Woolf describes, though often without her accompanying ambition to find a self that will make the flux cohere.

For this reason, the categorical nature of Jung's psychology of the unconscious has often been one of its most compelling features for men. In the archetypal complexes that Jung was the first to identify as ingredients of personality, a man can recognize his part personalities—the roles and values that he might choose to take up when try-ing to adapt to living in the world in a masculine way. Men often focus their efforts in therapy on living up to one particular role. Part of the job of the psychotherapist in that situation is to see how the patient's psyche is responding to his unconscious decision to disregard the other identities and values that are available to him.

In this chapter, I name some of the archetypes that, in previous writings (Beebe, 1981, 1985, 2007), I have identified as key to the development of consciousness in both sexes, but here I emphasize them not as they more often appear in the psy-ches of women, that is, as different qualities of energy within a comfortably fluid holistic psyche, partly content to remain in a somewhat unprecipitated state, but rather as the more rigidly bounded roles with which men may be identified. To be sure, identifications with particular roles, for instance that of mother, do also occur in women, but more often, in our culture at least, it is on the masculine side of her personality that a woman will feel most driven to take up a particular role to the exclusion of the rest of her identity. In cultures that are not as patriarchal as ours, the need for men to concentrate on a single role might seem to be less urgent. Most cultures, however, given the central importance granted to the ways women can provide nurturance and shelter, are far more matriarchal than they may at first seem, and the women in them already know what they are supposed to do. The problem any culture faces, therefore, to paraphrase Margaret Mead, is finding interesting roles for the men. A similar search can govern the inner world of a man in analytical psychotherapy, where the archetypes tend to present themselves as options for ways of being in the world. As the reader explores the different arche-types that I present here, she or he should keep in mind that the role each implies could seem to some men like just the way a man is supposed to be.

The hero

We might start, as the study of archetypes usually does, with the hero. "The hero," Jung (1989) tells us, "is the symbol of the greatest value recognized by us" (p. 57). In our culture, with its patriarchal system of education modeled upon the Greeks and Romans, perhaps the greatest values imparted to men are achievement and responsibility. These standards cannot be met by someone who lacks autonomy, accuracy, and self-control—aspects of self-reliant agency that are exemplified in the myths of the hero (Segal, 1990). Stories of the hero continue to have wide appeal in our culture and to exert profound psychological influence. From the standpoint of depth psychology, the hero is the archetypal role model for ego-identity, described for his fellow psychoanalysts by Erik Erikson as "the accrued experience of the ego's ability to integrate all identifications with the vicissitudes of the libido, with the aptitudes developed out of endowment, and with the opportunities offered in social roles" (Erikson, 1963, p. 261).

What is significant for the psychology of a man's development as we encounter it in analytical work is how often the image of the hero will appear in the psyche of a client beginning to consolidate his identity out of the lost state of mind that has caused him to seek treatment. One of my clients first came to me when he was 19; he was recovering from a brief psychotic breakdown in college. His need to develop his own psyche separately from the excessive superego expectations of his parents soon became a theme of the therapy. After the first few months of our work, he dreamed he was at a political rally where a new leader was chosen by the vote of those present. After he had this dream, his life changed and it was almost impossible to believe that the patient had ever been psychotic. For years thereafter he consistently displayed a strong, decisively masculine ego, and soon moved forward into high levels of achievement, marriage, and a successful professional career. The hero figure, elected by the political party in his dream, evidently went on to take office in his psyche: in retrospect, it was the image of the emergence of ego strength in this patient.

Jungian theory offers a way of understanding the hero figure in a man's psyche that is even more precise: the hero symbolizes what Jung calls the *dominant* function of consciousness and is thus an image of the cutting edge of the ego. For Jung (1939/1959), "Consciousness needs a centre, an ego to which something is conscious" (¶506). But this is not all. Will is perhaps the most characteristic attribute of the ego once it assumes its place at the center of consciousness, and I could certainly see that strong will emerge in my patient, who effectively took charge of his therapy after having this dream, by asking me to hurry up, be more concise, get to the point, and so on.

There are, according to Jung, various functions of consciousness that the ego may decide to differentiate to varying degrees in the course of deploying the will. These ego functions, specified in Jung's theory of psychological types, can be named *thinking*, *feeling*, *sensation*, and *intuition*, and each can be deployed in either *extraverted* or *introverted* ways (Jung, 1921/1971, ¶¶556–671). My patient's leading function, once the election held in his unconscious fostered its emergence in his actual life as his ego's 'chief executive,' was extraverted thinking.

The patient, like many another extraverted thinking type, became adept at planning out his life. At first I feared he was replacing his formerly weak, depressed ego with a set of manic defenses, according to a pattern of bipolarity, but years of subsequent contact with the patient confirmed that he was simply taking charge of his own life. His planning, which even included directing his therapist's approach to his treatment, was part of assuming his own rightful use of his superior function. In time, he was also able to develop his feeling side in a normal way. When I last saw him in his early thirties, he was no longer overbearing at all and could express appropriate gratitude for the work we had done when he was a college student. His ability to take heroic precedence over me in directing the therapy permitted him to develop a dominant ego that would free him from his parents and allow him to become his own man.

The *puer aeternus*

How different this client was from another young man that I saw, also a college student who had suffered a brief psychotic episode, and who throughout our work was much more identified with the archetype that Jung and his followers call the *puer aeternus*. This name, which in Latin means eternal youth, was used in antiquity to refer to the child god Iacchus in the Eleusinian Mysteries, who was identified with the new birth these rites promised to individuals who partook in them. Iacchus was a younger version of Bacchus (Dionysos) with overtones of Cupid (Eros). In our time, the term *puer aeternus* has staged a return in Jungian psychology to indicate a man who "remains too long in adolescent psychology" (von Franz, 1970, p. 1) and, although charming and promising, is ultimately unreliable.

When I first saw him, around the time he was about to turn 20, this patient was rather clearly identified with the high-minded, godlike side of this archetype. He was obviously highly intelligent and well read and sported a verbal style that recalled the nineteenth century English romantics. He looked like a young Lord Byron, and his air, in the outpatient clinic where we met for psychotherapy, was imperious and dismissive. Far from trying to direct what I had to say, as my heroic patient had done, he simply didn't listen to it. I had the sense that he felt superior to anything I had to offer and that he found the ritual of psychotherapy a bit ridiculous. He spoke of getting 'PhDs' and having romantic relationships with both men and women as if all that were easy. In fact, he was a college dropout with a budding homosexual orientation and no relationship or job. He dreamed that we were walking together on the clouds above Mt. Olympus. My job, with this patient, was to deal with his *inflation*, which was getting in the way of authentic ego development.

The *puer aeternus* we meet in clinical practice is someone who trumpets "a kind of false individualism" (von Franz, 1970, pp. 1–3). Since he is special, he sees "no need to adapt." He evinces an:

> arrogant attitude towards other people due to both an inferiority complex and false feelings of superiority. Such people also usually have great difficulty in finding the right kind of job, for whatever they find is never quite right or quite what they wanted.

In relationships, too, the right partner is never found, because no one can match the ideal person the patient is looking for:

> There is always a 'but' which prevents marriage or any kind of definite commitment. This all leads to a form of neurosis . . . the "provisional life," that is, the strange attitude and feeling that one is *not yet* in real life.
>
> *von Franz, 1970, pp. 1–3*

Whatever one undertakes is accompanied by the feeling that it is not the real thing, and therefore there can be no real commitment to it.

One way to help such a person is to engage his feelings about the therapeutic relationship. In my patient's case, getting him to express his anger at having to be in therapy at all helped to ground the work and move it in the direction of real adaptation. It turned out that he was irritated with the power imbalance of therapy and that this was why he was treating me with such disdain. Our work finally addressed this reality when I insisted that he show a measure of respect for my role as therapist. Predictably, this made him furious, but his fury brought his human ego into the relationship. In Jungian terms, the centerpiece of his ego was introverted feeling, which is very sensitive to imbalances of power. He told me in no uncertain terms that it was I who was being pompous. It would have been tempting to put this down as projective identification, but accepting his resentment of my assertion of power was the more helpful course.

Discriminating the appropriate and inappropriate uses of power is something people with strong introverted feeling are good at; this function is often symbolized in dreams as the judge. As the patient became less 'above it all' and more directly confrontational with me, he gradually began to make more realistic judgments as to what he needed to do in his own educational, vocational, and romantic life.

This bit of case illustrates how first recognizing the archetype effectively possessing the person and then identifying the psychological type of the patient's real ego, which has been buried in the archetypal presentation, can be ways for the Jungian therapist to more deeply empathize with the nature of a patient's struggle in life. Although I could see, early in our work, that he was identified with the archetype of the *puer aeternus* and that his ego had become inflated by this identification, he would not have tolerated my telling him so. In responding to the archetypal quality of this young patient's initial presentation, my goal was to loosen his excessive identification with the godlike *puer*. I needed to help him disidentify with that role and gradually take on the risk of becoming more humanly vulnerable in my presence. But he needed to take that risk before he could receive this interpretation. In fact, it only became possible to communicate my view of his *puer* problem when he had begun to outgrow it and could be more direct with me. And for him, the process of discovering that an identification with the *puer aeternus* archetype does not finally release a competent masculine identity would have to be mutual: I was a young therapist when I began to work with him, and I was similarly inflated by first exposure to Jungian theory. I came in for considerable criticism from this patient for what seemed to him like my arrogance in using the theory to make judgments about someone else. The dizzying height of the archetype we both had to climb down from within our relationship became the gauge of the distance he had to go to become more fully human.

The trickster

A third archetype that not infrequently makes its appearance in the psychotherapist's consulting room is the trickster. It is one that is problematic for analytical work, because the very ethos of this kind of psychotherapy is a commitment to being sincere and vulnerable. A man identified with the trickster archetype is anything but sincere and vulnerable. The archetypal thrust of the trickster's restless energy is to resist having to do things the way others think is right. The trickster toys with expectations, flouting rules that attempt to uphold standards of behavior and questioning the values of those who defend the standards (Radin, 1972).

Here's what that can look like in the consulting room. A graduate student of twenty-four came to therapy complaining of a dulling of his feelings. He revealed that he was gay and in a long-term partnership with another man that was going well. With his partner's consent, he was supporting his graduate education by working as a prostitute. I had to point out to him that it wouldn't be consistent with the goals of the therapy, which were presumably to help him overcome the dulling of his feelings, if I also simply allowed him to support his therapy, as he had done his graduate work, by turning tricks as a prostitute. I told him, therefore, that I would see him, but not if he paid for the therapy out of earnings as a sex worker. He told me that he thought that was elitist, but that he would do it.

After time to think about his remark, I told the patient that I felt a bit ripped off by it: that I wanted to be sure the change I was suggesting was one he wanted to make because he agreed it made sense, given his presenting symptom, and was not one he was making simply to meet my standards. He agreed that it was a change he wanted to make.

Then occurred some serendipitous boundary crossings, of the kind I do not find unusual when 'mercurial'[1] communications involving feeling risks have created disturbances in the interpersonal field with a client. My new patient happened to be taken by a friend of his to the home of a woman that unbeknownst to him was also a friend of mine. He told her that he had just started with a 'fantastic psychiatrist' and mentioned my name. The woman, somewhat naively, relayed this comment to me when by chance I saw her later the same week. Normally, I don't enjoy having any information from third parties about a client's feelings about me, but under the circumstances I found the information that the patient had apparently liked the limits I had set reassuring, and it gave me confidence to see what would happen next in the therapy.

The patient discontinued his work as a prostitute, and I believe from the communications he made to me over the next year and a half that he kept to this decision. He told me that the change involved a combination of finding other work and accepting more support from his living partner until he could get on his feet. But after the initial limit setting, I did not strictly monitor his behavior in this regard, out of respect for his moral autonomy. My point was to communicate that I felt that prostituting himself was incompatible with the goal of his therapy, as stated by him at the outset—to do something about the hardening of his feelings, which was what had led him to seek professional help.

It was this communication that impressed him and motivated him to change his life, and for more reasons than I could have known at the time. A year and a half into his therapy, he mentioned that when, in high school, he had told his stepfather that he dreamed some day of going to graduate school, the stepfather had coldly replied, "I don't care what you do; I don't care if you sell your body." In the therapy, the young man had finally met someone who didn't accept the terms of the double bind he had been placed in by the stepfather's remark, that the only way for him to get an education, including even a psychotherapy, was to disregard his own feelings.

When the trickster appears out of the psyche of a patient, its calling card is usually a display of the archetype's capacity to put both others and oneself in a double bind (Beebe, 1981, p. 38). The patron divinity of alchemy, the wily Roman god Mercurius, is often referred to as "*duplex* and his main characteristic is duplicity" (Jung, 1948/1967, p. 217). Contemporary men who have aligned their survival strategies with the trickster archetype can be quite duplicitous when urging their psychotherapists to support personal choices that are, in fact, highly untherapeutic. The analytical therapist will want to recognize that the trickster is operating in the patient, but that is not enough. The therapist will have to have integrated enough trickster of his or her own to be able to turn the double bind around and reverse the terms of the hard bargain that the trickster in the patient is trying to drive. When the patient initially told me that he could not pay for the therapy unless he went on working as a prostitute, I felt the cage of the double bind closing in around me. By making him see that he would not be able to have me as a therapist if he continued his prostitution, I managed to turn the trap back on him and by so doing signaled him as well that I was at least potentially equal to the challenge of being his analyst.

The shadow

With his deceptions, manipulations, and rule flouting, the trickster can be an effective archetypal force for self-defense in a dangerous world, but his is not the only available approach. Sometimes we fend off threats by pulling rank, by identifying and pointing out the opponent's weaknesses with chilling, withering remarks. This is the bailiwick of the *senex* archetype—the critical, saturnine, old man who, metaphorically speaking, paces up and down inside each of us, waiting for his chance to put troublesome people in their place. Or we may respond to perceived danger in still more unconscious ways, undermining and devastating a potential enemy through actions, formulations, and evaluations that are nearly as surprising and unexplained to us as to others. This is the work of a part personality, or archetype, that I call the demonic personality. Or, finally, we may defend ourselves through avoidant or passive-aggressive actions including seduction, or through direct attack, the realm of what I call the opposing personality. These four archetypes—trickster, *senex*, demonic personality, and opposing personality—comprise, in my judgment, the cast of characters that make up the enormous region of individual personality that is repressed by most people—what Jung called the shadow.

The shadow is repressed because it is felt to be incompatible with a person's moral values. It retains, and from time to time expresses, feelings, motives, desires, and ambitions that the person has long since decided are unworthy, because they do not accord with the individual's idea of how people should feel, let alone behave. Since it usually is not owned as part of the person, the shadow has a great deal of autonomy, which allows it from time to time even to escape repression, so that it can act out the very strivings that the ego has rejected as incompatible with its standards. I have found it helpful to think of the shadow as the 'ego-dystonic' part of our consciousness. Just as the 'ego-syntonic' personality will develop over time, so too does the shadow develop in the course of life, differentiating itself in ways that are decidedly contrary to the ideals associated with the ego's usual identity.

The types of consciousness deployed by the shadow are precisely the ones not preferred by the ego-syntonic parts of the personality. For example, in a person for whom extraverted thinking predominates, introverted thinking will be in shadow. If that person's second most preferred function of consciousness is introverted intuition then extraverted intuition will find expression in the shadow.

Since each of us can potentially deploy four types of consciousness through our ego-syntonic personality (sensation, intuition, feeling, and thinking—each in either an extraverted or introverted form), the other four possible types of consciousness (again sensation, intuition, feeling, and thinking, but now with the opposite attitude with respect to introversion or extraversion) express themselves through ego-dystonic, potentially destructive, shadow parts of the personality.

The opposing personality

One of these shadow archetypes of consciousness, the opposing personality, consists of a cluster of defenses of the self that are used to oppose, rather than unite and work with, others. The opposing personality fuels the defensive character styles—passive-aggressive, paranoid, avoidant, and histrionic—we sometimes see in our patients. Deployed internally, this consciousness can end up opposing one's own best interests in perverse ways.

Archetypally, the opposing personality is one of two places in a man's psyche where his contrasexuality, that is, his inner femininity, is likely to show up strongly. In the grip of the opposing personality, a man may make 'bitchy' remarks or unleash a seductive sexual charm whose purpose is to exercise control over others.

The other place in the psyche that has a contrasexual coloring is the *anima*, which Jung defines in *Psychological Types* as a soul figure representing a man's inner attitude (Jung, 1921/1971, ¶808) and in his later writings as "the archetype of life itself" (Jung, 1954/1959, ¶66). The anima, however, holds a potential for leading the man toward integrity. The same cannot usually be said of the opposing personality. We will return to the anima later, but we should note here that, when projected onto an actual woman, even one the man hardly knows, his veneration for the anima may lead him to idealize the woman and want to marry her. Projecting the opposing personality, by contrast, will cause a man to see the woman in a negative or troublesome light as she seems to embody the man's own antagonistic traits.

When projected, the opposing personality can also become intensely sexualized, but the relationship that ensues is usually characterized by arguments and confrontations. In the movie *Casablanca* (1943), the frequent face-offs between Humphrey Bogart (playing an introverted feeling hero) and Ingrid Bergman (as his extraverted feeling challenger) carry the quality of a relationship between a man and his opposing personality. Within a personality (and a film like *Casablanca* is like a personality, with the different characters its part personalities) the opposing personality is defined, typologically, as using the same function as the hero's (in Rick's and Ilsa's case, feeling) but with the opposite attitude (introverted in Rick, extraverted in Ilsa). It is not hard to see the motivation to bring these two attitudes together when the outcome is the wholeness of feeling in romantic love, the seductive subject of *Casablanca*. In real life the tension between the opposing personality and the dominant, heroic ego can become a matter for exploration in psychotherapy.

Though in a strict type sense, it is nothing other than the shadow of the heroic superior function of the ego, the opposing personality, as I have studied it in myself and my clients in analysis, turns out to be a highly complex state of mind. Because it has many facets, analysts who have tried to describe it usually end up doing so in partial ways only. Though they can see and focus upon the seductiveness, avoidance, passively enacted aggression, or paranoia they see in the person using the opposing personality, often they neglect to connect the dots and so lose the oppositional quality of the archetype as a whole.

Jungian analysts have frequently identified this oppositional quality in a man as his 'negative mother complex' or 'negative anima.' This neglects the fact that the opposing personality is so much closer to the man's own consciousness than either his mother or his anima. It can also reflect cultural factors, as when a gay man, put on the defensive by the culture's hostility to homosexuality, strikes back with the false-feminine opposing personality, defending himself against real or imagined 'straight' attacks on his identity by being campy, seductive, or bitchy. This passive-aggressive style of self-presentation covertly attacks patriarchal assumptions about masculinity. The bitchy opposing personality can take on a life of its own in any man, no matter how secure he seems to be in his masculine identity. Not that the man usually sees how his personality has been taken over by an oppositional attitude! Like Kevin Spacey's character in the film *American Beauty* (1999), he may feel he is simply asserting himself, reclaiming his masculine birthright, and should have done so long ago. But if the man can catch himself in the act of enacting his opposing personality in a way that is obviously not worthy of him and put a stop to it, the contrasexuality of the figure, its shadowy nature, and the reality that this is a part of himself that he would prefer to get past, will sometimes be made evident to him in a dream.

A professional man in the midst of a Jungian analysis in his early thirties noticed that he couldn't 'face' going through his bills and adding up his checkbook. A superficial reader of Jung, he thought, "Managing money is something an intuitive man shouldn't have to deal with." One day, his voice rising in a false-feminine way, with his spouse watching helplessly by, he threw the checkbook he was having trouble reconciling across the room. He was starting, in his most 'hysterical' mode, to make a scene that had been enacted before around the threat of scarcity of money. At such times he would assume a personality that was much more fear-driven than his normal 'can do' extraverted ego, which could always see some possibility for coping with any problem, large or small. Realizing, on the basis of previous analytic work, that he was in the grip of a complex, he stopped himself in mid-scene and instead went over to the discarded checkbook, picked it up, dusted it off, and started again to bring it into balance, which he managed to do half an hour later.

This setting of limits upon himself brought a decisive change in his attitude toward managing his money, a change duly recorded by the dream he had the same night: Looking at his hometown newspaper, he saw a headline that said, "New Attorney General Appointed." Underneath this banner was another story, "Woman Found Strangled." She was, the dream newspaper said, the daughter of Betty Grable, the favorite 'pin-up' for American soldiers in World War II, and Harry James, her trumpeter husband, who had led a famous band.

As a daughter of these Swing Era celebrities, the dream figure was not of his parents' generation, but of his own. She was not a celebrity and was also not as attractive as her parents had been: in the newspaper picture, she had a decidedly pig-like nose. I believe that this detail represents the unconscious greed that was hidden in the man's anxiety about money. This daughter was in fact, a symbol of the narcissistic entitlement of his own generation that was at the heart of his money complex. He privately held the opinion that he was a special person and that worrying about money was for ordinary people. What this man was avoiding was a reality that he had tried to throw as far from himself as possible: that expenditures need to be covered by income. The first step toward this goal was balancing his checkbook to see what he really had.

Mulling over the dream figure of the murdered woman with the aid of these self-reflective associations led the man to see that she was the image of his histrionic panics about money, the opposing personality to this man's dominant, heroic, resourceful personality. He brought the news from his dream of her having being strangled (which he associated to his having managed to choke off the oppositional histrionic panic he had begun to indulge himself in the night before so that he could determine on a realistic basis how much money he actually had) to his Jungian analyst who smiled and said, "I'm glad she's gone." The "new Attorney General" in his dream, then, represented a masculine superego more in line with his business-trained father's attitude toward money, which had involved the functions of extraverted thinking and introverted sensation in planning and accounting for how money was spent.

The father

Although the father is an archetype that needs little introduction to readers of masculine psychology, the Jungian understanding of how to work with it in psychotherapy has only infrequently been surveyed (Samuels, 1985). Aside from presentations of the father as one of the parent archetypes (Berry, 1973;

Wilmer, 1990), much of the Jungian literature on the masculine centers on finding the possibilities of the father archetype within (Henderson, 2005; Perry, 1970), becoming a father (Colman & Colman, 1988), and living up to the demands of a father role that is ever being redefined through cultural change (Neumann, 1954; Tatham, 1992; Zoja, 2001). Although writings that explore the working through of the father–daughter relationship can be found (Bolen, 1992; Dallett, 1991; Leonard, 1982; Woodman, 1992), Jungian analysts and psychotherapists have more often focused on the vicissitudes of the father–son relationship (Collins, 1994; Corneau, 1991; Sandner, 1987).

Whereas Freud emphasized the terrifying aspects of the father as potential castrator to the son who might grow up to be his rival, Jungian analysts, particularly of my own generation, have emphasized what the *I Ching*, the Confucian classic that focuses on archetypal human situations,[2] describes in its chapter on "The Family" (Hexagram 37), the Confucian ideal of the loving father in the traditionally patriarchal Chinese culture:

> Three of the five social relationships are to be found within [the hexagram of The Family]—that between father and son, which is the relation of love, that between husband and wife, which is the relation of chaste conduct, and that between elder and younger brother, which is the relation of correctness.
>
> I Ching, *1950/1967, p.144*

Carrying this idea of humanizing the father archetype so that it can be experienced in a personal way forward in relation to psychotherapy, my colleague Andrew Samuels has emphasized the importance in the psychological development of both boys and girls of what he calls "the father's body" (Samuels, 1993, pp. 135–143), and I have delineated the critical role played by "the father's anima" (Beebe, 1985) in the integration of the authority of the father. These are conceptions that point to a *patriarchal transmission* in the course of development in or outside of psychotherapy that can scarcely be accomplished without another person willing to play the role of father. This transmission, as Samuels makes clear with his postulate of a "father of whatever sex" (Samuels, 1993, pp. 133–135), can certainly take place within homes and in therapies where a woman must assume the father role. A lesbian or gay parent is just as able to convey the needed "father's body" and "father's anima" as a heterosexual father.

It is the absence of any transmission of father energy that creates the father hunger that leads a young person to seek an actual older male with something to transmit; hence the frequent conflation in young people's minds of the father with the archetype of the Wise Old Man. (In the seven-novel *Harry Potter* series by J. K. Rowling, we see something of this in the relationship between the student wizard Harry Potter and the headmaster Dumbledore.) The body of the father is not only his physical presence or his literal role as the source (if he is) of the child's genes but the body of knowledge about fatherhood that he has to transmit. An example of this occurs in the very long analyses that analytic candidates undergo, sometimes with older male analysts who are recognized in their communities as wise elders. Such analyses have often been compared unfavorably to indoctrinations, but the modeling that occurs in them can play an important role in transmitting to a younger psychotherapist the necessary confidence needed to assume the role of analyst. Such fathering in analytic training is frequently called mentoring, and the process initiation. There is a Jungian literature on the topic (Kirsch, Rutter, & Singer, 2007) that includes women, but here I will emphasize how the way its deployment by a male catapults him into a father role.

A vital part of a man's masculinity is caught up in how potent or impotent he feels as *a man with something to impart*, and that may be the archetypal definition of what a father is, since it applies equally to men who have never had children and to men who have. It is very important to recognize a man's need to involve himself in what might be imaged in the totem pole, which shows a vertical succession of ancestors, one standing on top of another. This totemic succession is a good image of the patriarchal transmission, which rests on the home truth that each generation of men stands on the shoulders of the last. This may be especially precious to men, because the notion of what a father is actually changes with each generation and so is in greater danger of getting lost than the idea of what a mother is, which seems to endure with less change across cultures over time.

To understand the father archetype and the role it creates for a man, we have to first recognize the man's need to participate in the archetype, to receive love and lore from a father, and to be able to transmit the same to a son or daughter. As psychotherapists, we have to recognize the absolute necessity for some men to work extraordinarily hard to be able to have something to transmit to their children, often along material lines. And we have to take very seriously the efforts of unmarried, unpartnered, childless men to offer valuable lessons they have learned to the next generation. Not infrequently, this comes into the analytic transference at times when the patient is trying to teach the therapist something. Such enactments are not resistances to the analyst's authority; they are the patient struggling to find a voice and an authority to participate in the transmission.

In the Jungian typology of a man's consciousness, the nurturing father archetype will be associated with the auxiliary function, not the dominant function, so that, as the father archetype comes into play and becomes important to the man, he must loosen his identification with the archetype of the hero. The hero is forever proving his own mastery. The father, by contrast, seeks to help *the people he mentors* to be, and feel, more competent. He cannot do that if he is in competition with them.

The *senex*

The shadow of such a father is the *senex*. Like other names Jung selected for unconscious archetypes, this one takes origin in Latin, where it means 'old man.' It is the root word of a more familiar borrowing from Rome: senator. Anyone who has listened to a confirmation hearing of a cabinet officer or Supreme Court justice in the United States Senate will recognize the questioning style of the archetype,

which regularly voices a depreciative and skeptical, if not frankly cynical, interpretation of nearly anyone's suitability to take the office for which he or she has
been put forward. In October 1991, during the extended hearings of the US
Senate's Judiciary Committee on the nomination of Clarence Thomas to the US
Supreme Court that brought in Anita Hill as a late witness, a trio of male senators
on the committee with names Herman Melville might have contrived—Simpson
and Specter and Hatch—so disparaged Hill's integrity that she finally would not,
though invited back to rebut others' testimony, return to the hearings. Thomas
was confirmed, and, in outrage, a new crop of voters avenged the way they felt
Hill had been mistreated in the next Congressional election, creating what the
media called the 'Year of the Woman.' In the fall of 1992, a record of twenty-
nine women, all Democrats, were elected to the US Congress, four of them to the
Senate to join the two women already there. The people of the United States had
sent its Congress a message that men are not automatically entitled to dominate
national discourse. It became common wisdom that, by questioning Hill as if the
committee hearings were theirs and theirs alone, the male senators had slipped into
the patriarchal shadow, where they could no longer listen, making it impossible for
any other voice, especially a female one, to speak and feel heard in their presence.

This is how a display of the *senex* by men often affects women in a working
situation. Interestingly, the *senex* archetype, when internally active as a withering
self-critic, has the same silencing and deadening effect on the feminine figure inside
the man, the anima. Since she is the "archetype of life itself" (Jung, 1954/1959,
¶66), all the vitality seems to drain out of the individual. Captured by the *senex*,
the remaining persona seems old, dry, and absent of animation; all that remains is
cynicism, a tendency toward depreciation, and despair. To hear the *senex*'s reitera-
tive insistence on life's lack of meaning, value, and future (at least for the person for
whom the *senex* is speaking) makes one realize how much this is the voice of major
depression. In the most extreme case, there can be the psychotic delusion that one
has actually died and one's guts are rotting.

Men identified with the *senex* are notoriously savage toward *puer aeternus*-
identified men (Captain Hook vs Peter Pan), but the more everyday games of
cat and mouse played by the *senex* are with the trickster. The *senex* takes a grim
pleasure in catching the trickster at chicanery, which of course upholds the *senex*
worldview that people are not to be trusted.

Owing to his saturnine presentation, the man in the grip of the *senex* can be
hard for a therapist to empathize with. It may help to realize that the *senex* is an
archetype that emerges when a personality feels itself to be going into decline. The
trio of Republican senators must have felt this way when the Senate confirmation hearings were extended by the Democratic committee chair to accommodate
Anita Hill, and then allowed to be televised, a series of steps that threatened to turn
a process in which they were used to some dignity into a circus.

At such times, when a personality feels itself to be losing control of the situations in
which it must continue to function, the *senex* archetype resorts to strategies that simu-
late heroism. This is epitomized in the madness of Don Quixote, during which the

protagonist models his entire heroic persona on fictions. Once people start to observe him in this role, the Don simply keeps on enacting what he believes, deludedly, he is already famous for and does so with monomania (Beebe, 2007).

The very same behaviors can be seen in any man in the grip of the *senex* archetype. Such a man is not above adding a measure of tricksterism to his act, to convince himself, and the world, that the hero archetype has in fact been revitalized by him. It is amazing how often others collude with the fiction that some real power has been revived. James Hillman has spoken to what the *senex* is finally seeking: "Longings for superior knowledge, imperturbability, magnanimity express *senex* feelings as does intolerance for that which crosses one's systems and habits" (1989, p. 208).

But doesn't this betray a sense within the person that his life is *actually* futile, and that all that remains to the former hero is to extract from others a measure of respect for the fantasy that he continues to mean something? Therapists working with depressed patients who are identified with the *senex* find themselves in a paradox. The ever self-critical patient can run his life down in a relentlessly punitive way, but the therapist is usually not allowed to breathe a word that might expose the fictions by which the patient is living. In my work with men in the grip of the *senex* archetype, if I am given anything like a chance to intervene in their lives, however, I take the opportunity to challenge these fictions.

Here is an example of what I mean. At the outset of my psychiatric career, I had as a patient a 55-year-old plumber with a chronic depression, who at that time was seeing me in an outpatient clinic only for refills of an antidepressant.[3] During our monthly sessions, I kept hearing from him how his wife was always 'on him.' The only evidence the patient could muster, however, was a mildly sarcastic remark she had made. But asked if he ever dreamed, he responded with more animation:

> Why, yes. Last night I had a dream about my little dog. I was holding him up in my arms, and he was looking up at me every so tenderly, when suddenly he seemed to droop his head like he was going to die.

I asked the patient to tell me about his dog. It turned out that he loved his pet above all other things because the dog was always sweet and cheerful. I then asked the man if this dog might not be his own cheerful disposition, which had faded into despondence after his wife's sarcastic remark. My patient seemed to like this idea.

At the next monthly session, the patient related another dream. "The dog was there again, sitting at my feet and looking up at me. As I watched, its face turned into a vicious wharf rat." The patient told me that he had seen wharf rats in his younger days when he often worked on the harbors "around people that were hardly better than wharf rats they were so mean." Pursuing the lead of the previous month's session, I asked my patient if he was ever mean, if he ever lashed out. "Well if you put it that way, doctor, I guess I do. Oh I don't like that dream. I hate to think my little dog would turn into a wharf rat."

"Yet that's what seems to happen to a good disposition when a person gets mean," I responded.

It was not easy to confront this patient, already depressed, with the reality that he could be the perpetrator as well as the victim of meanness, but this is what the dream seemed to be saying. This was the first picture this patient ever had of his mood problem, and he marveled at the insight it gave him. Then, for the first time, he allowed himself to tell me that he launched nightly into verbal attacks against his wife, not unlike the content of his monthly sessions, when he would belittle her to me. His wife's occasional barbed remarks turned out to be her weak defenses against the things he said.

"I can be pretty cruel, doctor," he admitted.

The following month, the patient brought his wife to the medication clinic with him. She turned out to be a quiet, timid woman, somewhat frightened of her husband. She reported that he upset her with his critical remarks, but lately there had been some improvement. For the first time, she had been curious to see his doctor, and the patient had been willing to bring her. This contact opened the door to some much needed couple work.

The demonic personality

If the transformation in this patient's dream of the sweet dog into something as unequivocally beastly as the wharf rat suggests more than just a shift from ideal mood to depressed mood, what other shift is implied? The image has something to do with good and bad character. Dreams in which figures associated with the ideal are juxtaposed with images of the beastly also suggest a mythologem that involves just this coincidence of opposites, which we know today as the fairy tale of "Beauty and the Beast." This is a tale that goes to the heart of a paradox we find in the demonic personality—that though it is an image of undermining pathological narcissism, it can, when confronted and contained with integrity, start to make an effort to be unusually compassionate.

My hope is not to be sentimental in presenting this possibility, but to present the evidence for it. Clinical observation has shown me that the function of consciousness that is most distant from our ego consciousness can be deployed in both terribly undermining and in surprisingly positive ways. In a man whose hero consciousness expresses itself through extraverted sensation, for example, the function of extraverted intuition tends to take on a perversely destabilizing role, leading him to embrace the wrong possibilities and reject the right ones, except when, very occasionally, it is the source of a moment of unexpected good sense. Likewise, if introverted feeling is the man's leading, heroic function, then he tends instinctively to use introverted thinking to undercut himself and other and only occasionally 'gets it right' with that function.

Looking through the lens of typology at the figure of the Beast in the Disney version of the tale (*Beauty and the Beast*, 1991), I see an extraverted feeling character, locked into a demonic presentation of his caring for Belle. Belle, however, seems to operate with introverted feeling, so like Ilsa and Rick in *Casablanca*, they stand in shadow relation to each other. (The rather unattractive heroic figure in the story, Gaston, embodies extraverted thinking, as he is always making plans for everyone and is blind to the feelings of others.) But, if Beast is Belle's shadow, her visit to the castle of the Beast, then, is not just to rescue her father; it is also to engage in a transaction with this other side of feeling. In gratitude, Beast, who has been enchanted so that he cannot love, falls in love with her and both their lives are transformed.

A live action film that perfectly conveys the psychological idea I find in this story is James Brooks's *As Good as It Gets* (1997). It presents Jack Nicholson as Melvin Udall, a severely obsessive-compulsive man who is a misanthrope, and Helen Hunt as Carol Connelly, who in her humble job as a waitress at the corner restaurant he frequents brings an ethic of care to all her transactions.

For Melvin, she is an image of perfect integrity. Melvin, by contrast is classically demonic—absolutely undermining to others. The opening sequence of the film shows him pursuing his neighbor's messy dog, which has somehow gotten loose in the hall of the apartment building, so that he can throw the dog down the trash chute to the furnace in the basement.

It is hard for most audiences to recover from this display of Melvin's cruelty, made no less palatable by the sweet voice Melvin uses to cajole the dog to let him pick it up. Their ambivalence toward Melvin is mirrored by Helen Hunt's Carol, who thinks of him as an impaired person. What we all miss about Melvin, however, is the emotional intelligence buried in his pathological presentation. He is the only person who realizes the difficulty Carol has seeing her integrity. Melvin's place in her life turns out to be to mirror it to her. So in this variant of the tale, it is not just Melvin's Beast who needs somehow to be transformed into a sensitive partner, but it's Carol's Beauty, who needs to think out of the box of her own perception. In fact, it takes love from someone she assumed was pathologically narcissistic (Melvin) to bring the beauty of her soul home to her. The great strength of Jack Nicholson's performance is that his Melvin credibly does so.

In Melvin's case, the same extraverted feeling function he was using in a pathologically narcissistic way at the outset of the film is by the end being used in a constructive, relationship-building way. The reason for the change is that he has been engaged by the integrity Carol commands. If we interpret these characters on the intrapsychic level, as part personalities, they demonstrate that pathological narcissism in a man can be overcome if the anima is empowered to engage constructively with the most demonic personality. Melvin begins to use his extraverted feeling to mirror Carol's integrity, and she is profoundly touched. In this way, the spirit of love enters her psychological world through the shadowy Melvin. And when Melvin says, "You make me want to be a better man," it has a ring of truth.

To get to this truth in outer life, it has to be experienced in an intrapsychic way first. Otherwise the narcissistic man will repeatedly set up people to imagine that they can easily save him from his pathological narcissism by carrying for him the integrity his demonic personality craves and then he will disappoint them.

Instead of a dependency on other people who have integrity, I am imagining the pathological narcissist finding the place of his *own* integrity, and I know that this is possible because I have found repeatedly in my years of working in depth with men that this is what they most appreciate discovering from psychotherapy.

The more integrated the person is, and the higher functioning, the harder the time he may have recognizing the demonic side of his personality. A man in his early fifties had been in psychotherapy for several years with a male analyst for help with a pathologically narcissistic father, whose demands on him had escalated when the patient had entered midlife and started to become successful in his work. The patient's whole psyche would be set vibrating simply by his father's ringing him up on the phone. At first, however, the patient did not know that his psyche was vibrating: his wife had to tell him, when she picked up the 'vibes,' which she experienced as physically painful force fields coming from him that were intolerable to her.

Here, the wife was like Helen Hunt in *As Good as It Gets* saying to Melvin, "I can't do this" when he tries to walk with her while obsessively avoiding stepping on cracks in the sidewalks. The patient was, metaphorically, trying to walk around the crack in his own psyche, and his wife was feeling the pain that emanated from it.

Her integrity in confronting him was soon matched by his integrity in identifying the dissociated mental state for himself, verifying that he was, in effect, 'vibrating,' with both fear and rage at his father's intrusiveness. He figured out that what upset him about the calls was his father's habit of heaping abuse on other family members in a way that allowed no possibility of coming to their defense. By the end of each call, this son would be literally shaking. He found a way of explaining to his father that he could no longer take calls from him, the symptom of terrified agitation subsided, and the wife pronounced him far easier to live with. With the father under control and the relationship with the wife moving out of the danger zone of her limits of tolerance, the man felt that he was ready to leave psychotherapy.

Within a few weeks of doing so, however, he noticed that he was experiencing an entirely different level of difficulty. Now it was not with his father: it was with himself. He would find himself in certain situations, particularly at work, when he was sure people were feeling contempt toward him. He became so upset at those times he could barely do his work: he wanted to go away and hide from those who could see how utterly incompetent he was. If people were nice to him, he suspected that it was out of pity. Using the technique he had learned from his wife, however, of attending very closely to the affects inside him, he began to be aware that these painful feelings were accompanied by a sort of voice, low and insinuating, not really audible, but present nonetheless. It was 'saying,' "You're nothing. You're just nothing!" He knew, this time, the problem he was having was not with his father any longer, but perhaps with the kind of self-depreciation his father had had to struggle with.

Father and son were Jewish, so the patient wondered if it was an internalized anti-Semitism that the father could only handle by thoughtlessly running down others and never even recognized as an attitude he was carrying. That seemed close, but the patient realized that the voice wasn't saying "You're Jewish!" in a damning way. It was saying, "You're nothing!" If he hadn't been Jewish, it would have used something else to level him to unimportance. He found that by paying attention to the feeling of unimportance, he could always tell when the voice was active. It was *his* demonic personality, no one else's, and his integrity lay in being willing to own it.

At the same time, he had to admit his utter vulnerability when the voice was speaking, noting the same agitated, anguished vibrations that had made his wife so miserable when she was the only one picking them up. In this way, he began to get in touch with his anima for the first time. Up to then, he had thought that you just had to endure certain unpleasant states of mind that didn't seem to go away, and you did so by distracting yourself as much as possible with work. That way, you always got what needed to be done finished, and you could have at least that measure of accomplishment, even if you were miserable much of the time.

The patient could reason that way in part because introverted sensation was his dominant, heroic function and he could use it as a stoic defense. But his heroism went beyond stoicism: it lay in an ability to give himself to any task that he was assigned. The person who carries introverted sensation as his dominant ego function can generally understand how any process works and by attending to very small details can verify whether the correct procedures are being followed by those charged with getting work done using that process. Being good at verifying that things are matching up with what should be happening during each present increment of time as the job advances makes a man with this dominant function a good manager, in the sense of keeping accurate work flowing within budget, but his inferior extraverted intuition may often fail to deliver the larger picture to him of where things overall are going.

Now, he was beginning to see what his extraverted intuitive wife had long known. Nothing good could come of this way of operating, dissociating from his feelings and simply soldiering on, over time. As long as the voice was still free to come whenever it wanted, he continued to be undermined from within. The patient decided to return to therapy.

In therapy, the patient was advised to establish a relationship to the voice by imagining that it was a real voice and then having a discussion with it. Their dialogues would take the form of him saying, "I can't really accept your effect on me. What good will it do either of us to have you telling me I'm nothing?" The answer came back, "You just are, that's it. You're a Jew and you will go to hell, so what's the point of talking to you now. You aren't going to amount to anything." The patient came to realize that the voice belonged to a part of himself he had virtually avoided his whole life, his introverted intuition, which made these global, archetypal assessments, to which there was no right of appeal. So he asked the voice to tell him its story, and it turned out that the soft-spoken voice belonged to a Christian man who had violated the tenets of his faith by frequenting massage parlors where women offered him sexual favors. He was sure that God, no matter how merciful, would never forgive him, even if his wife could. The patient responded by saying, "What you've done may be far from ideal, but I don't think you're going to burn in Hell for it. You need to get a grip: it's too hard for you always to carry such a load of guilt." As this psychological work progressed, the patient's bouts of feeling that he was nothing began to decrease. Instead, he had come to appreciate what such a feeling might be made of, a reaction to self-betrayal. With the example of the broken Christian very much in his mind, he began to become aware of ways in which he was betraying himself at work by failing to assert his own values. For the first time in a very long time, he took a look at the big picture of his career, rather than the individual challenges, and saw that it no longer had the meaning and rightness for him that it once had. He made a career change into a kind of work that freshly expressed his values and gave him an opportunity to contribute more meaningfully. In this way, the introverted intuitive demon that had plagued him became a daimon, guiding him to a higher level of integration within his own ethical perspective. At the heart of all this was a vivid felt sense of his integrity as something that must not be compromised.

The anima: from roles to Self

The place of a man's integrity, as I have been hinting throughout this chapter, is the anima. (Anima is Latin for 'soul.') Here the man can be taken beyond his usual set of masculine roles. When asked by men to define the anima, the British Jungian analyst Michael Fordham (personal communication, 1979) used to say, "It's the woman you are." When he first said it to me, I was amused, but not convinced. But as I have mulled over dreams of men who have found the anima, his statement has made more and more sense to me.

One such dream was related to me by a young man who had come to see me a couple of years after finishing college. He was working out his acceptance of his homosexuality and starting to 'come out.' This patient had a persona indistinguishable from many young heterosexual men of his age, and he liked to present himself as a hipster. He allowed people close to him, including me, to believe that he had used drugs frequently. That was certainly plausible: at that time and place, the early 1970s in Northern California, antiestablishment, middle class youths with good educations were testing the boundaries of their upbringings. In the second year of his therapy with me, he dreamed that he met 'his old lady,' which in hip parlance meant a romantic partner close to him in age. In the dream they were living together, and he came home to her. She had an unpretentious, real face that he found wonderful. He kept saying how good she looked to him—not because she was beautiful (she wasn't) but because she was so real.

Coming upon his 'old lady' this way, 'at home,' and really liking her just as she was was an amazing experience for this young man. He did not use the word, but I realized that she was his anima. Being comfortable with her meant that he was at home with himself.

It was around this time that he made the great confession of his analysis, which was that the persona of drug aficionado that he had so carefully cultivated, even to the extent of making me believe that he had been 'using' up to the time he began working with me, was essentially a sham. He had in fact not gone very far with drugs at all. Shortly after making this confession, he had another dream: a James Bond figure was seen departing from his psychic landscape, off on another adventure with other people, never to return. "I wonder what he'll do next," was the last thought of my patient as he watched him depart. I knew I too was witnessing the departure of a false self.

It seemed clear to us both that locating his 'old lady,' the anima figure that represented his reality, had exploded the hipster pretensions of the fictitious persona he had been hiding behind to make himself more glamorous. Not long after these dreams, my patient began to engage seriously and no longer theoretically with his homosexuality and to talk about how he wanted to live that. He had a dream that his and another man's bodies fitted perfectly together, and it was clear to him that if he found the suitable partner he would be entirely comfortable in a homosexual partnership. Not long after this was clear, he felt ready to terminate. He had a final dream in which he suffered an injury, called for a medic, and got his wound healed. A follow-up contact nearly 15 years later revealed that shortly after terminating with me, he entered into a long-term love relationship with a man that had lasted over a decade, followed by a break up, and now, he told me, he was in another long-term relationship with a man that seemed destined to last even longer. He was clearly comfortable with his life.

The anima, then, is a place in the psyche where a man can transcend his propensity to play roles, including the various archetypal roles we have been exploring in this chapter. When the anima is reached, rigid roles begin to give way to a deeper connection with oneself that is beyond role. Jungian psychology has classically described the anima as the mediatrix to the Self, and as a personification of the ego–Self axis. (See the Frontispiece to Edinger, 1973 for an illustration of this idea.) Another way to say this is that the anima is the place in a man's psyche where the dream of integrity of personality can become a reality. The plumb line of personhood that develops between superior function hero and inferior function anima establishes the spine of personality, making "integrity in depth" possible (Beebe 1992, pp. 106–107).

When this happens, a personality can bloom, and the personal self will acquire more affective coloration, cohesion, and temporal stability than before.[4] If it doesn't happen, the anima will be like a flower that hasn't opened. Occasionally a dream will show just this image. Jung calls the anima the "archetype of life" because she gives a man the feeling that he is alive. Hill (1998) points out that the anima is different from the ego in many ways, starting, in a man, with the gender difference. Then there is the fact that she is associated with the inferior function of a man's typology and is thus often clumsy where the heroic function would be smooth. Hill feels she should be regarded as the archetype of *otherness*. Hillman (1985) in his exhaustive survey of the ways in which Jung conceptualized the "personified notion" of the anima, concurs, and suggests that the purpose of having a part of the mind that is so different from the ego is that, as a soul, it serves the instinct for reflection, our ability to consider our lives from another standpoint (Hillman, 1985, pp. 85–87).

In his *Red Book*, begun in the midst of a midlife crisis that he compared to primitive "soul loss," Jung (2009) seems to agree. There, he makes it clear that he must connect with his soul and even enter a kind of dialogue with her to be able to reflect adequately on how, in the course of making a name for himself in the world ("the spirit of this time") he managed to lose touch with "the spirit of the depths" (Jung, 2009, p. 229). Before the book is through he will even have apologized to his soul for having abandoned her while pursuing a dazzling persona.

Jung recommends getting to know one's anima as well as possible. That is his therapy for the numerous anima problems to which men, particularly, are prey: bad moods, resentments, obsessive longings for attachment, uncontrolled emotional outbursts. All of these, he says, are symptoms of "faulty adaptation to the inner world" (Jung, 1966, ¶319). Since the anima is concerned with how the man is relating to his deeper psyche, she will call attention to problems by sending symptoms from dread and depression to obsession and depersonalization. Through these manifestations, the anima moves the ego to acknowledge the reality of the psyche. These symptoms tend to moderate when the anima is recognized as the bridge to the unknowable self, which the man must learn to respect.

At any stage of a man's life, finding the anima can be a great boon to his subsequent development. The feminine archetype opens up a man to the notion of individuation beyond conventional roles. Once secure in the anima, a man can begin to appreciate what Virginia Woolf described her mind to be like—living from a place where the different roles that the archetypes provide are not so much ends in themselves, as fragments of a greater wholeness. Then the real thing becomes simply to stay with oneself in an ongoing, related way, drawing upon all of the archetypes that can make this possible, but without being trapped in any of them.

Notes

1 Mercury's Greek analogue was Hermes, and at the boundary lines of the ancient Greek city-states, phallic monuments were set up in his honor, suggesting the charged nature of boundary crossings.

2 Jung's efforts to make this book of wise advice in typical situations available in an English-language translation (*The I Ching*, 1950/1967) that speaks to a Western psychological audience must count as his mature contribution to the understanding of the father archetype.

3 This case is also discussed in Rosenbaum and Beebe (1975, p. 394).

4 Followers of Kohut's self psychology will recognize these as signs that the self is getting what it needs, which suggests that, once located, the anima operates as an internal self-object providing affect regulation to the psyche so that it can function optimally.

References

American beauty. (1999). Cohen, B. & Jinks, D. (Producers) & Mendes S. (Director). USA: Dreamworks. [Motion picture].

As good as it gets. (1997). Brooks, J., Johnson, B., & Zea, K. (Producers) & Brooks, J. (Director). USA: Tri-Star Pictures. [Motion picture].

Beauty and the beast. (1991). Hahn, D. (Producer) & Trousdale, G. & Wise K. (Directors). United States: Walt Disney Pictures. [Motion picture].

Beebe, J. (1981). The trickster in the arts. *San Francisco Jung Institute Library Journal, 2*(2), 22–54.

Beebe, J. (1985). The father's anima. In A. Samuels (Ed.), *The father: Contemporary Jungian perspectives* (pp. 95–110). New York: New York University Press.

Beebe, J. (1992). *Integrity in depth.* College Station, TX: Texas A&M University Press.

Beebe, J. (2007). The memory of the hero and the emergence of the post-heroic attitude. *Spring Journal, 78*, 275–296.

Berry, P. (Ed.). (1973). *Fathers and mothers.* Zurich, Switzerland: Spring Publications.

Bolen, J. (1992). *Ring of power.* San Francisco, CA: Harper San Francisco.

Casablanca. (1943). Wallis, H. (Producer) & Curtiz, M. (Director). United States: Warner Bros. [Motion picture].

Collins, A. (1994). *Fatherson: A self psychology of the archetypal masculine.* Wilmette, IL: Chiron Publications.

Colman, A. & Colman, L. (1988). *The father: Mythology and changing roles.* Wilmette, IL: Chiron Publications.

Corneau, G. (1991). *Absent fathers, lost sons.* Boston, MA: Shambhala.

Dallett, J. (1991). *Saturday's child: Encounters with the dark gods.* Toronto: Inner City.

Edinger, E. F. (1973). *Ego and archetype.* Baltimore, MD: Penguin.

Erikson, E. H. (1963). *Childhood and society,* 2nd Ed. New York: W. W. Norton.

Henderson, J. L. (2005). *Thresholds of initiation,* 2nd. Ed., rev. Wilmette, IL: Chiron Publications.

Hill, G. (1998). Men, the anima, and the feminine. *San Francisco Jung Institute Library Journal, 17*(3), 49–62.

Hillman, J. (1985). *Anima: An anatomy of a personified notion.* Dallas, TX: Spring Publications.

Hillman, J. (1989). Mythology as family; father: Saturn and senex. In T. Moore (Ed.), *A blue fire* (pp. 208–216). New York: Harper & Row.

I Ching or book of changes, The (1950/1967). 3rd Ed., R. Wilhelm & C. Baynes (Trans.). Princeton, NJ: Princeton University Press.

Jung, C. G. (1921/1971). Psychological Types. In *Cw 6.*

Jung, C. G. (1939/1959). Conscious, unconscious, and individuation. In *Cw 9, i* (pp. 3–41).

Jung, C. G. (1948/1967). The spirit Mercurius. In *Cw 13* (pp. 191–250).

Jung, C. G. (1954/1959). Archetypes of the collective unconscious. In *Cw 9, i* (pp. 3–41).

Jung, C. G. (1966). *Two essays on analytical psychology,* 2nd Ed., R. F. C. Hull (Trans.). Princeton, NJ: Princeton University Press.

Jung, C. G. (1989). *Analytical psychology: Notes of the seminar given in 1925.* W. McGuire (Ed.). Princeton, NJ: Princeton University Press.

Jung, C. G. (2009). The way of what is to come. In S. Shamdasani (Ed.), *The red book: Liber novus* (pp. 229–231). New York: W. W. Norton.

Kirsch, T., Rutter, V. B., & Singer, T. (2007). *Initiation: The living reality of an archetype.* London: Routledge.

Lehrer, J. (2008). *Proust was a neuroscientist.* Boston, MA: Houghton Mifflin.

Leonard, L. S. (1982). *The wounded woman: Healing the father–daughter relationship.* Athens, OH: Swallow Press.

Neumann, E. (1954). *The origins and history of consciousness.* R. F. C. Hull, (Trans.) New York: Bollingen Foundation.

Perry, J. W. (1970). *Lord of the four quarters: Myths of the royal father.* New York: Collier.

Radin, P. (1972). *The trickster: A study in American Indian mythology,* with commentaries by Karl Kerényi and C. G. Jung. New York: Schocken Books.

Rosenbaum, P. C. & Beebe, J. (1975). *Psychiatric treatment: Crisis, clinic and consultation.* New York: McGraw-Hill.

Samuels, A. (Ed.). (1985). *The father: Contemporary Jungian perspectives.* New York: New York University Press.

Samuels, A. (1993). *The political psyche.* London: Routledge.

Sandner, D. (1987). The split shadow and the father–son relationship. In M. A. Mattoon (Ed.), *The archetype of shadow in a split world.* Proceedings of the Tenth International Congress for Analytical Psychology, Berlin, 1986. Einsiedeln, Switzerland: Daimon.

Segal, R. (Ed.). (1990). *In quest of the hero.* Princeton, NJ: Princeton University Press.

Tatham, P. (1992). *The making of maleness: Men, women and the flight of Daedalus.* London: Karnac.

von Franz, M.-L. (1970). *The Problem of the puer aeternus.* New York: Spring Publications.

Wilmer, H. A. (1990). *Mother/father.* Wilmette, IL: Chiron Publications.

Woodman, M. (1992). *Leaving my father's house: A journey to conscious femininity.* Boston, MA: Shambhala.

Woolf, V. (1989). *A room of one's own.* New York: Harvest.

Zoja, L. (2001). *The father: Historical, psychological, and cultural perspectives.* Hove, England: Brunner-Routledge.

5

THE WIZARD OF OZ

A vision of development in the American political psyche

The Wizard of Oz, the 1939 MGM color musical starring Judy Garland, Bert Lahr, and Ray Bolger (*Wizard of Oz*, 1939), has been reissued so often that its presence within the American psyche has the quality of a recurrent dream. As nearly everyone knows, it is about a little farm girl Dorothy who, in what may or may not be a dream, is blown with her little dog Toto from Kansas by cyclone to the fairyland of Oz. With the help of a Scarecrow, a Tin Man, and a Cowardly Lion whom she meets along the Yellow Brick Road that leads to Oz's capital, she must persuade the country's ruling Wizard to develop a way for her to return home. In the course of these adventures, Dorothy kills two Wicked Witches and secures the invaluable protection of a Good Witch, who in the end proves to be the mentor who will guide her safely home.

This sentimental mythology is made to work because of the sure vaudevillian touch with which the transcendental meanings are delivered—as if Ralph Waldo Emerson were being pantomimed by a troupe led by Ed Wynn—right up to the end, when the players gather for a curtain call. After years of simply enjoying its magic, I have thought to reflect on the film's political consciousness because it seems to address the American psyche, and particularly its politics, directly. As the title of this chapter suggests, I think this movie about a journey across incommensurable realms offers a vision for bridging other opposites of the kind that divide the US nation in its ongoing crisis of value.

An analysis of the film by Salman Rushdie (1992) indicates the high estimation this seeming child's entertainment has achieved in its many decades of repeated rerelease. In the fall of 1998, a restored, color-and-sound-corrected digital print won new respect not only for the high achievement of the film's various components—script, acting, cinematography, special effects, music, dance, costumes, and sets—but for their integration into a meaningful whole. As Rushdie notes, this integration is all the more remarkable because "it's extremely difficult to say who the artist was"

(Rushdie, 1992, p. 13). *The Wizard of Oz* had a producer and associate producer with strongly creative personalities, four successive directors, at least two sublime stars and, by the filming's bumpy end, three charismatic supporting actors, as well as an exceptional team of expert scriptwriters and a remarkable lyricist and composer to shape the meaning of its story (see also Harmetz, 1998). A newspaperman and early specialist in marketing techniques L. Frank Baum had first told the story at the turn of the century to his own children (Traxel, 1998, pp. 140, 300–303). He developed it into a best-selling children's book that quickly became the basis for a stage musical—the first of the major reconfigurings by other than the original author's hands (Gardner & Nye, 1994, p. 26). Yet we will not be misled if we linger awhile with the problem of Baum's original intention in creating this profitable property.

Baum himself said in his April 1900 preface to the first Chicago edition of *The Wonderful Wizard of Oz* that it "was written solely to pleasure children of today" and that it "aspires to being a modernized fairy tale, in which the wonderment and joy are retained and the heartaches and nightmares are left out" (Hearn, 1973, p. 2). But it seems clear that he also took the opportunity to playfully limn the political reality of his turn-of-the-century America. As Henry M. Littlefield first suggested in the similarly turbulent year of 1968, the cyclone that Baum envisages as hitting Kansas was likely to have been his allegory for the Populist movement. By the time Baum began to compose *The Wizard of Oz*, this coalition had swept the entire Midwest into its vortex and had propelled the "silver-tongued orator" Nebraska Senator William Jennings Bryan into his crusading 1896 run for the Presidency against the Eastern financiers' favorite (and eventual winner) William McKinley. The animus Bryan, a Democrat, held against the Republican Establishment 'monometallists,' who wanted America's paper currency to be backed up only by gold bullion, was enunciated by his famous "Cross of Gold" speech at the Chicago Democratic Party Convention ("You shall not crucify mankind upon a cross of gold"). His aim was to protect the farmers who preferred a loose, even inflationary monetary policy, since they had frequent need of credit. The Populist solution that he had appropriated for his party was to continue to use silver as well as gold to back the currency, a strategy that also appealed to silver mining interests in the West. Bryan won the nomination, and L. Frank Baum participated in his torchlit parades. Bryan's rhetoric may have moved Baum to imagine, in his American fairy tale, the Republican approach to economics as a mythical Yellow Brick Road leading America toward an illusory Emerald City of centralized affluence, where McKinley would be presiding as humbug Wizard (Littlefield, in Hearn, 1973, pp. 221–233).[1]

Of the passionate, yet stubbornly abstruse twenty-five-year political debate over Free Silver versus the Gold Standard, historians Samuel Eliot Morison and Henry Steele Commager made a classic assessment:

> We can see now that the issue was both deeper and less dangerous than contemporaries realized. It was deeper because it involved a struggle for the ultimate control of government and of economy between the business interests of the East and the agrarian interests of the South and the West—a

struggle in which gold and silver were mere symbols. It was less dangerous because, in all probability, none of the calamities so freely prophesied
would have followed the adoption of either the gold or the silver standard
at any time during these years. When the gold standard was finally adopted
in 1900, the event made not a ripple on the placid seas of our economic life.
When the gold standard was abandoned by Great Britain and the United
States, a full generation later, the event led to no untoward results. Historical
parallels and analogies are always dangerous, but we are safe in saying that in
light of the experience of the 1930s much of the high-flown discussion of
the 1890s was fantastic.

Morison & Commager, 1950, p. 249

Today, with the tools of Jungian psychology, we might better recognize why
the idea of a Gold Standard elicited such an angry response from the political
unconscious at the end of the nineteenth century. As an image symbolic of the
metal that in alchemy was the earthly counterpart of the sun (Sol), an exclusive
privileging of gold suggested the predominance of solar masculine values within
the ruling establishment. In the grip of religious fervor unaccounted for by his
economic argument, Bryan was urging his party to balance the Gold Standard
with that of Silver, a metal that we know from Jung's alchemical researches to be
the terrestrial representative of Luna and thus a symbol of the Feminine Principle.
Already, through the charismatic leadership of the 'silver-tongued orator,' the
Democratic Party's twentieth-century matriarchal stance, with its Eros toward the
economically less fortunate, was taking shape in opposition to the more traditionally patriarchal Republican position emphasizing self-reliance.[2] But although
such an interpretation of Bryan's movement was fully compatible with the pre-
eminence that Baum gives to the feminine in the narrative structure of the Oz
books as a whole,[3] its full implications would not have been conscious for Baum
at the time. The often whimsical Baum probably turned his fancy to the politics of
his day as part of a more general strategy to amuse children by exposing the pretensions of their elders, but this move gave his intuition its chance to explore the
American political psyche in a way that continues to fascinate. Littlefield, who has
shrewdly deciphered the allegorical level of the text, believes that the Scarecrow,
with his anxiety over his intelligence, originally reflected the lack of intellectual
self-confidence of many Midwesterners in Baum's time, when they were still reel-
ing from the accusation recently leveled against them by William Allen White in
an 1896 article, "What's the Matter with Kansas?" White, asserting that Kansas's
farmers were ignorant, irrational and generally muddle-headed (Hearn, 1973,
p. 227), had suggested they should be worried about their thinking. The Cowardly
Lion, according to Littlefield, is Bryan himself, with his mighty oratorical roar,
his underlying chronic insecurity, and his ultimate courage in taking on the East
Coast establishment. The rusted Tin Woodman's unwilling immobility represents
the fate of the unemployed workers in the East after the depression of 1893. The
pair of Wicked Witches might refer to the threats posed, on the one hand, by the

environment (i.e. drought, the traditional witch 'of the West' that can only be 'put out' by water) and, on the other hand, by the market (traditionally under the negative control 'of the East'). These adversaries, Baum's allegory argues, can be defeated by the energy provided by the Populist cyclone if only farmers can learn to think for themselves, mobilize their potential allies among the politically rusty East Coast workforce, and muster their courage in standing up to the hypocrisy of central government. Otherwise, the soul of traditional agrarian America must remain, like Dorothy, lost and unable to find its way home.

Although this first detailed political reading of the tale has much to recommend it, we cannot reduce the meanings of this perennially popular story to these topical references of the time of its creation or even to the probable intentions of its creator, L. Frank Baum. Rather, Littlefield's exposure of the election-year subtext serves us best if it enables us to grasp that *The Wizard of Oz*, like so many works that have captured the American imagination, derives a good deal of its energy from a primary concern for the political health of the nation.

In the case of *The Wonderful Wizard of Oz*, this concern survives in the later constructions that have been placed on the tale. When the story was made into a film forty years after Baum first wrote it out, for instance, the allegory's point of reference seemed to have shifted to Midwestern anxiety over America's turn to internationalism on the eve of the Second World War. Its 1938 script certainly trumpets the message so often sounded by the isolationists at that time: "There's no place like home." In the 1970s, with the advent of women's liberation and the feminist and gay rethinking of the constrictions of traditional gender roles for men and women, the film began (in Jungian terms) to signal a triumph of matriarchal values over the threatening patriarchal anima (witch) and the pompous patriarchal animus (wizard). A liberated gay man, for instance, might describe himself as a "friend of Dorothy" and locate his own individuation story in hers (Hopcke, 1989). Today, two decades after winning the Cold War against Soviet Russia, Americans watch *The Wizard of Oz* knowing that their young nation's fate, inevitable as Dorothy's in the face of the cyclone, has too long been to be swept onto the international stage in the uncomfortably prominent role of peacekeeper, the destroyer of all world wickedness. From that last perspective, the film can now seem to my compatriots like a warning dream coming from some prescience in the American psyche of 1939, urging us to stiffen our integrity lest we lose our national center in the inflation of becoming the world's leading power, one indeed "not in Kansas anymore."

The Wizard of Oz, however, is more than a warning, for it resolves the tensions it creates. The anxiety is beautifully brought to life by Judy Garland, who is an image less of Baum's little Dorothy, as captured by W. W. Denslow's original drawings, than of a growing, insecure nation on the verge of its debut as a mature world power. But the film moves its heroine, and our sense of ourselves as a nation, toward the mature integrity we feel at the end when Dorothy, in a closing set piece suggestive of wholeness, is back from the dream and nightmare of Oz, and finds herself safe in her own bed, surrounded by seven of the Kansas characters. This final scene is like the coda of a human symphony, making explicit an eightfold structure of consciousness in the relation of these characters to each other and to Dorothy. With this tableau as a key to the structure of the film, it is possible to trace how Dorothy's individuation proceeds through her links to the other characters.

The interaction of eight characters is one way to visualize the differentiation of consciousness in an individuating psyche.[4] Within such a polyphonic arrangement, the distinct consciousnesses represented by the characters have, like so many voices in a democracy, a potential for harmony, but one that will be either undermined or achieved by the particular political process which the film records. I call that process *political* because it involves alliances, contending parties, and struggles for audience and power, all revealed by the way the characters in a film play out their psychological roles—their different consciousnesses—in relation to each other. In a film with particular resonance such as *The Wizard of Oz*, these roles can be specifically metaphoric of the political developments emerging in the American psyche at the moment of the film's construction.

A natural starting point in elucidating this political structure within *The Wizard of Oz* is with Dorothy herself. In terms of the film's idiosyncratic politics of American consciousness, the little girl's standpoint is privileged. She emblematizes a form of what nowadays is called 'emotional intelligence' (Goleman, 1995). As played by Judy Garland, who is ever poised to react to the feelings of the other characters (including her little dog Toto) and make them her concern, this standpoint is what C. G. Jung has called *extraverted feeling*.[5] It is in relation to this apparent strength of her character that we can understand her special relationship to the Scarecrow, the first of the fantastic companions she picks up on the Yellow Brick Road. The Scarecrow, who famously starts their acquaintance by singing and dancing Harburg and Arlen's "If I Only Had a Brain," is a marvelous depiction of the insecurities captured by Jung's term, 'inferior introverted thinking.' According to Jung's theory of psychological types—that is, types of psychological consciousness, or what present-day cognitive psychologists call 'intelligences' (Gardner, 1983; Thompson, 1985)—*introverted thinking* is at the opposite end of a rational axis from extraverted feeling.

There is also a power differential in these arrangements. If extraverted feeling is the superior, dominant function, introverted thinking will regard itself as inferior. And indeed, the Scarecrow has an inferiority complex and gives image, with his comical physical incoordination, to the inherent unreliability of any 'inferior function.' The character's movements are not entirely under his conscious control due to the flimsy quality of his embodiment as a cloth man stuffed with straw. But his connection with Dorothy gives him a 'spine' to replace the beanpole she helps him down from. We can visualize the two characters together as the backbone of the movie itself. Their relationship is central to the integrity of the film. Figure 5.1 illustrates what I mean.

In parenthesis, I have identified each character in Jungian terms according to the typical form of consciousness that that character displays throughout the film. The *position* of the characters in relation to the other is also important if we want

Dorothy (extraverted feeling)

Scarecrow (introverted thinking)

FIGURE 5.1   The relationship between Dorothy and the Scarecrow

to understand the consciousness politics of the film. In relation to the Scarecrow on the spine or axis of integrity of the film, Dorothy is in the superior position. We have already suggested as much by saying that throughout the film her kind of intelligence is privileged. Although Dorothy describes herself as "the Small and the Meek" when introducing herself to the Wizard (who with characteristic puffery has described himself as "Oz, the Great and Terrible"), there is little doubt that she trusts her feeling responses more than does any other character. In the end, it is just an uncensored spontaneous reaction that allows her to accomplish the heroic deed of melting the witch by throwing a bucket of water over her. Dorothy is related to as a superior person, not only by the Munchkins whose Mayor and officials greet her as a visiting dignitary, indeed their 'national heroine,' but also by all the other characters. She is thus a perfect image of Jung's 'superior function' of consciousness, a political designation that I have elsewhere described as the locus of the hero archetype in any psyche (see Harris, 1996). Similarly, the Scarecrow—a marginally adapted even if magical figure with whom most people would not want to be seen in public—is a good personification of the way the animus (in relation to a woman's more comfortably dominant superior function) is forced to carry the 'inferior function' role.[6] We could therefore draw our diagram again with new labels that emphasize the political relationship of archetypes in this arrangement of consciousness (Figure 5.2).

Dorothy (heroine)

Scarecrow (animus)

FIGURE 5.2   The political relationship between Dorothy and the Scarecrow (1)

Putting the two types of construction—hierarchical status and archetype—together, the political relationship of these characters is summarized in Figure 5.3.

When we start to introduce the other characters around this 'spine' that defines the politics of consciousness within *The Wizard of Oz*, we can also identify an axis of 'auxiliary' functions that set out to assist Dorothy in mature and less mature ways. This much more 'irrational' axis is defined by Glinda the Good and the Cowardly Lion. Glinda represents a very motherly, and I would say introverted, intuition, which 'knows' the right magic to protect Dorothy but largely keeps her knowledge of its workings to herself, until the time seems right to share it. The Yellow Brick Road that she asks Dorothy to follow is itself an image of intuition, which Jung notes is frequently symbolized in fantasy by the color yellow (Jung, 1950/1959a, ¶588, 1950/1959b, ¶697). On the other hand, the Cowardly Lion, in his physical size, his bullying swagger, and his need to impose his body on others ("Put 'em up, put 'em up!" he demands, as he thrusts forth his clenched fists and swings his tail) is defined in terms of extraverted sensation. This type of consciousness, according to Jung, can be a formidable intelligence too, the inverse of introverted intuition in its immediate attention to present realities, but here it is in a primitive level of development. In contrast to Glinda's implied parental position within the story as Great Mother, he has the status of the Great Baby, whom the other characters must chide or reassure. He oscillates between boastful omnipotence ("I'll be King of the Forest") and cowering terror ("Why'd you have to do that?" he blubbers, when Dorothy slaps him across the nose for growling at Toto). Indeed, part of the comedy of the Lion, as played by Bert Lahr, is that his intuition is so inferior that, for all his tearfulness, he never seems to anticipate the real danger he invites by the physical (extraverted sensation) abandon with which he wades into each new situation. It is not so much that he lacks courage as that his courage is of the *puer aeternus* type. Bert Lahr's Lion displays an inflated sense of what he can pull off that is easily punctured by reality, at which point he falls into despair over his own cowardice. The *puer aeternus*, like the Great Mother, is an archetype that Jungian psychology has reintroduced to Western culture. The Latin (from Ovid) means eternal, or perpetual, boy. This certainly seems to define the Cowardly Lion. And so we can draw an auxiliary character axis for these two opposed consciousnesses that bring their strength to Dorothy (Figure 5.4).

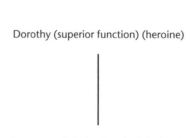

Dorothy (superior function) (heroine)

Scarecrow (inferior function) (animus)

FIGURE 5.3 The political relationship between Dorothy and the Scarecrow (2)

Glinda (Great Mother)   Cowardly Lion (*puer aeternus*)
(introverted intuition)   (extraverted sensation)

FIGURE 5.4 An auxiliary character axis

Locating these characters now around Dorothy and the Scarecrow, we get a basic quaternity of figures that defines the particular pattern of consciousness that emanates from the story itself (Figure 5.5).

If, however, we remove the particular character names and the archetypal roles they occupy in the story by a political designation to suggest their relative *power* within the story, our diagram would resemble Figure 5.6. Figure 5.6, as aficionados of Jungian type theory will recognize, defines the consciousness of the extraverted feeling type with auxiliary introverted intuition, or what the Myers–Briggs Type Indicator (a standard assessment for determining the consciousness preferences in individuals) scores as ENFJ. A recent description of ENFJ in the type literature follows: "On the great highway of life, . . . ENFJs are . . . like road rangers, patrolling life's detours and alternate routes, rescuing lost drivers, giving them decent maps" (Thomson, 1998, p. 357).

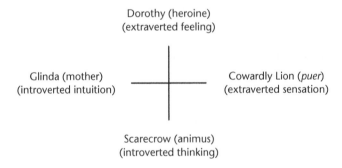

Dorothy (heroine)
(extraverted feeling)

Glinda (mother)   Cowardly Lion (*puer*)
(introverted intuition)   (extraverted sensation)

Scarecrow (animus)
(introverted thinking)

FIGURE 5.5 The pattern of consciousness emanating from the story

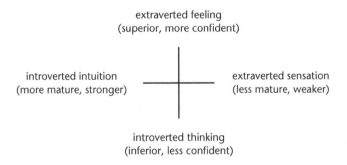

extraverted feeling
(superior, more confident)

introverted intuition   extraverted sensation
(more mature, stronger)   (less mature, weaker)

introverted thinking
(inferior, less confident)

FIGURE 5.6 Consciousnesses and their political designations

Thomson's simile echoes the sensibility of *The Wizard of Oz* taken as a whole. The consciousness of the characters and their relative positions combine to give the film itself a definite consciousness—that is, a certain set of concerns that define it not only as a psychological, but also a political space. By establishing the positions of the characters in relation to each other in terms of the way they feel about themselves, how the other characters relate to them, and the degree of emotional development they display, we can understand the consciousness politics of the film.

Movies, of course, do not depend only on functions of consciousness to get their effects. They also, notoriously, depict forms of unconsciousness that challenge the more conscious characters with life's threats, dangers, and complications, as well as their own defenses against moving forward. Unconsciousness itself is a political force in *The Wizard of Oz*, as we see in the remarkable scene where the enchanted poppies put the flesh-and-blood characters to sleep and threaten to stop this particular road movie in its tracks. And of course the entire film (unlike Baum's novel) is cast as a dream experienced by Dorothy in a coma, after a blow on the head by a window loosened in the cyclone. That the unconscious presents itself to Dorothy and her conscious helpers in the form of various personalities who represent a system of threats and defenses suggests that the film expresses a reaction to trauma itself. As Donald Kalsched has demonstrated, such shadow figures play a major role in the psyche's response to being traumatized, and they are both ambivalent sources of further complication as well as unexpected sources of help from within. What Kalsched has written about therapeutic work is also true for our struggle to make sense of the psyche in art and politics:

> We encounter here a supreme irony in our work with the psyche. The self-same powers that seem so set on undermining our . . . efforts—so ostensibly devoted to death, dismemberment, and annihilation of consciousness—are the very reservoir from which new life, fuller integration, and true enlightenment derive.
>
> *1996, p. 62*

From the standpoint of Baum's allegory, the trauma from which Dorothy is seeking to recover is the split in the American political psyche itself, its historic, tragic tension between populist and plutocratic interests. It is from this 'basic fault' in the American political psyche that the characters in the Oz story first drew life, and their tensions survive the later retellings of the tale.

We will now examine figures in both the novel and the film that are truly shadowy, in that neither their potential for good nor for evil is entirely clear, even when it seems to be. Rather, they participate in the murky ambivalence of the unconscious itself, as something not just to be overcome but to be faced and learned from. The most obvious of these characters is the Wizard. When he is unmasked at last by Toto, who pulls aside the curtain, revealing the humbug, as the Scarecrow correctly names him, Dorothy is moved to offer one of her spontaneous, forceful feeling evaluations: "Oh, you're a very bad man!" The Wizard replies, "Oh no, my dear, I—I'm a very good man. I'm just a very bad wizard" (Langley, Ryerson, & Woolf, 1994, p. 62). Yet the same man, who with callous opportunism sent Dorothy and her friends to bring back the broomstick of the Wicked Witch of the West (a politically 'smart' move, since the Witch had already sky-written with that broom her command to him to "surrender Dorothy"), proceeds to use his rhetoric to show them how best to think about themselves. In other words, he serves initially to undermine the confidence of the ultimately prevailing characters, but ends up supporting it. He is an image of the power of the unconscious to be used in both mean and generous ways. Such ambivalence is characteristic of a psychological intelligence used demonically, and the Wizard as described by Baum in the novel resembles a demon in the way he assumes different shapes. To Dorothy he appears as a great Head, to the Scarecrow, a lovely Lady, and to her other, more sensitive companion the Tin Woodman as a "most terrible Beast." (This last demonic avatar reminds us that the remarkable ability of a demonic figure to be "cruel and kind at the same time" was perhaps first remarked upon, as Joseph Henderson has noted [Jung, von Franz, Henderson, Jacobi, & Jaffé, 1964, p. 138], by Beauty's father in the quintessentially psychological fairy tale *Beauty and the Beast*.)

In the film, however, it is the Scarecrow who is in the best position to stand up to the Wizard's impressive iconography and rhetoric by saying, "You humbug," a choice of words Frank Morgan's extraverted thinking Wizard for once does not correct and subvert ("Yes, that's exactly so, I'm a humbug"[7]). This is a crucial moment in the politics of the film when the integrity of the Scarecrow's incisive introverted thinking succeeds in standing up to the obfuscations of the Wizard's demonic extraverted thinking. This confrontation near the end of the film is reminiscent of the moment before the cyclone trip to Oz when Dorothy rebukes Almira Gulch (who is trying to have the biting and cat-chasing Toto destroyed) by exclaiming, "You wicked old witch!" In that earlier confrontation, our extraverted feeling heroine stands up to a strongly opposing will symbolized by another feeling standpoint, the antagonistic introverted feeling[8] of Miss Gulch, who is so concerned with protecting her own interests that she doesn't care enough about the feelings of others.

Like Dorothy, we are being initiated into the politics of confrontation, where consciousnesses encounter opposing attitudes, with respect to introversion and extraversion, in the form of figures they experience as shadowy. The characters that give the film its spine of integrity can be diagrammed in relation to their antagonists, naming the psychological types associated with each character. We should understand that even a figure of the unconscious can exhibit a characteristic type, implying that there is intelligence in the unconscious, although it is typically used in an unconscious and frequently unethical way, hence the description of such functions of potential but problematic consciousness as 'in shadow' (Figure 5.7). In this scheme, we can see that Dorothy's heroic extraverted feeling is opposed by the introverted feeling of Almira Gulch, and that the Scarecrow's righteous indignation, expressing an animus demand for a higher standard of integrity, is directed against the pompous obfuscations of the Wizard.

The connection of the extraverted feeling Dorothy to the introverted thinking Scarecrow is an axis of integrity created by their love for each other. By contrast, the introverted feeling Almira Gulch and, at least initially, the Wizard, are mere deployers of power, tyrants in their respective realms. We need to look more closely at these characters who define a shadow axis that poses a political threat to the integrity of Dorothy and the Scarecrow.

Although played by the same actress, Almira Gulch does *not* correspond in every psychological detail to the Witch she becomes in Dorothy's 'dream'. Margaret Hamilton's performance is in fact a dual role no less extraordinary than the twin sisters played a few years later by Bette Davis in *A Stolen Life* (1946) and Olivia de Havilland in *The Dark Mirror* (1946), films which make explicit this Hollywood convention. The challenge to an actress playing two sharply contrasting characters in the same picture is traditionally posed in classic American film by one character being (in the language of psychological type) extraverted and irrational, and the other introverted and rational. The political preference within the traditional American psyche for women who are introverted and rational, usually introverted feeling, can readily be noticed here. In terms of traditional American values, this has the psychological implication of asking women to take up the position of anima figures, supporting and granting the legitimation of their approval to the heroic extraverted thinking of its ruling men.

In the world of *The Wizard of Oz*, everything is topsy-turvy. The extraverted thinking 'ruling man' is the humbug Wizard in Oz, and the introverted feeling Almira Gulch owns "half the county" in Kansas, in which Aunt Em's farm is located. Far from being represented as an anima figure supporting the integrity of the power structure, she is presented as an opposing personality threatening the rule of care in governing human relationships. Yet even though her 'better' character is already shadowy, Margaret Hamilton runs true to the dual role genre in which her performance falls, in being asked to play an even more wicked character who is extraverted and irrational. Her magnificently menacing Witch, who is constantly threatening Dorothy with what she is *going* to do to her, is a sharply etched

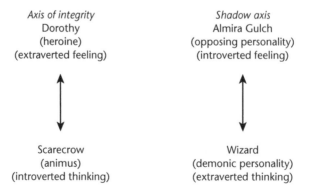

FIGURE 5.7 Dorothy and the Scarecrow in relation to their antagonists

example of the shadowy (negatively witchy) use of the psychological consciousness which Jung calls extraverted intuition, the function which concerns itself, in any situation, with future possibilities. She discloses this promise of bad things to come not just with specific frightening suggestions but with the anticipatory delight of her evil cackle.

And, unlike Hamilton's Almira Gulch, her Witch finds her typological opposite in the film not in Dorothy, but Glinda. Glinda the Good Witch (who almost never discloses her designs) and the Wicked Witch of the West (who always does), take opposite attitudes toward the irrational intuitive power (the ability to perceive and conjure by way of the unconscious) that is traditionally the province of any witch. Again in the language of Jung's typology of character, Glinda the Good's attitude is that of the introverted intuitive, and the Wicked Witch of the West's attitude is that of the extraverted intuitive. The Wicked Witch's winged monkeys rather perfectly embody an intuition used to terrify others with its unexpected ability to get to them, just as the Witch is always inserting herself into Dorothy's private spaces and thoughts—for instance, in the crystal ball sequence in the Witch's castle when she elicits and then mocks Dorothy's anxieties about Aunt Em. This is the opposite of Glinda's reassuringly self-contained, bubble-enclosed, introverted intuition used to solace and focus Dorothy without intruding on the girl's autonomy.

We find a similar pair of opposed attitudes in the two animal characters in the film, who together occupy the other pole—sensation—of the irrational axis. Toto and the Cowardly Lion are opposed from the moment the Cowardly Lion makes his first appearance. When the Lion growls and threatens Dorothy, the Scarecrow, and the Tin Man, Toto barks. The Lion goes after Toto, but Dorothy slaps the larger beast, reducing him, as we have seen, to a sort of whimpering baby. Toto's role here is to facilitate the exposing of the reality behind the bluster. That is precisely what the little dog again does when the Wizard of Oz tries to put off keeping his promise to reward Dorothy, the Scarecrow, the Tin Man, and the Lion after they succeed in bringing him the broomstick of the Wicked Witch of the West. This time it is the Wizard who roars, "Do not arouse the wrath of the Great and Powerful Oz." At this point, Toto runs to the background of the big screening room on which Oz's propaganda image surmounts the throne and pulls aside a curtain hanging to one side. That is when the human Wizard is finally revealed, talking into a microphone.

Toto, who is normally rather still and never charismatic, is really the character to expose what Rushdie calls the Great Humbug. Rushdie confesses that he "cannot stand" Toto, finding even the purposive bit with the curtain "an irritating piece of mischief-making" (Rushdie, 1992, pp. 17–18). Toto, who works behind the scenes, is personally unprepossessing, does not usually call attention to himself, and makes few wasted movements, is an effective image of *introverted sensation*, a consciousness close to intelligent animal sense that concerns itself with identifying what is real. In the final scene of *The Wizard of Oz*, when Aunt Em's rational solution to Dorothy's account of the journey to Oz is to tell the girl, "We dream lots of silly things," Dorothy cries exasperatedly to the Kansans assembled around her bed, "Doesn't anyone believe me?" and Toto jumps up beside her, as if to say he can vouch for the reality of her experience. Introverted sensation, as Jung (1921/1971, ¶650) emphasized, is an irrational function, which can appreciate the reality of the psyche even against rational considerations, because it trusts the evidence of its own senses.

But Toto is also a trickster, who consistently moves the plot forward by creating some kind of mischief that breaks with an established order of things (biting Almira Gulch, growling at the Lion, jumping out of the hot-air balloon just as the Wizard is about to take Dorothy back to America). The effect is usually to subvert an inflated use of power and force Dorothy, out of her feeling for Toto, to take a stronger position in defense of caring generally. In other words, Toto galvanizes Dorothy's instinctive courage, the very quality that the Cowardly Lion lacks. The puerile Lion therefore reflects something immature in Dorothy's character that Toto is helping her to grow beyond.

By adding the shadow functions carried by the (Wicked) Witch and trickster, we can now more fully illustrate the interplay of consciousnesses that gives energy to the auxiliary axis between intuition and sensation, which drives the irrational plot of the film, forcing Dorothy through their cross-fire to develop her integrity as a character (Figure 5.8).

The Witch's role in bringing out Dorothy's courage is obvious; that portion of the tale is a nineteenth-century hero story, with a nod to Dumas. Dorothy becomes, perhaps, d'Artagnan (although she has to share this role with Toto), and the Lion, the Scarecrow, and Tin Man become the Three Musketeers (Dumas, 1844/2007). This is the side of political effectiveness that is celebrated by successful restorations of legitimate governments, holy wars, and being on the 'right' side in elections. It leaves out the deeper part of the shadow to catalyze political individuation, a development that can only take place when the shadow is included and appreciated as part of one's own political consciousness, rather than simply defeated or repressed as belonging to an Other who is 'wrong.' Heroic victories generally result in inflating the winner's standpoint beyond its true value. Here it really is up to the trickster to take the story of one's political development beyond simply 'putting out the Witch.' Anyone studying what Samuels has called "the political development of the person" (Samuels, 1993, pp. 53–61) should take heed of the way Toto forces even the victorious Dorothy to rethink her own values.

Glinda the Good (mother) (introverted intuition)	————————	Lion (*puer*) (extraverted sensation)
The Wicked Witch of the West (witch) (extraverted intuition)	————————	Toto (trickster) (introverted sensation)

FIGURE 5.8 The interplay of auxiliary consciousnesses

Nowhere in the film is Toto's shadowy role in forcing Dorothy to think and feel for herself made more evident than in the final scene of the Technicolor (Oz) portion of the film, when, as a consequence of Toto jumping out of the balloon basket, Dorothy is advised to turn to Glinda for help getting back home. When Glinda in her introverted way finally discloses to Dorothy the secret of the ruby slippers, she does so by leading Dorothy herself to articulate what she has learned in Oz about her 'heart's desire.' It's only then that Dorothy is able to utter with full heart the magical feeling thought, "There's no place like home." This is introverted feeling and extraverted thinking emerging at last from the extraverted feeling heroine, and this expression of her shadow functions in such an affirming way is what directs the slippers to grant her wish and return her to Kansas, where she can to take up her now fully realized American identity.

The deep red of the slippers would alone have justified the decision of the producers at MGM to film *The Wizard of Oz* in color, for the hue imparts a value, and a psychological meaning, that Baum's allegorical Silver Shoes could not convey. The 'power' in the slippers is not just the force of the feminine principle, but the power of conscious introverted feeling to deepen and ground love. This explains the role of two important characters in the film which I have left until now to discuss: Aunt Em and the Tin Man. They are linked in Dorothy's fantasy by her shared concern for their hearts. In the Tin Man's case, the problem with his heart is simply his feeling that he lacks one, a problem that Dorothy takes on as if it were her own. In Aunt Em's case, real heart trouble is at issue. Or so Dorothy believes, for in the first crystal ball vision, related to Dorothy while she is still in Kansas by Professor Marvel shortly after she runs away with Toto to escape Miss Gulch, the fortune teller has seen Aunt Em putting her hand on her heart and falling onto a bed. Both Aunt Em and the Tin Man induce Dorothy to begin to reflect on the problem that lies within her own feeling, a deficiency that is masked by the abundant empathy she shows for all the other characters and the appreciation they bestow on her for it. Dorothy's feeling, despite its privileged, even valorized, status in the film, is somehow too unthinkingly, and too one-sidedly, extraverted.

It was not just Almira Gulch who was annoyed by Dorothy in Kansas. Aunt Em, that kindly, reserved keeper of order on the farm, whose caring for everyone is always held in reserve, is driven to ask Dorothy early in the film to "just help us out today and find yourself a place where you won't get into any trouble!" That place, of course, is "Over the Rainbow"—in Oz, where Dorothy is put magically in touch with the deeper value of harmony with her surroundings that Aunt Em is trying to convey to her.

One of the neatest psychological touches in the film is how the quietly kind Aunt Em and the noisily mean Almira Gulch are, on the inside, so similar. Both are concerned with property, proper order, and propriety, and both Kansas women, I think, exhibit introverted feeling in their brief but memorable onscreen appearances. Miss Gulch, recognizing that others may not understand where she is coming from, buttresses her introverted feeling with an extraverted thinking animus (personified by the Sheriff, whose order to have Toto seized she brandishes). The sincere Aunt Em shows the vulnerability of introverted feeling more openly when she says:

> Almira Gulch . . . just because you own half the county doesn't mean you
> have the power to run the rest of us! For twenty-three years I've been dying
> to tell you what I thought of you . . . and now . . . well—being a Christian
> woman—I can't say it!

Interestingly, Miss Gulch can't find the words to respond to Aunt Em, either.
The inability to articulate emotion that is nonetheless strongly felt is a particular
hallmark of introverted feeling. But both women, with their apparently different,
nicer and nastier styles of doing so, are united in wanting to oppose Dorothy's
heedless extraverted feeling willfulness with strong feeling wills of their own coming from another direction.

Introverted feeling, as Jung was the first to get us to see, is a valuation function
that works at the archetypal (not the personal) level, taking the deepest possible
sounding of a situation. It not only enables but compels us to feel the rightness and
wrongness of images, arrogating from its very closeness to the archetypal a bench
of judgment that grants it the power to decide what is appropriate and what is not
(see Chapter 15).

This theme is carried forward in the Oz section of the film, when Dorothy
happily starts to pick apples off an inviting-looking tree. The tree (an introverted
feeling type) turns out to have other feelings than the extraverted generosity
Dorothy instinctively expects. It asks, "How would you like to have someone
come along and pick something off of you?" At this point in the film, Dorothy is
no match for such an attitude; she simply fails to understand it. The feeling value
concealed in this standpoint is conveyed by the deep red of the apples on the tree,
which 'rhymes' visually with the ruby slippers. The overtones of the Garden of
Eden in the forbidden apples suggest a Knowledge of which Dorothy is psychologically innocent. And this, of course, is the political issue at the heart of the
film: the tension between extraverted feeling and introverted feeling. The value of
introverted feeling is unavailable to extraverted feeling because of the latter's blind-
ness toward it. The tree is thus a personification of the consciousness (and political
problem) that I have already identified as the opposing personality challenging the
heroine. It actually starts to throw its apples at Dorothy when manipulated to do
so by the clever Scarecrow, who sees a way to get Dorothy her snack. But this
comedic interlude, which culminates in Dorothy happily scrambling to pick up
the apples, turns suddenly serious when her hand (that is, her extraverted feeling)
presses into the hard, still foot of the Tin Man. The figure is rusty and immobile,
and even after she oils him, so that he can talk, he quickly opposes her cheerful
assurance that he's "perfect now" with a sarcastic retort: "Oh, bang on my chest if
you think I'm perfect." Then the Tin Man explains that his chest is hollow because
he hasn't got a heart.

In the ensuing song sequence, part of which is a duet, Jack Haley's Tin Man
seems almost effeminately competitive with Garland's Dorothy. Like Almira
Gulch, Aunt Em, and the Grouchy Apple Tree, the Tin Man embodies a feeling
attitude that is opposed to Dorothy's. His appearance on the scene creates within

the vaudeville show business leitmotiv of the film a political complication between the actors (upstaging) that was absent from Garland's previous duet with Bolger. From his sentimentality, moreover, it is obvious that the Tin Man doesn't exactly lack a heart; what he lacks (as the Wizard shrewdly figures out) is a testimonial, that is, an extraverted attestation of his feeling (which the Wizard gives him in the form of a heart-shaped watch). That the Tin Man is, moreover, all armor suggests that his introverted feeling is somehow rigid. By now, the audience will already have noted that stiffening up is one of Dorothy's most characteristic defenses, conveyed perfectly by Judy Garland's self-referential double takes. The narcissistic side of this defense does in a way lack 'heart,' because it cuts the character off from appreciating the introverted feeling of others. For all Dorothy's vaunted empathy, where is her feeling for Miss Gulch's concern over cat and garden, and for Aunt Em's desire for order on the farm?

One can trace a whole chain of figures and images representing the opposing personality type which Dorothy is gradually coming to terms with in the film— from Almira Gulch and Aunt Em, through the Grouchy Apple Tree and the Tin Man, and on to the Witch's Cossack-like guard. The series is punctuated by, and culminates in, the most mysterious of all these images of introverted feeling: the ruby slippers.

These slippers, which once belonged to the 'sister' of the Wicked Witch of the West, that is, to the Wicked Witch of the East, are, I think, meant to represent the concealed introverted feeling standpoint of Almira Gulch, which, in a more appealing presentation, is that of Aunt Em as well. In running away from both of these women, and then being swept up by the cyclone—the objectified force of her own instinctive repudiation of their standpoint—Dorothy has in effect 'killed' introverted feeling and has to accept the psychological consequences. Herein lies a complication in the assertion of power that Jung understood better than any other psychologist, one that very few contemporary politicians are subtle enough to grasp. Jung tells us that, when someone succeeds in killing, that is overcoming, the *mana* of another person (Jung defines this Polynesian word for charisma as the "bewitching quality of a person"), the conqueror then automatically [acquires] that mana (Jung, 1966, pp. 227–228). This, Jung tells us, is in accord "with the primitive belief that when a man kills the mana-person he assimilates the mana into his own body." Our extraverted feeling heroine must therefore accept the mana of what she has defeated, which is the introverted feeling standpoint not just of Almira Gulch but of Aunt Em as well. That is why the ruby slippers, carrying the power she has arrogated, appear on her feet and seem almost to be attached to them, so that the Wicked Witch of the West realizes that she will have to kill her to get them back. Dorothy does not learn how to use the slippers' power, however, until the end of the film.

Again, we can illustrate these stations in Dorothy's political development, which gradually transform her character from someone who is merely a partisan of her own standpoint to someone who is truly able to appreciate the value of a standpoint that is completely opposed to her own (Figure 5.9).

It is an appreciation for the introverted side of feeling that Glinda the Good is able at last to bring out in Dorothy when she gets her to articulate the value that the film calls "There's no place like home." This is the part of the script which many dismiss as sentimental or cynical, including Rushdie (1992), who calls it "a conservative little homily," and Zipes, who says it "is all a lie" since the point of Baum's Oz stories is that "home cannot be found in America" (Zipes, 1998, p. ix). What Zipes calls this "Home Sweet Home" ending can easily seem to lock onto the isolationist Republican discourse of the America Firsters, who were opposing Franklin Roosevelt's increasing interest in the problems of Europe at the time the film was made. Indeed, its introverted feeling was not at all a popular message by the time the film was released. Several re-releases were needed before the film made a profit, and only a series of annual television showings secured its status as a classic. America, after 1939, moved on to its manifest destiny to make the world safe for democracy, and extraverted feeling values were to predominate— that is, the values associated with selling and promoting 'the American way of life.'

We watch the film today in an age that has almost forgotten what introverted feeling is (could Gary Cooper be a star today?), and so the return home to Aunt Em can strike an uncanny chord even among those who are politically opposed to a return to traditional values. If one lets the magic of Judy Garland's performance work on one's American political sensitivities, one can see how extraordinary it can be for a liberal extraverted feeling to make a gesture toward the other, more conservative, feeling standpoint. (Just as conservative introverted feeling in American politics perennially dismisses extraverted feeling empathy as 'bleeding heart liberalism,' so liberal extraverted feeling routinely discounts introverted feeling's emphasis on individual responsibility as selfish and judgmental.) It is much more common, in American films, for a cold, introverted feeling to warm up and make a concession to extraverted feeling. Garland's Dorothy, realizing as her own the power implied by the ruby slippers, really reaches out to Aunt Em, and we want to embrace her for it. On the part of the character, this is a step beyond maintaining the consistency of her own attitude, and also beyond the way she

Extraverted feeling	(stance toward)	Introverted feeling
Dorothy	initially opposed to	Aunt Em
	kills	Wicked Witch of the East
	doesn't understand	Ruby Slippers
	is attacked by	Grouchy Apple Tree
	oils and helps to heal	Tin Man
	wins over	Witch's Guard
	learns to use	Ruby Slippers
	finally appreciates	Aunt Em

FIGURE 5.9 Stations in Dorothy's political development

sharpened her integrity in Oz with the support of her magical helpers. Her final gesture, without disavowing her Oz experiences, is a stunning acknowledgment of a value beyond the heroic. Her political development and, indeed, achievement in the film is finally not about justifying her own standpoint, but about finding common ground for the continuity of value.

Dorothy's ability, back in Kansas, to move herself into the territory originally pre-empted by Almira Gulch is paralleled by the Scarecrow's ascendance to the rulership of Oz when the Wizard abdicates in his favor. Together, Dorothy and the Scarecrow seem to represent a new, more conscious order with the integrity to supplant the patriarchal anima (Miss Gulch) and animus (the Wizard), who simply disappear from the story, like the totalitarian Wicked Witch of the West who melts away. This is of course the wishful level of Baum's fairy tale, carried forward by the film. The Scarecrow, with his newly legitimized introverted thinking, promises to be a truly loving philosopher king, but this is in Oz, and ironic, because empathic introverted thinking has rarely prevailed in American politics. Even more rarely does the extraverted thinking that dominates America's discourse yield the power it wields by having control of the nation's image of itself. That power is satirized here in the portrait of the media-manipulating Wizard, Oz (he even bears the same name as the country he rules). This Wizard, however, is at best a well-intentioned purveyor of persona, at worst a propagandist, and his gracious surrender of power is exactly what we don't observe in this aspect of the American political character.

And just as ironic, in its distance beyond what we usually see, is the development of Dorothy's feeling. In an America whose dominant consciousness is extraverted thinking, extraverted feeling as robust as Dorothy's comes as a bit of a shock. Extraverted feeling is the function most often educated as if it needed a road map (the latest is the notion of 'emotional intelligence') and thus asked to operate through rigid polarities of gratuitous charm and relatively adolescent condemnation of what it does not understand. John Travolta's character Vincent Vega in *Pulp Fiction* (1994) is a far more usual presentation of this side of the American character than Judy Garland's Dorothy. But, that leaves out shadow development. What is America's extraverted feeling, finally, but political feeling? And in that area we keep getting breakthroughs, such as the recognition of marriage equality for same sex couples by the United States Supreme Court and the taking down, at last, of Confederate flags in the American South, finally recognizing how offensive these have been to the feelings of African Americans. Other countries, to be sure, often complain about America's lack of grace in world affairs, its failure to stand by the values that once defined it. These are lapses of introverted feeling. Yet what often concerns the citizens of America, of which I am one, most about our political life is that our extraverted feeling is so often put on the defensive (Gormley, 2010).

Ever since Ronald Reagan's presidency, extraverted feeling in America has been summoned as if it might heal us, but in an increasingly cynical culture, and often with disastrous consequences for the political health of the nation.

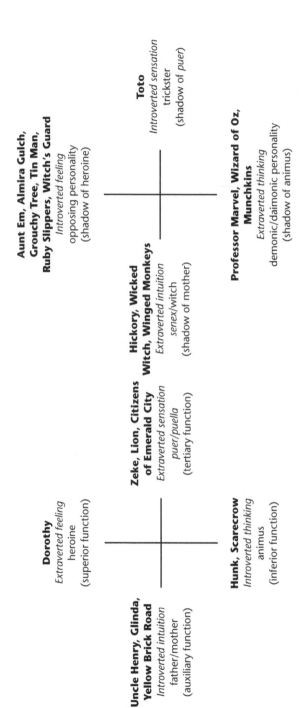

Toto
*Introverted sensation
trickster
(shadow of puer)*

**Aunt Em, Almira Gulch,
Grouchy Tree, Tin Man,
Ruby Slippers, Witch's Guard**
*Introverted feeling
opposing personality
(shadow of heroine)*

**Hickory, Wicked
Witch, Winged Monkeys**
*Extraverted intuition
senex/witch
(shadow of mother)*

**Professor Marvel, Wizard of Oz,
Munchkins**
*Extraverted thinking
demonic/daimonic personality
(shadow of animus)*

Dorothy
*Extraverted feeling
heroine
(superior function)*

**Zeke, Lion, Citizens
of Emerald City**
*Extraverted sensation
puer/puella
(tertiary function)*

Hunk, Scarecrow
*Introverted thinking
animus
(inferior function)*

**Uncle Henry, Glinda,
Yellow Brick Road**
*Introverted intuition
father/mother
(auxiliary function)*

FIGURE 5.10 Archetypal complexes carrying the eight functions of consciousness as seen in *The Wizard of Oz*

The contempt Americans so often and so publicly display toward each other became the major theme of the country's films in the 1990s, some of the best of which explore the possibility of extraverted feeling's eventual redemption. For instance, in *Groundhog Day* (1993), a sourly citified Bill Murray discovers that he won't be able to escape the extraverted feeling demands of small-town life in which he is repetitively forced to attend to the feelings of others; indeed he grows into them. In *As Good as It Gets* (1997), Jack Nicholson plays an even more cynical, characterologically wounded man whose sarcastic extraverted feeling is led to reinvent itself to earn the love of the introverted feeling waitress played by Helen Hunt. The happy endings these films managed to eke out for their challenged extraverted feeling protagonists in the 1990s are still poignant when seen today, but they also seem a bit naive. In America today, there is little evidence of what they promised. Recently, apart from the movie screen, dramatized antagonisms are shared on radio and television news. America, not so evolved from the shrill debates over metals that divided Bryan and McKinley, continues to engage in a vitriolic argument over the passage of essentially moderate health insurance reform, a controversy in which an introverted feeling insistence on privacy and self-reliance has repeatedly undercut any satisfaction that might be felt around having joined together to insure our mutual health. Within such a climate, Dorothy's Oz-born readiness to join arms with an assortment of opposed and like-minded companions to create an at-home feeling for all seems more than ever a foreign sentiment.

Notes

1 See also Hearn (1973, p. 69) for a critique of these ideas, including the suggestion that, since the grandiloquent Wizard is originally from Omaha, Bryan may really have served as the inspiration for the character.

2 James Hillman, in his magisterial essay on the alchemical, archetypal meanings of silver (Hillman, 1980, 1981), has noted that "the total collapse of the values of silver came during the heyday of western materialism, between 1870 and 1930, a debasement of silver that cannot be accounted for wholly in terms of new mines and mining methods" (1980, p. 36). This was a time during which fact became divorced from value in many other areas of life. See especially Hillman, 1980, pp. 35–37.

3 As the novelist Alison Lurie, an expert on subversively adult elements in children's literature, has argued (Lurie, 2000), this may have also reflected the status in Baum's life of his mother-in-law, the American feminist Matilda Joslyn Gage (1826–1898), who had served as president of the National Woman Suffrage Association from 1875 to 1876.

4 For a discussion of my work on the differentiation of consciousness, see Harris, 1996, pp. 39–85, and Chapter 3 of this book. In *The Wizard of Oz*, eight individual functions of consciousness are depicted: extraverted feeling (Dorothy), introverted feeling (Aunt Em, Almira Gulch, the Tin Man, the ruby slippers, the grouchy Apple Tree, the Witch's Guard), extraverted thinking (Professor Marvel, the Munchkins, the Wizard of Oz), introverted

thinking (Hunk, the Scarecrow), extraverted intuition (Hickory, the Wicked Witch of the West, the Winged Monkeys), introverted intuition (Uncle Henry, Glinda, the Yellow Brick Road), extraverted sensation (Zeke, the Cowardly Lion, the Citizens of the Emerald City), and introverted sensation (Toto). Note that two of the actors (Margaret Hamilton and Jack Haley) exchange psychological type when they move between the Kansas and the Oz sections of the film. Although particular characters are left behind in Oz, in the last scene the eight *consciousnesses* come together in a final tableau. The archetypal complexes, i.e. subpersonalities, that I think structure this particular arrangement of functions and attitudes are shown in Figure 5.10, where the relationship of the types to each other in *The Wizard of Oz* is illustrated.

5 "The extraverted feeling function concerns itself with other people's emotions – especially those that lie on or near the surface and are easy to sympathize with. Placing a value on people's feelings, extraverted feeling relates to them with discrimination, empathy, and tact . . . In its shadow aspect, extraverted feeling tends to discriminate against feelings that are less easy to identify with, and therefore less socially acceptable" (see Chapter 15).

6 Ann Ulanov has interpreted Dorothy's story as "a paradigm of a young girl's series of encounters with the animus function and with her ego's integration of the contents that the animus brings to it" (Ulanov, 1971, pp. 277–285). The animus, in Jungian psychology, refers to the support the unconscious gives to a woman's authority and is usually symbolized by contrasexual, i.e. male, figures. (The corresponding supportive and tutelary figure in the male unconscious is the anima.) From this standpoint, the Tin Man, the Cowardly Lion, the Wizard, and even Toto would be animus figures for Dorothy. I prefer, however, to reserve the term 'animus' for the figure most closely associated with the inferior function, who, when brought into relationship with the standpoint of the superior function, creates a plumb line of sufficient depth to allow the ego access to the ground of being (Jung's deep Self). This ego-Self axis associated with the animus is symbolized, in *The Wizard of Oz*, by the beanpole from which the Scarecrow attempts to give Dorothy directions when she has lost her way. Their ensuing contact succeeds in replacing this rigid, archetypal delineation of his potential to guide and ground her with a living, human relationship that suggests the integrity Dorothy achieves through her connection with this "other." She later confesses that he is [the] one she thinks she'll "miss most of all" when she leaves the transformative Land of Oz.

7 The dialogue quoted from *The Wizard of Oz* is as given in the movie script published on the fifty-fifth anniversary of the film's release (Langley et al., 1994).

8 "The introverted feeling function concerns itself with the values expressed in the archetypal aspects of situations, often relating to the actual situation by measuring it against an ideal. When the actual is found wanting, introverted feeling can become intensely disappointed. Although it often finds it hard to articulate its judgments, or simply prefers to keep them to itself, introverted feeling also tends to ignore social limits regarding the communication of critical responses, to the point of appearing to depreciate others. It may withhold positive feelings as insincere and fail to offer healing gestures to smooth over difficult situations. In its shadow aspect, introverted feeling becomes rageful, anxious, and sullen. It may withdraw all support for attitudes it has decided are simply wrong, even at the risk of rupturing relationship and agreed-upon standards of fellow-feeling" (see Chapter 15).

References

As good as it gets. (1997). Brooks, J. L. (Producer & Director). USA: Tri-Star Pictures. [Motion picture].

Dark mirror, The. (1946). Johnson, N. (Producer) & Siodmak, R. (Director). USA: International Pictures. [Motion picture].

Dumas, A. (1844/2007). *The three musketeers.* 1844 English translation (anon). Mineola, NY: Dover Thrift Edition.

Gardner, H. (1983). *Frames of mind: The theory of multiple intelligences.* New York: Basic Books.

Gardner, M. & Nye, R. B. (1994). *The wizard of Oz and who he was.* East Lansing, MI: Michigan State University Press.

Goleman, D. (1995). *Emotional intelligence.* New York: Bantam.

Gormley, K. (2010). *The death of American virtue: Clinton vs Starr.* New York: Crown Press.

Groundhog day. (1993). Albert, T. (Producer) & Ramis, H. (Director). USA: Columbia Pictures Corp. [Motion picture].

Harmetz, A. (1998). *The making of* The wizard of Oz. New York: Hyperion.

Harris, A. S. (1996). *Living with paradox: An introduction to Jungian psychology.* Pacific Grove, CA: Brooks/Cole Publishing Co.

Hearn, M. P. (Ed.). (1973). *The annotated wizard of Oz.* New York: Clarkson N. Potter.

Hillman, J. (1980). Silver and the white earth (Part One). *Spring:* 21–48.

Hillman, J. (1981). Silver and the white earth (Part Two). *Spring:* 21–66.

Hopcke, R. (1989). Dorothy and her friends: Symbols of gay male individuation in *The wizard of Oz. Quadrant 22*(2), 65–77.

Jung, C. G. (1921/1971). Psychological types. In *Cw 6.*

Jung, C. G. (1950/1959a). A study in the process of individuation. In *Cw 9, I* (pp. 290–354).

Jung, C. G. (1950/1959b). Concerning mandala symbolism. In *Cw 9, I* (pp. 355–384).

Jung, C. G. (1966). *Two essays on analytical psychology* (2nd ed). Princeton, NJ: Princeton University Press.

Jung, C. G., von Franz, M., Henderson, J., Jacobi, J., & Jaffé, A. (1964). *Man and his symbols.* Garden City, NJ: Doubleday & Company, Inc.

Kalsched, D. (1996). *The inner world of trauma: Archetypal defenses of the personal spirit.* London: Routledge.

Langley, N., Ryerson, F., & Woolf, E. A. (1994). *The wizard of Oz.* Monterey Park, CA: The Movie Script Library, O. S. P. Publishing, Inc.

Lurie, A. (2000). The Oddness of Oz. *The New York Review of Books 47*(20), 16–24.

Morison, S. E. & Commager, H. S. (1950). *The growth of the American republic,* Volume Two. New York: Oxford University Press.

Pulp fiction. (1994). Bender, L. (Producer) & Tarantino, Q. (Director). USA: Miramax. [Motion picture].

Rushdie, S. (1992). *The wizard of Oz.* London: British Film Institute.

Samuels, A. (1993). *The political psyche.* London: Routledge.

Stolen life, A. (1946). Warner, J. L. (Producer) & Bernhardt, C. (Director). USA: Warner Bros. [Motion picture].

Thompson, K. (1985). Cognitive and analytical psychology (Review of Howard Gardner's *Frames of mind*). *The San Francisco Jung Institute Library Journal 5*(4), 40–64.

Thomson, L. (1998). *Personality type: An owner's manual.* Boston, MA: Shambhala.

Traxel, D. (1998). *1898: The birth of the American century.* New York: Knopf.

Ulanov, A. B. (1971). *The feminine in Jungian psychology and in Christian theology.* Evanston, IL: Northwestern University Press.

White, W. A. (1896). What's the matter with Kansas? *Emporia Gazette,* 15 August, 1896. Online at https://www.kshs.org/kansapedia/what-s-the-matter-with-kansas/16717. Consulted 07/27/2015.

Wizard of Oz, The. (1939). LeRoy, M. (Producer) & Fleming, V. (Director). USA: Metro-Goldwyn-Mayer. [Motion picture].

Zipes, J. (Ed.) (1998). Introduction. In L. F. Baum, *The wonderful wizard of Oz.* New York: Penguin.

6

THE STRETCH OF INDIVIDUAL TYPOLOGIES IN THE FORMATION OF CULTURAL ATTITUDES

To write this chapter in the story of where typology can lead is to pay homage to a father. I went into analysis with a father complex and was lucky enough to find a psychological father in my third analyst, Joseph Henderson, who was himself analyzed by Jung. To work with Jung, Henderson had sailed for Europe in 1929 just before the stock market crashed—fortunate timing because his family's money was to disappear soon after. Henderson was able to get a year of analysis with Jung. He then studied medicine—at Jung's recommendation—in England, where he married Helena Cornford, a great granddaughter of Charles Darwin. With their young daughter, the couple later came to New York; Henderson began a practice of Jungian analysis, counting among his analysands the then unknown artist Jackson Pollock. A bit later the family relocated to the San Francisco Bay Area. Joining with Joseph Wheelwright and several others, Henderson helped to form and guide the first Jungian training group in the world, now known as the C. G. Jung Institute of San Francisco, where I took my own training starting in 1970. By the time I met him, Dr. Henderson was quite evidently a man used to living and adapting to many different cultures, and he brought a kind of psychological urbanity to the exploration of individual complexes, including the type complexes that I have been sketching in this book.

Cultural attitudes

In his book, *Cultural Attitudes in Psychological Perspective*, published after two decades of work in 1984, Henderson identified four contrasting stances that he saw as traditional orientations to culture, describing them as attitudes that explain much about how different individuals choose to engage with the culture in which they live. In this context, 'culture' can be thought of as the expressions and products of the shared, rarely examined assumptions and values of a group of people. These four stances that Henderson defined were the social, the religious, the aesthetic, and the philosophic.

In that book, Henderson says that the *social attitude* is concerned with "maintaining the ethical code of the culture" (1984, p. 17), but his meaning turns out more precisely to be that the social attitude sustains a culture's *ethos*—everything from its political principles to its social fabric. The social attitude seeks to keep the uniting spirit of a culture alive, and therefore attends to the ways people in that culture come together to enact its spirit, whether at play or at work. He cites Virginia Woolf's character Mrs. Dalloway as an example of a person with a developed social attitude, because she is conscious of trying subtly to influence others in ways that will benefit their belonging in English culture and at the same time allow them to be themselves in it (pp. 20–21).

Distinguishing the *religious attitude,* Henderson says that it can "appear only when the rewards and comforts of a parent–child relationship, or dependence upon testimonials of other people's faith, have been outgrown" so that there can be "an awakening [of] consciousness to that principle of Self to which the ego willingly submits." Henderson notes that this "initial submission of the ego to a superordinate power" is characterized by T. S. Eliot (in *The Waste Land*) as "that moment of surrender that a lifetime of prudence can never retract." A hallmark of the religious attitude is "the immediate conviction that spirit permeates all life" (p. 27).

The religious attitude need not be associated with organized religion. Henderson shrewdly cautions that the religious attitude may be impersonated or commandeered by the social attitude, because of the latter's readiness to intrude into the public beliefs and practices of others.

The *aesthetic attitude* is grounded in the individual experience of beauty and the often exuberant conviction that emerges from such an experience that the beauty one has glimpsed is united to the perception of something beyond it that is so true that it opens up infinite possibilities for one's own life. This is the stance that, as Henderson remarks, informs the controversial exclamation, only apparently philosophic, of the great English Romantic poet Keats while contemplating, in his "Ode on a Grecian Urn," the train of thought that can be experienced when studying an ancient Greek vase: "Beauty is truth; truth beauty—that is all/Ye know on earth and all ye need to know." Henderson writes that, unlike the social and religious attitudes, the aesthetic attitude exists "without any sense of duty whatsoever" (p. 45).

The *philosophic attitude,* by contrast to the aesthetic, is cooler, more thoroughly checked-out. As Henderson puts it, "When I meet the philosophic attitude, either in patients or in friends, I am impressed by their scrupulosity in getting to the truth of things" (p. 59). The philosophic attitude needs not only to know, but also to weigh what it knows. It is building a system of understandings that it must test before they can be trusted to offer support as a bridge to knowledge. Henderson therefore saw the philosophic attitude as a prerequisite to the rigors of a scientific method (p. 77).

Recognizing the cultural attitudes

One way to recognize these four attitudes, which Henderson believes are amply represented by people in any culture, is to notice how differently people choose to spend their optional cultural time. One can start by asking oneself, "How did I spend my weekend?" Did I party or volunteer for a collective social cause or participate in watching or playing a team sport? Did I to go to church to commune in my own favorite way with God, or to a yoga class, or to a meditation retreat? Did I go out of my way, perhaps in lieu of social interaction, to see an art show at a museum or a film by a director whose approach to filmmaking I have been following and want to savor or share? Did I go and give attentive concentration to a thoughtful lecture or spend hours reading a work of nonfiction that lays out a new idea to clarify the basis of an unsolved cultural problem?

Sources and antecedents of Henderson's theory

Henderson (1984, p. 10) identifies William James as a principal inspiration of the theory of cultural attitudes, citing James's *Pragmatism*:

> Against rationalism as a pretension and a method, pragmatism is fully armed and militant. But, at the outset, at least, it stands for no particular results. It has no dogmas, and no doctrines save its method. As the young Italian pragmatist Papini has well said, it lies in the midst of our theories, like a corridor in a hotel. Innumerable chambers open out of it. In one you may find a man writing an aesthetic volume; in the next someone on his knees praying for faith and strength; in a third a chemist investigating a body's properties. In a fourth a system of idealistic metaphysics is being excogitated; in a fifth the impossibility of metaphysics is being shown. But they all own the corridor, and all must pass through it if they want a practicable way of getting into or out of their respective rooms.
>
> *James, 1907/2008, p. 30*

As Samuel Kimbles (2003) has clarified, Henderson's conception of the cultural attitudes germinated in 1929–1930. Kimbles cites these lines from a paper by Henderson:

> When I was in Zurich as an analysand of Doctor Jung, I noticed in other analysands . . . a certain kind of transference commonly made upon Jung himself or upon his method, consisting in a certain cultural preference or bias which caused us to find in the analytical situation the same cultural disposition we preferred from our inherent background derived from education in the broadest sense of the term . . . In accordance with the cultural preference . . . one person found Jung's analysis acceptable because he was so religious, another because he was so scientific, another because he was philosophical.
>
> *Henderson, 1964, cited in Kimbles, 2003, p. 53*

In the same paper, Henderson recalls that the idea of the four cultural attitudes came up in a conversation in the 1930s with Friedrich Spiegelberg, a professor of philosophy and religion who had participated at the Eranos conferences, and again in

Henderson's reading of the book, *Four Ways of Philosophy,* by Irwin Edman (1937). Recognizing the degree to which the complexities of our contemporary multi-cultural civilization preclude these attitudes emerging very often in their purest cultural forms, or even being present at once in a fully integrated way (as we some-times imagine them to have been in the archaic cultures we idealize), Henderson at a later point in his long engagement with the idea, was able to say: "The original integrity of these cultural modes of expression is lost in any large civilization, but they emerge as individual modes handed down from one group of individuals to others through culture-contact and the creation of historical records" (1977, p. 126).

Jung's own strong interest in the history and world-views of religious culture (Jung, 1969) is another wellspring of Henderson's work on cultural attitudes. Henderson was to conclude that a psychological perspective emerges in analysis that affects the way traditional cultural attitudes are appropriated and used (for instance by taking from traditional religions mainly what is psychologically rel-evant to the person, rather than accepting entire a particular dogma just to be able to express authentically a newfound religious attitude (Henderson, 1982, pp. 127–138)). This conception of the psychological perspective or attitude made all the difference in how the new science of analytical psychology was received and taught at the Jung Institute of San Francisco. There, complex theory, as a key to approaching the unconscious, and Jungian typology, as a theory of conscious mind, were emphasized equally as a basis for an analytical practice that, however deep it went, would be solidly grounded in a grasp of the subjective individual psyche making the journey. Securing the personhood of a 'little-s' self was thought to be essential before an analysand could be encouraged, within therapy, to consider the contributions archetypes might make to that self's realization of the perspective of a more objective, transpersonal Self.

Thus Henderson knew he was approaching the traditional attitudes with which educated, adult persons had always related to their cultures through the lens of the pragmatic relation to psychological experience pioneered by William James and applied to psychoanalysis by Jung with a sense of the pluralism of approaches that individual differences, such as typological differences, demanded. Henderson's approach to culture had a democratic slant from the start that was quintessentially American as well as Jungian. For instance a supporting antecedent was American cultural anthropology as taught in relation to the psychology of personality by Harvard professors Clyde Kluckhohn and Henry Murray, in their seminal text-book, *Personality in Nature, Society and Culture* (1948). This book became basic to Henderson's recognition of the need to factor culture into any analysis of personal-ity (Henderson, 1985, personal communication).

Henderson's formulation of the cultural attitudes is a Jungian parallel to the work of an earlier student of Murray's, Erik Erikson, whose integrative psychoanalytic text, *Childhood and Society* (1950), offers cultural and developmental perspectives seamlessly woven together. Henderson's work, however, adds the idea of different attitudes toward culture itself as a way of guiding individual consciousness through its assimilation of what culture has to offer and tries to exact from each of us.

More than any other analyst of his generation, Henderson emphasized the presence of real individual choice in this matter, based on the attitude toward culture that is natural to the given person.

The relationship of cultural attitude to psychological type

It doesn't take very long, if one stops to look, to recognize the degree to which different people presenting themselves for analysis manifest different cultural attitudes. As a psychological theorist, Henderson did not bother himself with how these attitudes were formed, since, for him, in an extraverted sensation way that he liked to let rule him (extraverted sensation being the language of his anima), these characteristic attitudes just *were*. They were the basis of how patients use analysis. He did, however, conclude that the people he was working with manifested different cultural attitudes in a conscious manner that seemed to him separate from their psychological type. He writes, for instance, taking Jung's own conclusions on the matter as his authority:

> It sometimes seems that Jung's four typological functions, taken separately, subtend the cultural attitudes. In *Psychological Types*, he speaks of two kinds of intuition in an introvert: that which tends toward an aesthetic attitude, and that which inclines one toward a philosophic attitude (Jung, *Cw 6*, ¶¶661–662). In other places, Jung seems to regard aestheticism as the product of the two 'perceptive' functions, intuition and sensation, while the philosophic or social attitudes become identified with the two 'rational' functions, thinking and feeling.
>
> *1984, p. 75*[1]

Henderson continues:

> In his later work, however, Jung disclaims any identity between cultural attitudes and psychological function. . . . No matter how faithfully we develop the four functions or understand them in other people, they do not account for the existence of religious, philosophic, aesthetic or social values. Hence there is a remarkable difference between people of identical personality type and function if they are differently oriented to culture.
>
> *pp. 75–76*

Cultural attitudes analyzed typologically

I agree with Henderson that there is not a direct correspondence between a person's psychological type and his or her relation to the cultural attitudes, but I believe that the eight-function, eight-archetype model will allow us, nevertheless, to learn much more about the formation of cultural attitudes based on what we have discovered about type development and type dynamics.

From its name alone, we might guess that the *social attitude* involves the extra-verted feeling function, since extraverted feeling is concerned with mutual trust and the harmonious working of groups. However, anyone who has ever tried to keep a group united and operating according to a given ethos by relying on extraverted feeling alone will have learned that a culture cannot be sustained in that way for very long. It turns out that a shared rhetoric is needed: foundational principles of the culture must be articulated so simply and clearly that they seem to be 'self-evident' and beyond question. Rules or laws are also needed and must be applied consistently, regardless of the individual personalities involved. In short, extraverted feeling must be combined with extraverted thinking to make a social attitude that is effective. Thus, for example, in politics, extraverted feeling may impel us to want to address a particular social problem, but we will soon turn to extraverted thinking to plan and organize a solution. Similarly, a military officer deploying troops according to an extraverted thinking plan of attack will have to stretch into extraverted feeling to insure that the plan does not falter because the morale of the troops and their social cohesion have been overlooked. The power and flexibility of any effective social attitude lies in the combination and balance of these two extraverted, rational functions.

The *religious attitude* is one that I associate with introverted intuition because this attitude privileges and trusts one's own perceptions of what is real, funda-mental, and of lasting importance over what others may see and think. When introverted intuition is operating well, an image of the deeper reality compel-lingly presents itself. But I would argue that something more than introverted intuition, with its ability to move beyond uncanny knowing to a convincing divining, is needed to turn the predilection to notice the religious dimension of life into an effective cultural attitude. This something more is introverted sensation with its instinct for specificity and its attention to what *is* and can be factually verified rather than just to a mystery that has been glimpsed through a transient epiphany. For example, Henderson cites the work of the alchemists, bearing witness to the changes of color and form during the long process of cooking the primal matter that is being chemically transformed, as an exercise of the religious attitude (1984, pp. 31–33). Anyone who has studied the allegorical images the alchemists made as analogies for processes they observed will notice the degree of illumination they are able to bring to the workings of nature within their alembics. I would say that it was the combination of introverted intuition, with its unbounded, symbolic literacy, and introverted sensation, with its observant clarity, that imbued the study of alchemical transformation with religious vision.

In a paper on dream interpretation (1972), Henderson described the combina-tion of these two functions in getting to the meaning of a dream:

> Introverted intuition perceives the variety and the possibility for develop-ment of the inner images, whereas introverted sensation perceives the specific image which defines the psychic activity that needs immediate attention.

If now we apply this kind of functioning to the perception of a dream, we meet both of these functions in a state of collision. . . . The intuitive function sees many things the dream might mean and is highly productive in summoning forth a wide variety of free associations, especially of the kind Jung has called amplifications. . . . But no amount of amplifications can give the true meaning of a dream. This must come from introverted sensation which can single out from all the possible meanings that one meaning which tells us what is the specific psychic activity behind the dream and how it can be brought into the foreground of consciousness.

Although Henderson does not use the word 'religious' to describe how he sees this process, I would say, having been his patient, that that is what it was for him. I recall, for instance, his reading some typed dreams I had left behind in a session in which I had not left us enough time to get to them. He told me at the start of our next session, "There was a baby born in those dreams you left behind last time." This signified a rebirth of my attitude toward the work we were engaged in in analytic practice (Beebe, 1984). By helping me draw together introverted intuition and introverted sensation, when I was in danger of neither accounting for all my inner material nor divining its significance, he managed to illuminate the value of both functions for me, and sparked an insight that was almost magical in its effect, going far beyond what either function could have done on its own, even if I had been able to command it. Studying the dream, which involved a baby whose foot had a distinctive outline being presented to Jung on his deathbed, as if a new addition to the family, I realized that I had identified my own Jungian standpoint. But to get to this insight required not just Henderson, with his reliable, dominant introverted intuition to guide me to this dream, but Jane Wheelwright, my control analyst supervising my cases at the time, to clarify with the specificity and groundedness of her introverted sensation that the baby's foot was really a standpoint, the very one I needed to finish Jungian training and be my own man. It was that real to her. So this insight, which has informed all my subsequent work, took two actual analysts, both of whom knew how to link introverted intuition and introverted sensation, coming from the opposite sides of this balance in their own personal typologies, but each supporting in a living way the Jungian attitude that was still undeveloped in me, so that their different type perspectives could come together with enough punch to make me realize that this special child was in fact my own way to carry forward the religious care that in his life Jung had brought to the inspection and analysis of psyche.

The beauty of this insight was not lost on my already better-developed *aesthetic attitude*, which even before I came to analysis was a place where opposite functions could come together and center me. In medical school at the University of Chicago, I often found the energy to sustain my morale against the extraverted sensation demands of the training that as an extraverted intuitive I was ill-equipped to meet, by going to the Chicago Art Institute, which inevitably connected me to extraverted sensation through beauty in a totally satisfying way. To experience life with an *aesthetic attitude* must surely involve extraverted sensation, since we know that that function is concerned with getting stimulation and enjoyment from sensory experience. Extraverted sensation on its own, however, might lead merely to thrill-seeking or hedonism, were it not combined with something else. Such an other thing, I would propose, is what I brought to looking at art, *extraverted intuition*, which spots the still unrealized possibilities in things, including the things on display at a museum.

A splendidly realized depiction of the aesthetic attitude in action can be found in Jacques Tati's film, *Mr. Hulot's Holiday* (*Les Vacances de M. Hulot,* 1953). On the last night of his vacation, the hero, a likeable, bumbling, extraverted intuitive lights a match in a dark shed that turns out to be a storehouse for fireworks. The pandemonium that ensues is some of the most thrilling, exquisitely choreographed chaos one could ever hope to experience. Tati's spectacular scene is an example of what Samuel Taylor Coleridge's biographer Richard Holmes presents in his book, *Darker Reflections* (1998), as Coleridge's conception of beauty: "Beauty as an explosion of energy, perfectly contained."[2]

Expertly portrayed by Tati himself, with his demonic extraverted sensation on full display, Mr. Hulot imagines at first that he will be able to gain control over the fireworks. He attempts to extinguish them by opening a nearby hose bib, but the hose is firmly attached to the spigot. The hose's other end is coupled to a rotary sprinkler, which our hero chases in a circle as it spins. The bursting fireworks light up the sky around the hotel where other vacationers are staying and even fly in through an open window. Everyone is awakened; the energy soon ignites their enthusiasm. A Victrola is inadvertently started up and begins playing loud jazz, at which point, we experience, in common with the vacationers, a cultural form that actually can contain the energy Hulot has brought to their on-holiday boredom. The entire community is somehow able to join in creating a cultural attitude that is receptive to this eruption. This is the aesthetic attitude.

Tati cuts back to Mr. Hulot, who now carries, without harm, a linked pair of Catherine Wheel fireworks as they twirl. They are like two sparkling centers of consciousness, but also like a bicycle, a new vehicle for him. We recognize Mr. Hulot, the persona employed by Jacques Tati, as a character who has become an artist, lit up by the possibility of being conscious of his effects. At that point, we can say that the director's aesthetic attitude has been completely constructed. Indeed, it was with this film that Jacques Tati became recognized as a cinema auteur.

The reader will appreciate that I have used typology as a kind of critical theory to explain an aesthetic effect. In doing so, I have ventured into my own other most differentiated cultural attitude, the *philosophic*. In the effort to construe philosophically, as a critic of culture must do, both thinking and feeling participate, and both are used with near ruthlessness in an introverted way, as I have used my thinking and feeling here, to get at core meanings that are mined not just as understandings in themselves but as valuable benchmarks against which to measure all future thought-discoveries in the realm of culture. The way I saw this scene in Tati's film has been a key to other movies as well, and to my own philosophy of film art.

And here, Coleridge, as perhaps the greatest, most psychological philosopher of art, anticipates my argument just as surely as he anticipated Tati's effect, writing in 1814, about the effect of "the sportive wildness of the component figures" in Raphael's fresco *Galatea* which he had viewed with his painter friend Washington Allston. As biographer Richard Holmes recounts, "together they had discovered Raphael's principle of harmony, a monumental circular structure within the central group (the old coach wheel), geometrically controlled by a 'multiplicity of rays and cords.'"

> Coleridge used a striking scientific analogy to sum up the harmonious beauty of Raphael's composition, in one of his most original pieces of art criticism. He praised the "balance, the perfect reconciliation, effected between these two conflicting principles of the FREE LIFE, and of the confining FORM! How entirely is the stiffness that would have resulted from the obvious regularity of the latter, fused and (if I may hazard so bold a metaphor) almost *volatilized* by the interpretation and electrical flashes of the former."
>
> *Coleridge, 1814, p. 373 cited in Holmes, 1998, p. 361*

Thus Holmes tells us,

> The chemical image was recalled from Davy's method of isolating primary elements with charges from a voltaic battery. It emphasized the dynamic, almost explosive, concept that Coleridge had of Beauty; or rather Beauty as an explosion of energy perfectly contained.
>
> *p. 361*

This gets at the alchemical quality of the energy-releasing union of the opposed principle of free life—extraverted intuition, with its sense of endless possibility—and the principle of realism—extraverted sensation, with its limiting focus on the actual forms of things. Coleridge's wheel and electrical flashes fully anticipate what Tati would realize on the screen as improbably joined opposites of containment and energy, which for him too is the essence, and the deeply comedic capacity, of the aesthetic attitude to release from the shock of the unexpected a congenial joy.

There is a similar pleasure in introverted thinking and introverted feeling combining to produce the happy thought that this is what makes it possible for us to appreciate art so much. That pleasure inheres in the *philosophic attitude* that permits criticism that is as acutely understanding as Coleridge's to be perennially relevant to actual poetic practice.

Rilke's famous sonnet, "Torso of an Archaic Apollo," rescued by William H. Gass (2000) from nearly a century of translations that led away from the dynamics of the poem itself, is a paean to the god's power to evoke the philosophic attitude. The premise of the poem is that all that is left of an original image of Apollo, sculpted in the archaic period of Ancient Greece, is its torso, but what we can now see implies everything we can no longer see. The poet conjures the statue's head with its eyes like the dual globes of the gas streetlamps that illuminated the night at the time of the poem's publication. The poet tells us of this old, yet new Apollo, "Yet his torso glows as if his look were set above it.... Otherwise the surging breast would not thus blind you . . . there's no place that does not see you. You must change your life" (Rilke in Gass, 2000, pp. 92–93).

It is not simply the god's ability to see through us with his penetrating gift of introverted thinking, defining all of what we are; it is our ability to feel the rightness of his insight that gives his gaze its transforming power. This is the trajectory that emerges in the construction of the philosophic attitude—the force of our values moving us to see the way thought develops. The architectural layout of this old Greek statue of Apollo was planned, with extraverted thinking, as carefully as an Austro-Hungarian empire streetlamp. The architecture allowed the eyes of the god, if we follow Rilke's phantomatic summoning of them, a piercing insight into the nature of the thing observed. This is philosophy's relevant subtlety personified, for the thing so fully perceived is some habit of thought within ourselves. And once philosophy has seen through what is fictional in our soul's very logic, we cannot but agree to transform the life it has led us to live. Such is the consequence of the Apollonian gaze of philosophy, which also oriented Freud, Rilke's Nietzsche-informed analyst. The philosophic attitude, when adopted by an introverted feeling type such as Freud (Jung, 1975, pp. 346–348 and 349–350), forces reflections on the truth of what we are. It is driven by a truly daimonic introverted thinking that undermines all our fictions. Then introverted feeling has to bow to that rush of insight. As Alfred Adler realized for individual psychology, when reflective thought can makes us feel how much our illusions have led us astray, we have to cease to live by them.

The stretch

Not everyone, in my experience, develops a cultural attitude, but when one is present, it offers an enormous advantage to the person possessing it. Consulting in close proximity two functions that normally do not cooperate, such as introverted feeling with introverted thinking, or extraverted intuition with extraverted sensation, is a bit like harnessing to the same wagon two very independent, rather headstrong horses that, in the past, have not particularly trusted each other. Perhaps they can pull together, but it doesn't happen without effort and missteps!

To engage a consciousness that is more comfortable and familiar to us with one that feels quite Other—especially in a combination that we usually experience as an 'either/or' rather than a 'both/and'—is a daunting innovation for the psyche. But once we are able to make that stretch, to be truly respectful and attentive to the kind of consciousness that feels so foreign, it seems that we also become more open to other non-preferred types of consciousness too. This budding openness to the other types of awareness is entirely applicable in interacting with culture because all eight types of consciousness are bound to be expressed, in some way, in a culture, some more openly than others. To have a cultural attitude, therefore, is to be prepared to engage effectively with what is Other to the self we know.

The need to relate to otherness has become the requisite skill for living in the twenty-first century. Henderson's four traditional cultural attitudes, which make sense within just about any culture, are very suitable for managing self–Other interactions. For this reason, individuating people starting with an agenda of defining personal identity often end up stretching that identity to achieve, for the first time as their own, one or more of these four cultural attitudes.

We can see the stretch symbolized in *The Wizard of Oz* (see Chapter 5) as extraverted-feeling Dorothy finally manages to enlist the extraverted-thinking Wizard to join with her to help her Oz friends. As I have argued in the previous chapter, this unexpected cooperation could hardly have happened had Dorothy not had the friendship of the Scarecrow and the help of her other companions, Toto, the Tin Woodman, and the Cowardly Lion. But it was particularly the Scarecrow, self-proclaimed as a case of inferior thinking, whose introverted thinking could label the Wizard a "humbug" when Dorothy could only tell the Wizard that he was "a very bad man." Together, Dorothy and the Scarecrow defined at that moment an axis of integrity that enabled them to stand up to the demonic Wizard, who had been doing everything possible to undermine them, and redirect him to use his extraverted thinking in a helpful way.

This rectification is applicable to any eighth function, which is in the archetypal position of being characteristically undermining, unless it is held to a standard of integrity, in which case it can become daimonic, an opportunity for spirit to enter the psyche from a shadowy place that had once only been an occasion for fear. We could say that prayer has the same effect with regard to a deity; the integrity that accompanies the humility of praying to a power Other enough to be potentially destructive, and which may in its own way have already visited destruction on some aspect of the life of the person now praying, often moves the very same deity enough to offer illumination, compassion, and a transformative intervention. We see this in the Wizard of Oz in a more secular way when he uses his extraverted thinking like a therapist, to reframe and transform through the magic of collectively sanctioned words what has been low self-esteem about thinking, feeling and courage into an internalized authorization for the Scarecrow to go on thinking, the Tin Woodman to use his introverted feeling, and the Cowardly Lion to realize the courage that has always been his. But it is Dorothy's ability to appreciate the Wizard's effort, as we viewers do, seeing the changing situation from Dorothy's viewpoint, that convinces us that a new attitude has been born within the film as a whole, and within Dorothy as its leading character. Her extraverted feeling affirmation of the Wizard's self-redemption through the healing use of extraverted thinking is the stretch that Dorothy—and we in the audience—have to make. We are glad to make it because of the cultural attitude that results. Rightly, the citizens of the Emerald City gather soon after to see this pair on to further adventures in America!

Yet the eighth function remains an Other that cannot totally be trusted: the Wizard does not know how to control the inflation of the balloon that results, and he ends up going off without Dorothy when she has to attend, briefly, to her tricky little dog. And we can say, more than three-quarters of a century after this movie was released, that America too has not been able to sustain the cultural attitude that the Roosevelt years, with their extraverted feeling, promised to the country that historically had emphasized and trusted extraverted thinking. America's imperial strategizing has often exceeded its compassionate good will, and so the democratic social attitude has had only varying success on the world stage. But it remains the cultural attitude that is most truly compatible with American individuation, and we long for it still, more than just the integrity of an extraverted thinking country in touch with good introverted feeling values. The return to these, by Dorothy, at home at last with Aunty Em, is a psychological achievement, but not quite the same thing as a fully realized and sustained cultural attitude.

Without such a stretch into what is normally seen as beyond the self, the personality, however capable it is of managing its own life, may be dangerously uncomprehending of the life experience of other people—especially of people who are not 'type-compatible.' A person stuck in a dominant function and unable to see why a stretch beyond it might be worth attempting is often perceived as rigid. Some amelioration of this overreliance on the dominant function comes normally after midlife, when a connection is made to the anima or animus that carries the inferior function. This is a shock at first, but it promises the potential for renewal.

Elsewhere in this book (Chapter 11), I argue that Salome, whom Jung met in the active imaginations he recorded in the *Red Book*, and who presented herself as the soul he was searching for, embodies extraverted sensation, an opposite to Jung's more native introverted intuition. As she intercedes in his psychic life, they end up defining together an irrational standpoint. After his encounter with her, we see that Jung is much more ready to transcend the rigidity of his original dominant function. At this point, Jung becomes Jung, and that means that he has achieved a 'little-s' selfhood that will enable him not only to imagine, know, and divine but also encounter, experience, and enjoy the many parts of his psyche. Now he is in a position to stretch into the psyche in new ways.

For instance, the demonic function of his psyche is not necessarily just undermining or threatening, and he has the humility to let it become a daimon. Witnessing the demonic function become a tutelary figure, as it can in long-term psychotherapy, a typologically minded observer can see that when the dominant and daimonic functions start to span the enormous differences between them, self and other come together to create a cultural attitude big enough to allow the self to live in the world. We see this play out in the *Red Book* after Jung has accepted the invasion of the ghost Anabaptists into his home as a reality he has to deal with (Jung, 1963, pp. 189–191) and applies himself to the strangely specific and concrete concerns that the spirits express (Shamdasani & Beebe, 2010, pp. 426–427). To harness spiritual introverted intuition in service to embodied introverted sensation is to form a religious attitude (Beebe, 2014, p. 117; see also Chapters 11, pp. 175–178, and 12, pp. 186–187, of the present book). Jung's articulate alter-ego Philemon expresses this attitude clearly throughout the *Seven Sermons to the Dead*, which is in effect a first draft of Jung's later analytical psychology, with its distinctive take on psyche itself as a discovery of the sacred living in us in astonishingly specific ways (Jung, 2009, pp. 346–354, including notes).

A different stretch between functions that do not ordinarily cooperate is that between the auxiliary, parental function and the trickster. In *The Wizard of Oz*, this pairing is between Glinda the Good, depicted as a motherly introverted intuitive, and Toto, the trickster, whose type seems to be introverted sensation. Between them they oversee Dorothy's spiritual development, helping her to rely on her own consciousness of a duty to her loved ones, the Christian attitude of sacrifice, and self-reliance in the service of what is good, despite the curves that loved ones throw.

This is not, however, the second most developed cultural attitude in *The Wizard of Oz*. That honor goes to the Witch in relation to the part of Dorothy that is not a budding adolescent heroine but still a little girl, cowering in fear at the heroic feats her individuation journey requires of her. The extraverted intuitive Witch's ability to instill terror in the part of Dorothy that is locked into the present—the extraverted sensation *puella*, the female counterpart to the frightened little boy that is the Cowardly Lion—produces extreme aesthetic pleasure in anyone who watches the movie. The Witch acknowledges as much after Dorothy throws a bucket of water on her. As she melts away, she cries, "Oh, what a world! What a world! Who would have thought a good little girl like you could destroy my beautiful wickedness!" (Langley, Ryerson, & Woolf, 1989, p. 119). This sounds like the aesthete's lament for the fact that artistically beautiful forms, for all the wicked skill with which they are contrived, cannot finally survive a world that has other, more urgent priorities.

A number of the principal actors in *The Wizard of Oz* play dual roles—portraying one character in Kansas and another in Oz—but, in depicting the frightened, impulsive child so distinctly from the heroine, Judy Garland makes it possible in her scenes in the witch's castle for the film to let us feel the stretch between extraverted intuition and extraverted sensation that creates the movie's aesthetic attitude. These scenes recall cliffhanger suspense movies such as *The Perils of Pauline* (1914); they also help us to appreciate all the other vaudeville entertainments with which the film is filled.

The cultural attitude that is not well developed in the film is the philosophic attitude. Dorothy's efforts to explain what she has learned ("If I ever go looking for my heart's desire, I won't look any further than my own backyard, because if it isn't there I never really lost it to begin with") seem strained and muddled, both as logic and as value, as does her homily, "There's no place like home." The introverted thinking really seems as inferior as the thinking the Scarecrow complained of, perhaps unfairly, in himself. We can see that, without any depicted interaction suggesting a genuine connection with introverted feeling as might have been demonstrated by a genuine friendship between the Scarecrow and the Tin Woodman, who embodies oppositional introverted feeling in Oz, it's not surprising that Dorothy's attempt at philosophy rests shakily on thin ground.

It is rare in most films for the anima or animus figure to connect to the figure representing the opposing personality, yet it is only when that happens that a hero or heroine is truly challenged by a different cultural attitude than he or she would normally use. Something like this does happens in the movie *Broadcast News* (1987) when the overconfident heroine, a producer of TV news from Washington, D.C., played by Holly Hunter as an extraverted thinking type, is confronted by a duel between two reporters over the philosophy of how the news is told. One reporter is a smart, critical, introverted thinking type, the film's opposing personality, this heroine's best male friend. The other is a seductively handsome introverted feeling type who is her current love object. This somewhat vulnerable introverted feeler is not above falsifying the reporting of a story to enhance its emotional effect. Like Jung trying to reconcile two types of truth, the heroine and the audience are torn by the ethical question of which of the two has the greater integrity. In *Broadcast News*, the philosophic attitude reveals a deep split in the American character. None of the characters is able to establish a relationship with each other in which anyone feels 'at home.'

The Wizard of Oz and *Broadcast News* offer the promise and the shadow of the evolution of American culture, showing how much a nation individuates through the generation of effective cultural attitudes. One of the pleasures of American cinema is the degree to which cultural attitudes are constructed in them, which enable us to reflect on America herself.

How much can we expect individuals, as opposed to nations, to construct cultural attitudes? Some individuals seem to function adequately without any cultural attitude, in part by steering clear of engaging too deeply with culture. For example, they may focus more on their immediate family, hobbies, and work and avoid getting into political, religious, philosophical, or aesthetic discussions and concerns.

Other people find fault with the dominant cultural attitude that surrounds them and, rebelling, seek a different attitude to live by. Such people generally develop for themselves a new cultural attitude out of the traditional four that Henderson described, and for a time rather insist upon it. In time they will often discover from the reactions of others that this new cultural attitude, formed out of combinations such as extraverted feeling and extraverted thinking, or introverted intuition and introverted sensation, being exclusively extraverted or introverted, and also exclusively rational or irrational, is insufficient. For this reason, many people find that they need to develop a second cultural attitude to balance the one-sidedness of their first.

Something like this happened with me, when I found my first self-achieved cultural attitude, which was aesthetic, was not enough to carry me through life. I had become an intense irrational, extraverted, aesthetic snob. I could sense that I needed a more prudent, rational, and reflective attitude as well—though not yet articulating the limitation of the aesthetic attitude in those psychological terms! By instinct, I stumbled toward the development of a philosophic attitude. The Harvard English major became the medical student studying science to qualify for psychiatry where I would take up a psychological theory. Yet I have chosen, often enough, to ground that theory in the aesthetic elaborations of culture, finding that rational, introverted theory comes alive when applied to the irrational extraverted exuberance of art. Less easy for me to come by is a stable relationship to either the social or the religious attitude. But what I have of these has given me a way into the world that I am grateful for, and that completes my typology, always a source of development of self, as something that can extend itself to relate to the consciousness of others.

A psychological attitude

At a presentation in San Francisco in 1991, Henderson said:

> After having written several papers about cultural attitudes some years ago, I realized that I had been observing them from another point of view entirely. I would not have thought of making this classification (of religious, social, aesthetic and philosophic attitudes), if I had not been a psychologist. This made me realize that there is another attitude, not just mine, which is also acquiring widespread attention in our time that can only be described as 'psychological.' So I decided to add another cultural attitude to my list, a Psychological Attitude.
>
> *Henderson in Benveniste, 2000, p. 44*

Elsewhere he has remarked that "psychology, in a Jungian sense, if properly valued, lays the foundation for a psychological attitude which has an identity of its own, while in no way challenging the other cultural attitudes or falsifying them" (Henderson, 1977, p. 142).

We can understand the psychological attitude as a stance taken toward psyche itself that can blossom once the presence of a self that knows what is good for itself begins to be palpable. This self, spelled with a 'little-s' to recognize its intermediate position between ego and Self (Beebe, 1979, 1981, 1988), is formed when the eight functions come together to create their alembic, providing a personal container to hold the self experience that is born of the relations between the functions. The Jungian analyst Charles Klaif (personal communication, 1986) once called this integrative area "the person in the psyche." In *Being a Character: Psychoanalysis and Self Experience,* Christopher Bollas (1993, pp. 64–99) describes the agency that is released at such times as "psychic genera," places of creative incubation that, in contrast to the traumas that sunder the spirit (Symington, 2002, pp. 131–140), bring new links to the mind and thus create the morale that is needed for healing and further individuation. Our typology, then, can be seen as a reservoir of consciousness that works within changing conditions of culture, capable of generating the cultural attitudes to do so. The psychological attitude provides flexibility for this system to stretch between its parts to generate cultural attitudes as needed to enhance self's basic function, which is to maintain an adaptation to inner and outer reality.

Notes

1 We are referred, here, by Henderson to Chapter 10 of Jung's *Psychological Types* to explore this understanding of sensation and intuition as perceptive functions, perception being regarded by Jung as an essentially "irrational" process and thinking and feeling as "rational" functions because their process, even when accompanied by emotion, involves reason, reflection, and the application of objective values (Jung, 1921/1971, ¶¶785–787).
2 I am indebted to John O'Donohue (2005) for introducing me to this way of putting how the experience of beauty, which is so core to the aesthetic attitude, is constructed.

References

Beebe, J. (1979). Review of James Hillman's *The Dream and the Underworld*. *The San Francisco Jung Institute Library Journal, 1*(1), 11–13.

Beebe, J. (1981). Heinz Kohut: 1913–1981. *The San Francisco Jung Institute Library Journal, 3*(1), 1.

Beebe, J. (1984). A Jungian perspective on interpretation. *Quadrant, 17*(2), 53–59.

Beebe, J. (1988). Primary ambivalence toward the Self: its nature and treatment. In N. Schwartz-Salant & M. Stein (Eds.), *The borderline personality in analysis* (pp. 97–127). Wilmette, IL: Chiron Publications.

Beebe, J. (2014). The *red book* as a work of literature. In T. Kirsch & G. Hogenson (Eds.), *The red book: Reflections on C. G. Jung's Liber Novus* (pp. 108–122). London: Routledge.

Benveniste, D. with Henderson, J. L. (2000). *Thinking in metaphor: Summaries of Joseph L. Henderson's ARAS lectures 1985–1998.* (Unpublished compilation in library of C. G. Jung Institute of San Francisco).

Bollas, C. (1993). *Being a character: Psychoanalysis and self experience.* London: Routledge.

Broadcast news. (1987). Brooks, J. L. (Producer and Director). USA: Twentieth Century Fox. [Motion picture].

Edman, I. (1937). *Four ways of philosophy.* New York: H. Holt & Co.

Erikson, E. (1950). *Childhood and society.* New York: W. W. Norton & Co.

Gass, W. H. (2000). *Reading Rilke: Reflections on the problems of translation.* New York: Alfred A. Knopf.

Henderson, J. L. (1964). The archetype of culture. In A. Guggenbuhl-Craig (Ed.), *Der Archetyp/The archetype* (Proceedings of the Second International Congress for Analytical Psychology, Zurich, 1962) (pp. 3–14). Basel: S. Karger.

Henderson, J. L. (1972). The psychic activity of dreaming. *Psychological Perspectives, 3*(2), 104–105.

Henderson, J. L. (1977). Individual lives in a changing society. *Psychological Perspectives, 8*(2), 126–142.

Henderson, J. L. (1982). A religious dilemma in a multicultural society. *Psychological Perspectives, 13*, 127–138; also in Henderson, J. L. (1990) pp. 131–141.

Henderson, J. L. (1984). *Cultural attitudes in psychological perspective.* Toronto: Inner City Books.

Henderson, J. L. (1990). *Shadow and self: Selected papers in analytical psychology.* Wilmette, IL: Chiron Publications.

Holmes, R. (1998). *Coleridge: Darker reflections, 1804–1834.* New York: Pantheon Books.

James, W. (1907/2008). *Pragmatism: A new name for some old ways of thinking.* Rockville, MD: Manor.

Jung, C. G. (1921/1971). Psychological types. In *Cw 6.*

Jung, C. G. (1963). *Memories, dreams, reflections*. New York: Pantheon.

Jung, C. G. (1969). Psychology and religion: West and east, 2nd Edition. In *Cw 11*.

Jung, C. G. (1975). *Letters, vol. 2: 1951–1965*. G. Adler & A. Jaffe (Eds.), R. F. C. Hull (Trans.). Princeton, NJ: Princeton University Press.

Jung, C. G. (2009). *The red book: Liber novus*. S. Shamdasani (Ed.), M. Kyburz, J. Peck, and S. Shamdasani, (Trans.) New York: W.W. Norton.

Kimbles, S. (2003). Joe Henderson and the cultural unconscious. *San Francisco Jung Institute Library Journal*, *22*(2), 53–58.

Kluckhohn, C. & Murray, H. (Eds.) (1948). *Personality in nature, society and culture*. New York: Knopf.

Langley, N., Ryerson, F., & Woolf, E. A. (1989). *The Wizard of Oz: The screenplay*. New York: Delta.

Mr. Hulot's holiday (Les vacances de M. Hulot). (1953). Tati, J. (Director) France: Discifilm [Motion picture.]

O'Donohue, J. O. (2005). *Beauty: The invisible embrace*. New York: Harper Perennial.

Perils of Pauline, The. (1914). Gasnier, L. & MacKenzie, D. (Directors) USA: General Film Company. [Film serial.]

Shamdasani, S. & Beebe, J. (2010). Jung becomes Jung: A dialogue on *Liber novus* (*The red book*). *Psychological Perspectives*, *53*(4), 410–436.

Symington, N. (2002). *A pattern of madness*. London: Karnac.

Wizard of Oz, The. (1939). LeRoy, M. (Producer) & Fleming, V. (Director). USA: Metro-Goldwyn-Mayer. [Motion picture].

PART II
Type and the MBTI

7

EVOLVING THE EIGHT-FUNCTION MODEL

Eight archetypes guide how the function-attitudes are expressed in an individual psyche

There's much talk in the type world nowadays about the Eight-Function or Whole Type Model, and my name is sometimes brought up as a pioneer in this area. This chapter establishes the historical context of what I've contributed, and explains in my own words what my innovations have been.

Historical background: Jung's eight functions

It was C. G. Jung, of course, who introduced the language we use today: words such as function and attitude, as well as his highly specific names for the four functions of our conscious orientation (thinking, feeling, sensation, intuition), and the two attitudes through which those orientations are deployed (introversion and extraversion).

Establishing the rationale for this language as a helpful basis for the analysis of consciousness was the purpose of his 1921 book, *Psychological Types*. Toward the end of that book he combined function types and attitude types to describe, in turn, eight function-attitudes. Regrettably it wasn't until Dick Thompson published his 1996 book *Jung's Function-Attitudes Explained* that we had that term for these cognitive processes,[1] so most Jungians have simply referred to them as eight 'functions.'

Nevertheless, for Jung the attitude type was the primary thing, and the function type a kind of sub-something that expressed that attitude in a particular way. Accordingly, he organized his general description of the types in terms of the attitudes, describing first "the peculiarities of the basic psychological functions in the *extraverted* attitude" and then going on to "the peculiarities of the basic psychological functions in the *introverted* attitude."

Jung started with extraverted thinking and extraverted feeling (which he called 'the extraverted rational types') and extraverted sensation and extraverted intuition ('the extraverted irrational types'), before turning to the introverted types: intro-verted thinking and introverted feeling ('introverted rational types'), and introverted sensation and introverted intuition ('introverted irrational types'). These were the eight psychological types in Jung's original description.

These functions–attitudes were nothing less than capacities for consciousness residing within any individual—though of course most people do not differentiate all these capacities for their own use. It was Jung who taught us that most people pair a rational function with an irrational one to develop a conscious orientation, or, as he put it, an *ego-consciousness*, that for most people involves just these two differentiated functions.

Despite Isabel Briggs Myers's later reading of a single sentence in Jung's long and often contradictory book (Myers & Myers, 1980/1995, p. 19; Jung, 1921/1971, ¶669), he never made clear that the attitude type of the two functions in this two-function model of consciousness would alternate between function #1 and function #2.

Jung did, however, open the door to the possibility of a further differentiation of functions, up to a limiting number of four: the *fourth* to differentiate being his famous 'inferior' function, which remains too close to the unconscious, and thus a source of errors and complexes.

Jung said relatively little about the *third* function. He expected that both func-tions #3 and #4 would, in most people, remain potentials only, residing in the unconscious, represented in dreams in archaic ways and relatively refractory to development except under exceptional circumstances—such as the individuation process Jung sometimes witnessed in the analysis of a relatively mature person in the second half of life, when the archaic functions would press for integration into consciousness.

Anima/animus: bridge to the unconscious

When Jung's close associate Marie-Louise von Franz published her Zurich seminar on the inferior function, in *Lectures in Jung's Typology* (1971/1998), I was already a candidate in analytic training at the C. G. Jung Institute of San Francisco. Her dis-cussion of the possibilities for development in this largely unconscious area of the mind was thrilling to read, and it opened up the four-function model for a whole generation of analysts.

Von Franz made it clear that we have a choice about developing function #3, but that the integration of function #4, the inferior function, is very much under the control of the unconscious, which limits what we can do with it. Nevertheless, this much of the unconscious belongs in a sense to the ego—and even provides the bridge to the Self that the other differentiated functions cannot.

I became aware that the inferior function was often thought by Jungian analysts to operate in this way because it is 'carried' by the anima or animus, archetypes of soul that can serve as tutelary figures, representing the otherness of the unconscious psyche, and also its capacity to speak to us to enlarge our conscious perspectives

(Jung, 1921/1971, ¶¶803–811).[2] The anima and animus are like fairy bridges to the unconscious, allowing, almost magically, a relationship to develop between the two parts of the mind, conscious and unconscious, with the potential to replace this tension of opposites with the harmony of wholeness. And it is through the undifferentiated, incorrigible inferior function that they do their best work!

Basic orientation: hero/heroine, father/mother, *puer/puella*

By then I thought I knew my own type—extraverted intuition, with introverted thinking as my second function—and I had taken the MBTI questionnaire, which scored me ENTP, in apparent confirmation of my self-diagnosis. It was in dreams that I met my anima as a humble, introverted-sensation type Chinese laundress, and it was she who could provide me a bridge to the practicalities of life that my conscious standpoint, ever theoretical, tended to leave out. I think it was also she who made me consider sorting out the rest of my consciousness. Which archetypes were associated with my other functions?

I began to watch my dreams. Gradually it became obvious that when they symbolized my extraverted intuition, it was in a heroic, rather grandiose way. (In a dream, I once saw President Lyndon Johnson, architect of the Great Society in my country, as an image of my dominant extraverted intuition, which gave it a high-handed, crafty cast, a bit out of touch with the actual readiness of those around me for the changes that I wanted to introduce in their lives, in the name of helping them progress.)

My introverted thinking was symbolized by a father in one dream that found him in conflict with an upset feeling-type son, whom I eventually recognized as an image of my third function. The particular son figure in the dream was a persistently immature man in analysis at the time, whose oscillation of woundedness and creativity fit well the description Marie-Louise von Franz had given in her classic study of the "Problem of the *Puer Aeternus*" (1970), the Latin term suggesting an eternal boyhood befitting an immortal. I decided that this dream was referring to an aspect of my own feeling that was inflated, vulnerable and chronically immature.

In this way, I began to evolve my understanding that the four functions are brought into consciousness through the dynamic energy of particular archetypes:

- Hero for the superior function
- Father for the second or 'auxiliary' function
- *Puer* for the tertiary function
- Anima for the inferior function.

My functions were carried into consciousness on the backs of those archetypes! A great deal of their functioning, even after they became conscious—that is, available to me as ways of perceiving and assessing reality—continued to reflect the characteristic behavior of these archetypes.

Later, I found evidence in the dreams of women for a heroine, a mother, and a *puella aeterna* (eternal girl), symbolizing the first three functions of consciousness in a highly analogous arrangement to the way my own were symbolized. I could also verify from their dreams what other Jungian analysts had already established, that the animus carries the inferior function for a woman—although I came to reserve that term for a spirit or soul figure operating as a bridge to the unconscious, and not simply to refer to an antagonistic or argumentative side of the woman, as some were doing in accord with the more normal English language use of the word animus, which does not include its Jungian, spiritual meaning (Emma Jung, 1957).

I went public with these ideas for the first time in 1983, at a conference for Jungian analysts and candidates at Ghost Ranch in Abiquiu, New Mexico. There I offered the first archetypal model for the various positions of consciousness that heretofore had been called 'superior,' 'auxiliary,' 'tertiary' and 'inferior' functions. I suggested that these should be thought of, respectively, as the heroic function, the father or mother function, the *puer* or *puella* function, and the anima or animus function, in accord with the nature of the archetype that had taken up residence in each of these four basic locations of potential consciousness.

Wow! Behind each typological position in the unfolding of conscious, an archetype was involved, guiding us to be heroic, parental, and even puerile and contrasexual, as part of what makes us capable of becoming cognizant of ourselves and the world around us.

The shadow personality: opposing personality, *senex*/witch, trickster, demonic personality

At the time I was too dazzled by the seeming completeness of the four-function model to see that even more delineation was needed to make sense of what Jung had said we could find in ourselves, if his vision of a wholeness to consciousness could be realized.

Four functions were still only half the story of how consciousness arranges itself. Jung said in *Psychological Types* that, if one takes into account the all-important attitudes, extraversion and introversion, we have to realize that there are in all eight functions, or, as we say now, function-attitudes.

Von Franz had postulated that the greatest difficulties that occur between people are on the basis of one using a function with a particular attitude (e.g. extraversion), and the other using the *same* function with the *opposite* attitude (e.g. introversion). I decided to apply that idea to the situation within a single psyche, in which the antagonism was not between two people, but between two functions with opposite attitudes, seeking to express themselves within the same person.

The result, I realized, was almost always a repression of one member of such a pair of functions, as a consequence of the conscious preference for the attitude through which the other member of the pair was expressing that function. In my own case, I had figured out that my tertiary function was not only feeling, but extraverted feeling, and that my inferior function was introverted sensation.

Where were my introverted feeling and extraverted sensation? Obviously, deep in the unconscious, kept there because they were shadow in attitude to the function-attitudes that I had differentiated.

Even more in shadow were the functions opposite in attitude to my first two functions—that is, the introverted intuition that my superior extraverted intuition tended to inhibit, and the extraverted thinking that my auxiliary introverted thinking looked down upon.

These four functions—introverted intuition, extraverted thinking, introverted feeling, extraverted sensation—continued to express themselves, however, in shadowy ways. What, then, were the archetypes that carried these repressed shadow functions?

Answering this question led me to take up the problem of the types in shadow, which has preoccupied me ever since. Work in this area has to be tentative, because we never fully see our own shadow, but in my case I began to identify typical, shadowy ways in which I would use the four functions that lie in the shadow of my more differentiated quartet of individuated function-attitudes. My introverted intuition, shadow in attitude to my superior extraverted intuition, has decidedly oppositional traits: it expresses itself in ways I could variously describe as avoidant, passive–aggressive, paranoid and seductive, in all cases taking up a stance that is anathema to the way my superior extraverted intuition wants me to behave. I decided to call the archetype carrying this bag of oppositional behaviors the opposing personality.

Similarly, my fatherly introverted thinking, a patient teacher of complex ideas, was shadowed by a dogmatic, donnish extraverted thinking that didn't listen to, or even care about, others' ideas. I decided to call this rather pompous, unrelated figure my *senex*, using James Hillman's (1967/1979) choice of name for an archetype that is coldly, arrogantly, judgmental, in an old-man-pulling-rank sort of way. (The Latin word *senex*, root of our word 'senator', means 'old man'.)

Gradually I realized that women I knew had a similar archetype carrying the shadow of their normally motherly auxiliary function, and that this archetype displays many of the 'negative mother' characteristics I had learned to associate with the witch figure in European fairytales (von Franz, 1972).

The shadow side of my eager-to-please but oh-so-vulnerable-to-the-feelings-of-others internal boy was the trickster, which, in me, with its confident introverted feeling, could reverse any expectation—to double-bind anybody who tries to ride herd on the child. (As a little boy, to taunt my mother when she expected perfection of me, I actually used to draw the two-faced god Mercurius, although I did not yet know his mythological identity.)[3]

Finally, I began to see my extraverted sensation, the shadow side of my anima introverted sensation, as a demonic personality that often operates as an undermining oaf, a beastly part of myself that nevertheless can occasionally be an uncanny source for the infusion of redemptive spirit into my dealings with myself and others.[4]

The four archetypes of shadow—opposing personality, *senex*/witch, trickster and demonic/daimonic personality—and the function-attitudes they carried for me—introverted intuition, extraverted thinking, introverted feeling, extraverted sensation—were all what a psychologist would call *ego-dystonic*. That is, they were incompatible with my conscious ego or sense of '*I*-ness'— what I normally own as part of 'me' and 'my' values. Nevertheless, they were part of my total functioning as a person, uncomfortable as it made me to recognize the fact.

In this way, using myself as an example, and my years of Jungian analysis as a laboratory, I eventually came to identify eight discrete archetypes guiding the way the eight function-attitudes are expressed within a single, individual psyche.

Although, for convenience of reference, and out of respect for the traditional numbering of the functions, I am in the habit of assigning numbers to the function-attitude 'positions' associated with these archetypes, I no longer view the type profile of an individual as expressing a hierarchy of differentiation of the various functions of consciousness.

Rather, I have come to regard the positions the types of function-attitude seem to occupy, when we construct a model of them in our minds, in a much more qualitative light. It is as if they form an interacting cast of characters through which the different functions may express themselves in the ongoing drama of self and shadow that is anyone's lived psychological life.

Although the actual casting of specific function-attitudes in the various roles will be governed by the individual's type, the roles themselves seem to be found in everyone's psyche. Hence I regard them as archetypal complexes carrying the different functions, and I like to speak of them as *typical subpersonalities* found in all of us.

I have spent many years verifying this scheme. Through observation of clients and others whose types and complexes I have gotten to know well, and through the analysis of films by master filmmakers in which archetypes and function-attitudes are clearly delineated, I have concluded that the relationships between these archetypes and the scheme of differentiation that results for the function-attitudes is not merely personal to me, but is actually universal.

The archetypal roles within this scheme are shown in Figure 7.1. An example of how the model distributes consciousness in an ENFJ is provided in Figure 7.2. A listing of how the consciousnesses are distributed in each of the 16 MBTI types is found in Table 7.1.

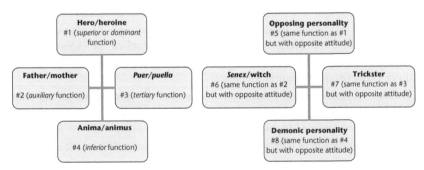

FIGURE 7.1 Archetypal complexes carrying the eight functions of consciousness

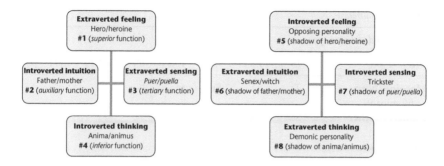

FIGURE 7.2 Archetypes associated with the eight functions of consciousness (using ENFJ as an example)

This model of the archetypal complexes that carry the eight functions of consciousness is my present instrument for the exploration of type in myself and others. It helps me to see, in just about any interaction, what consciousness (that is, which *function-attitude*) I am using at that given time.

More importantly, the model allows me to see what position that function-attitude inhabits, and thereby I am pointed to watch for the archetypal ways in which, as a consequence of being in that position, that particular consciousness expresses itself.

I am grateful that this model is leading present-day type assessors to take a second look at C. G. Jung's foundational eight-function description of the types. My hope is that their increasing comfort with a total eight-function, rather than a preferred four-function, model will enable them to begin to recognize the combinations of

TABLE 7.1 MBTI types showing pairing of archetypal roles and types of awareness

MBTI Type	ESTJ	ENTJ	ESFJ	ENFJ	ENTP	ENFP	ESTP	ESFP
Extraverted dominant types								
Heroine/hero (dominant)	Te	Te	Fe	Fe	Ne	Ne	Se	Se
Father/mother (auxiliary)	Si	Ni	Si	Ni	Ti	Fi	Ti	Fi
Puer/puella (tertiary)	Ne	Se	Ne	Se	Fe	Te	Fe	Te
Animus/anima (inferior)	Fi	Fi	Ti	Ti	Si	Si	Ni	Ni
Opposing personality	Ti	Ti	Fi	Fi	Ni	Ni	Si	Si
Senex/witch	Se	Ne	Se	Ne	Te	Fe	Te	Fe
Trickster	Ni	Si	Ni	Si	Fi	Ti	Fi	Ti
Demonic/daimonic personality	Fe	Fe	Te	Te	Se	Se	Ne	Ne

(continued)

TABLE 7.1 *(continued)*

Introverted dominant types

MBTI Type	ISTP	INTP	ISFP	INFP	INTJ	INFJ	ISTJ	ISFJ
Heroine/hero (dominant)	Ti	Ti	Fi	Fi	Ni	Ni	Si	Si
Father/mother (auxiliary)	Se	Ne	Se	Ne	Te	Fe	Te	Fe
Puer/puella (tertiary)	Ni	Si	Ni	Si	Fi	Ti	Fi	Ti
Animus/anima (inferior)	Fe	Fe	Te	Te	Se	Se	Ne	Ne
Opposing personality	Te	Te	Fe	Fe	Ne	Ne	Se	Se
Senex/**witch**	Si	Ni	Si	Ni	Ti	Fi	Ti	Fi
Trickster	Ne	Se	Ne	Se	Fe	Te	Fe	Te
Demonic/daimonic personality	Fi	Fi	Ti	Ti	Si	Si	Ni	Ni

Note: In the two-letter abbreviations, the first letter defines the function, the second letter gives its attitude, either introverted or extraverted. Code: E = extraverted; I = introverted; N = intuition; S = sensation; T = thinking; F = feeling.

type and role that emerge, both for good and for ill, as these consciousnesses differentiate themselves in human beings.

Notes

1 Linda Berens used the term 'cognitive processes' (1999) to refer to the eight types of consciousness that Jung discovered.
2 I have adopted Jung's use of Latin when speaking of the anima and animus (literally 'soul' and 'spirit') because that language allows for gender (the anima often being a feminine figure in a man, and the animus a masculine one in a woman), and because it conveys the archaic quality of these deep structures of the mind that Jung uncovered in his explorations of the unconscious.

   Jung called them *archetypes of the collective unconscious*, but when carrying function #4, the inferior function, I feel they also form part of the conscious mind's functioning. Hence I regard them as *ego-syntonic*—compatible with the ego and its preferred function-attitude—even though carrying values from the unconscious mind that compensate the attitude of the person's superior function.
3 In choosing the name trickster for this side of my shadow, I drew upon Jung's classic delineations of the trickster archetype (Jung 1948/1967, 1954/1959).
4 As with the opposing personality, the term demonic personality is my own creation. In developing my model I deliberately left these terms large and vague to convey the vast stretches of personality territory involved in these dark and largely unexplored areas of myself where my shadow typology expresses itself as character pathology.

References

Berens, L. (1999). *Dynamics of personality type: Understanding and applying Jung's cognitive processes.* Huntington Beach, CA: Telos Publications.

Hillman, J. (1967/1979). Senex and puer. In J. Hillman (Ed.), *Puer papers* (pp. 3–53). Dallas, TX: Spring.

Jung, C. G. (1921/1971). Psychological types. In *Cw 6*.

Jung, C. G. (1948/1967). The spirit mercurius. In *Cw 13* (pp. 191–250).

Jung, C. G. (1954/1959). On the psychology of the trickster figure. In *Cw 9, 1* (pp. 255–272).

Jung, E. (1957). On the nature of the animus. In *Animus and anima* (pp. 1–43), New York: Spring.

Myers, I. B. with Myers, P. (1980/1995). *Gifts differing: Understanding personality type.* Palo Alto, CA: Davies-Black.

Thompson, H. L. (1996). *Jung's function-attitudes explained.* Watkinsville, GA: Wormhole.

von Franz, M.-L. (1970). *The problem of the puer aeternus.* New York: Spring.

von Franz, M.-L. (1971/1998). The inferior function. In M.-L. von Franz and J. Hillman, *Lectures on Jung's typology* (pp. 3–88). Woodstock, CT: Spring Publications.

von Franz, M.-L. (1972). *Problems of the feminine in fairytales.* New York: Spring.

8

TYPE AND ARCHETYPE

The spine and its shadow

Archetypes associated with the superior and inferior functions form the personality's spine

The idea that each of us has the potential to access the full range of consciousnesses that Jung identified in *Psychological Types* is an appealing one, and one which, thanks in part to my own work, has been increasingly explored and accepted by a number of type practitioners in recent years (Berens & Nardi, 2004; Hartzler, McAlpine, & Haas, 2005; Haas & Hunziker, 2006).

Known as the eight-function model, the theory does not deny that each of us has just one superior and one auxiliary function on which most of us rely heavily; but it goes further, analyzing how our consciousness operates when we find that we must reach beyond these two favored ways of coming up with intelligent responses to life's demands.

The eight-function, eight-archetype model of psychological types is based on two observations that are fundamental to its understanding and application. The first observation is that, in the course of our lives, *we each actually make use of all the function-attitudes*, those eight options of consciousness that Jung originally described in *Psychological Types*: introverted thinking, introverted feeling, introverted sensation, introverted intuition, extraverted thinking, extraverted feeling, extraverted sensation, and extraverted intuition.

The second observation is that these function-attitudes, though having typical characteristics that a century of type research has repeatedly verified, are *not expressed in the same way by every individual who deploys them*. There is a normal variation, not only in the strength and reliability of the functions, according to the degree of preference and practice that the individual will bring to the expression of each type of consciousness, but also in the role the individual enters when expressing a particular consciousness.

This second observation moves type theory well beyond Jung's original discovery—clarified and amplified by Isabel Briggs Myers through her seminal insights into the nature of type development—that the function-attitudes arrange themselves as a series of numbered positions, implying a hierarchy of differentiation: i.e. dominant function, auxiliary function, tertiary function, and inferior function.

My own addition to type theory was to recognize that such a numbering of functions implies that there are, rooted in the structure of the psyche, eight positions, one for each function-attitude. This insight led me to postulate archetypal qualities adhering to each of the positions, rather in the way a local genius is said to preside over every town and city in Italy.

Figure 8.1 is a diagram that shows the archetypes that preside over the expression of the first four function-attitudes, in function positions from superior to inferior.

The diagram shows these relations for a person whose MBTI type is ENTP, but the archetypes associated with the different numbered positions would be the same for the other 15 types as well, even though the function-attitudes occupying the four positions vary according to the type.

In this chapter I will be concentrating on the pair of archetypes associated with the superior and inferior functions in Figure 8.1, which define an axis (the vertical line in the diagram) that I call the *spine* of personality, and adding to them two archetypes (not shown in Figure 8.1) of the function positions that form the normally invisible *shadow* to this spine. (Archetypes associated with the auxiliary and tertiary functions, which form the *arms* of the diagram, with *their* shadows, will be discussed in Chapter 9.)

The function positions I am concentrating on here (the superior and inferior functions and their opposite-attitude shadows), together with their associated archetypes, form the core of any personality, which structures how the person's consciousness is most characteristically used, for better and worse.

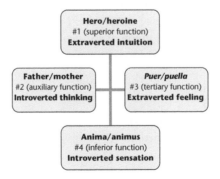

FIGURE 8.1   Archetypes associated with the first four function-attitudes (using ENTP as an example)

Most people who explore type start by locating their superior and inferior functions and develop a sense of how differently competent they feel when using one versus the other. They find it much more difficult to recognize when they are using these same functions with the opposite attitudes, however; for then, whether they realize it or not, they are drawing upon archetypes that serve not to realize the aims of the personality, but to defend it, usually by managing other people in oppositional and underhanded ways.

Before we can explore the archetypal characteristics of this core axis of the shadow, and of the spine of greater integrity that it shadows, we have to get better acquainted with how an archetype, a figure of the unconscious, can be associated with a function of consciousness, which seems to many people like a paradox. Let me trace my own history of developing this idea.

Early in my analytic training, I heard from older analysts, who seemed to have heard it from their analysts and supervisors—many close associates of Jung—if not from Jung himself, that the 'inferior function' is often associated with the archetype of soul in a man, and spirit in a woman.[1]

For a man, it was said, the inferior function was carried by the anima, the internal feminine figure that represents the instinct for soulful connection and reflection (Hillman, 1985). In a woman, the inferior function was said to be carried by the animus, the internal, masculine psychic figure that represents spirited standards (Jung, E., 1931/1957).

My teachers' expression 'carried by,' I came to understand as 'personified by,' 'embodied by,' or 'in the charge of.' This association of the inferior function with a contrasexual figure in the unconscious was implicitly contrasted by my Jungian teachers with the ego control that appears in relation to the 'superior function.'

My primary contribution to the deeper understanding of Jung's typology was to ask, and to try to answer, the question: "If the functions in these two positions—inferior and superior—are tied, as they seem to be, to specific archetypes within the psyche, to what archetypes are the functions in the other positions linked?"

By studying my own dreams, fantasies and behaviors, and those of my patients, over 50 years of practicing individual psychotherapy, and by using the films of visionary directors as a projection of the psyche, I have identified what seem to me to be convincing and reliable patterns of association. From these studies, I have found four positions of consciousness to be at the core of the individual self:

- the superior function
- the inferior function
- the shadow of the superior function
- the shadow of the inferior function.

By 'shadow,' a term Jung deliberately left imprecise, I mean having the same function but the opposite attitude. So, for example, when the superior function is introverted feeling, its shadow is extraverted feeling, the inferior function is extraverted thinking, and the shadow of the inferior function is introverted thinking.

Table 8.1 shows these relations for all the different types of superior function, as well as the archetypes associated with the different type positions involved. (These latter links will be explained later in the chapter.)

The *superior* function, not surprisingly, is the part of the ego we are most ready to claim ownership of, because it is associated with a sense of competence and potential mastery. The archetype that grants us this confidence in relation to the superior function (around which it is possible to develop a superiority complex) I have named the hero in a man and the heroine in a woman. This is a part of the psyche that welcomes facing challenges, that takes pleasure in recalling its past successful exploits, that revels in its unflagging reliability.

The differentiation of the hero/heroine is usually the work of childhood, and the more the original family recognizes and values the superior function, the more the child is seen (at least in this area) as remarkable, competent, and gifted.

The *inferior* function, in contrast, is a perpetual source of shame or embarrassment for most people. Acknowledging and accepting this shame with a measure of humility is a first, necessary step towards knowing oneself, finding integrity, and beginning to make a meaningful connection to the unconscious (Beebe, 1992).

But because the inferior function is usually so poorly developed, especially in a young person, to be forced to use it can be an agony, and even calls forth a yelp of complaint, a cry that is often high-pitched in a man, full-throated in a woman. This sonic quality gives us a glimpse into the contra-sexual nature of the archetype carrying the inferior function: the defensive, hysterical, helpless, irritated, bird-like

TABLE 8.1 Types of superior and inferior function and their shadows

Superior function	Shadow of superior function	Inferior function	Shadow of inferior function
Hero/heroine	Opposing personality	Anima/animus	Demonic/daimonic personality
Introverted feeling	Extraverted feeling	Extraverted thinking	Introverted thinking
Introverted intuition	Extraverted intuition	Extraverted sensation	Introverted sensation
Introverted thinking	Extraverted thinking	Extraverted feeling	Introverted feeling
Introverted sensation	Extraverted sensation	Extraverted intuition	Introverted intuition
Extraverted feeling	Introverted feeling	Introverted thinking	Extraverted thinking
Extraverted intuition	Introverted intuition	Introverted sensation	Extraverted sensation
Extraverted thinking	Introverted thinking	Introverted feeling	Extraverted feeling
Extraverted sensation	Introverted sensation	Introverted intuition	Extraverted intuition

whining in a man is the voice of the anima under pressure, while in a woman the growl of an animal cornered, embittered and at the end of its rope, can emerge from the pressed animus.

Despite its burden of shame, the inferior function, with its connection to soul or spirit, is also a place of great idealism in the psyche. The higher cause or mission that seizes our energy is often associated with this area of the psyche where we are ourselves rather weak and inept.

Thus, a person whose superior function is introverted thinking will often put a very high value on the goal of everyone in a group getting along together, although this person may lack any of the feeling skills to facilitate such an outcome. Conversely, an introverted feeling type may be drawn to champion the most abstruse strains of philosophy, even as he or she has to struggle to follow the more intricate twists of thinking.

The person who cares most passionately about the quality and safety of food may have superior introverted intuition and thus inferior extraverted sensation, while the person with superior introverted sensation may be the most concerned to maintain the quality of the future, for instance by acting now to reduce global warming, an extraverted intuitive precaution.

In Jungian psychology, anima and animus development are seen as the work of the second half of life, when the inferior function that is associated with anima and animus will start to appear in a much more creative and adapted way.

Sigmund Freud, whom Jung regarded as an introverted feeling type (1975), developed the extraverted-thinking psychoanalytic theory after the age of forty. It was originally a sexual theory, in which the anima value of connection was made biologically explicit. Freud even gave each of his closest supporters in Vienna a ring to wear, signifying their pledge never to be untrue to the sexual theory, at a time when Jung was already starting to deviate from this dogmatism. The analogy would be to Arthur's knights swearing fealty to Guinevere.

The Jungian analyst Jane Wheelwright, who identified as an introverted sensation type, began after the age of fifty to develop her creative animus as a writer, addressing among other things how to counteract the fears of women as they grow older and exploring the possibilities of psychological development even in the face of death. Wheelwright's writings at this stage of her life, reflecting her own animus development, had a strongly extraverted intuitive cast.

When there is development of both the superior and the inferior functions, we can speak of a 'spine' of consciousness that gives a personality backbone. (In Freud's case, the introverted feeling that made him a sensitive psychotherapist when that was still a very new medical subspecialty was combined with an extraverted thinking ability to clearly articulate a theory that made sense of the dynamics of the cases he treated.)

We know that the person's consciousness is organized around a core of identity and integrity and that it stands for something. On the other hand, such a well-differentiated consciousness will also cast a definite shadow. The 'spine' of personality and its shadow for an introverted feeling man is shown in Figure 8.2.

Applying this model to the analysis of Freud's consciousness, about which there is a considerable literature since his standpoint has been so influential in the development of depth psychology generally, we are led to examine how he seems to have used his extraverted feeling and introverted thinking. It has been frequently documented how fraught with accusations of disloyalty, and examples of unrecognized unfaithfulness on his own part, Freud's relations with colleagues were.

Recently it has come out that Freud was involved in a shadowy liaison with his sister-in-law, who lived with Freud and his wife. (Freud had begun 'living in abstinence' with his wife when he was thirty-seven, as she did not want to have another child (Gay, 1988).) The evidence that has surfaced of this long-rumored affair (which the sister-in-law may have confessed to Jung) is a hotel registration that indicates that the two registered as husband and wife when travelling together (Blumenthal, 2006). All this suggests shadow extraverted feeling.

What is the evidence for shadow introverted thinking? Introverted thinking involves naming things in fresh ways, in relation less to outer definitions already agreed upon than to an archetypal sense of the things' unconscious resonance. A non-shadowy introverted thinking can often find just the right name for something, but a shadowy introverted thinking may choose a name that gives the thing named a disagreeable association.

Thus Freud named the normal attachment that little boys have for their mothers the 'Oedipus' complex, and the normal interest we all have in our own self-image, 'Narcissism.' But Oedipus actually slept with (and even married) his mother, and had to blind himself for the transgression of looking at her naked. And Narcissus fell in love with his image in a river and drowned trying to kiss it.

Such archetypal names for normal processes of development seem to me misnomers that undermine our sense of the necessity of such processes for normal development. In fact, they slowed down psychology's sense of the role of attraction to the parent of the opposite sex in the course of developing a well-functioning sexuality, as well as the role of self-esteem in enabling any personality to flower. For generations, analysts warned their patients off interest in their parents and in themselves as signs of psychopathology, when they were not. This was the shadow that qualified the enormous therapeutic possibilities of the new discipline of psychoanalysis.

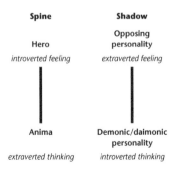

FIGURE 8.2 The 'spine' of personality and its shadow (for an introverted feeling man)

Today, we can speak of the archetypes involved in the way Freud used extra-verted feeling (the shadow of his superior function) and introverted thinking (the shadow of his inferior function). I have named them the opposing personality (the archetype that led Freud to regard former colleagues such as Adler and Jung as 'enemies'), and the demonic personality (the archetype that led him to distort and undermine the meaning of such universal aspects of child development as sexual interest in a parent, or intense fascination with oneself, that his scientific genius allowed him to discover in the fantasies and dreams of his patients—who assuredly were not dreaming of Oedipus and Narcissus).

I have found that the archetype I've named the opposing personality normally shapes the expression of its associated function-attitude in paranoid, avoidant, passive-aggressive and seductive ways. For the introverted feeling Freud, this was how his extraverted feeling tended to manifest, and a similar fate awaits each of us in the function-attitude that is the shadow of our superior one.

The opposing personality is a primary resource of defense, a part of us that tends to lurch forward first when we feel our heroic superior function and its most cher-ished values to be under attack.

We may also find ourselves thrown into the opposing personality when we are called upon to use the function-attitude that it carries. Thus, in writing about archetypes, which live most fully in the realm of introverted intuition, I, a per-son whose superior function is extraverted intuition, may find myself (as in this chapter) using somewhat negative, oppositional examples, as above in my Jungian reading of Freud.

The archetype I have chosen to call the demonic personality shapes the expres-sion of the function-attitude that shadows the anima or animus. We get a good image of the qualities of the demonic personality in the way Freud used language that twisted, in a pathologizing direction, our whole culture's understanding of some normal aspects of unconscious personality development, such that it has been the devil's own work to rescue these areas of ourselves from the tendency within depth psychology to think about them negatively.

Yet it would be ungrateful to Freud not to admit that he also uncovered the areas of infantile sexuality and basic self-esteem that no psychologist before him had explored nearly so accurately. I often use the term demonic/daimonic personality to convey that the archetype associated with the most unconscious of regions of the mind can deliver insights that are of the highest value, as well as depreciating and undermining ones. It is truly an area of ourselves that is both devil and angel.

The demonic personality is usually the locus of our most unyielding and uncon-scious flaws of character. When we act beastly, it is often through this archetype and its associated function-attitude.

I have interpreted the fairy tale *Beauty and the Beast* as a story of the struggle we all have with the worst part of our character (Beebe, 1998). Beauty is the anima, carrying the idealistic inferior function, with its burning concern for connecting in a quality way with others.

Beast is the demonic/daimonic personality, which in life, unlike the Beast at the end of most versions of the fairy tale, does not transform into a handsome prince. This most incorrigible of our function-attitudes stays a beast, but one that to some extent can be tamed through the anima's solicitous and energetic care.

Although we commonly feel excruciatingly self-conscious about the inferior function (the anima and animus can amplify that self-consciousness to the point of projecting that everyone is noticing our clumsiness in this area), it is important to realize that most of us are quite unconscious of the impact on other people of the functions carried by the opposing or demonic personality.

These less-inhibited parts of our functioning are among those that others experience negatively. They form the realistic basis of the 'unfair' judgments we sometimes experience ourselves receiving from others. It would be wiser for someone receiving such a judgment to say to him or herself, 'That person has seen my shadow.'

The question for the development of consciousness is, can we learn to see it, too?

Note

1 Jung (1921/1971, ¶306) suggests that "the soul is coupled with the less differentiated function," but for the most part this idea has been transmitted in the oral tradition of Jungian analytic training.

References

Beebe, J. (1992). *Integrity in depth*. College Station, TX: Texas A & M University Press.

Beebe, J. (1998). Toward a Jungian analysis of character. In A. Casement (Ed.), *Post-Jungians today* (pp. 53–66). London: Routledge.

Berens, L. & Nardi, D. (2004). *Understanding yourself and others: An introduction to the personality type code*. Huntingdon Beach, CA: Telos.

Blumenthal, R. (2006). Hotel log hints at desire Freud didn't repress, *International Herald Tribune*, 24 December 2006.

Gay, P. (1988). *Freud: A life for our time*. New York: W. W. Norton.

Haas, L. & Hunziker, M. (2006). *Jung's mental processes: Building blocks of personality*. Huntingdon Beach, CA: Telos.

Hartzler, M., McAlpine, R. W. & Haas, L. (2005). *Introduction to type and the 8 Jungian functions*. Mountain View, CA: CPP.

Hillman, J. (1985). *Anima: An anatomy of a personified notion*. Dallas, TX: Spring.

Jung, C. G. (1921/1971). Psychological types. In *Cw 6*.

Jung, C. G. (1975). Letter to Ernst Hanhart, 18 February 1957. In G. Adler & A. Jaffé, (Eds.), R. F. C. Hull (Trans.), *Letters, vol. 2* (pp. 346–348). Princeton: NJ: Princeton University Press.

Jung, E. (1931/1957). On the nature of the animus. In *Animus and Anima*, (pp. 1–43). New York: Spring.

9

TYPE AND ARCHETYPE

The arms and their shadow

In Chapter 8, I emphasized archetypal roles (hero and anima/animus) that are intimately associated with the experience of personal identity and showed their relationship to typology. I noted that these particular roles, centered as they are on the qualities of the superior and inferior functions, help to define the 'spine' of personality. Becoming conscious of this axis between the superior and inferior functions allows someone to know who he or she is and makes it easier for the person to hold to that identity with integrity in dealings with others.

When we turn to the auxiliary and tertiary functions, we find that they too define an axis, which is often diagrammed as a cross bar to the vertical spine. I refer to what is represented by this crossbar as the 'arms' of the personality. Functions creating this horizontal axis are concerned less with issues of identity than with ways of caring and being cared for by others.

In *Psychological Types*, Jung sketched eight fundamental options for consciousness: introverted thinking, introverted feeling, introverted sensation, introverted intuition, extraverted thinking, extraverted feeling, extraverted sensation, and extraverted intuition. Any one of these options can become a particular person's auxiliary or tertiary function. Knowing the type of consciousness that actually turns up in one of those places, however, does not by itself reveal the role the function will be playing in the person's life. That *role* is determined by the placement itself.

I have observed that there is a definite role that a person enters when deploying the auxiliary function, and another, different, role that a person takes up when trying to use the tertiary function. Consciousness seems to organize itself in such a way that different functions take up residence in different places in ourselves. The idea of 'place,' here, is a metaphor for the intrapsychic and intersubjective experience of a person who is moving, inside and in relations with others, between qualitatively very different areas of psychological functioning. Not all the qualities of the experience of consciousness in each new place can be accounted for by the nature of the function attitude in that place, because extraverted feeling in the superior (first) place feels different from extraverted feeling in the auxiliary (second) place, and extraverted feeling in the tertiary (third) place feels like something else again. The additional factor responsible for the felt qualitative shift is the archetype in that place. The archetype turns the place into a role we may take up in life.

The function-attitude occupying the auxiliary position is strongly developed in most adults, like the right arm of a right-handed person, which has long been used to do things to help and support others. The auxiliary function is parental; it takes the lead in fostering the development of other people, and it often serves as their role model. The tertiary function, by contrast, is more like the left hand of a right-handed person, sometimes original and creative, but always a bit unstable and at times even weaker in its reliability than the inferior function. Even when the tertiary function shows flair in what it does, it tends to be acutely aware of its need for the stabilizing influence of another person; this portion of our consciousness is thus more associated with vulnerability than with competence.

The auxiliary function is not so good at taking care of the third function in oneself, but it operates like a *good parent* to everyone else, offering its strength as protection to the more vulnerable parts of others. This is particularly attractive to the tertiary function in another person, which is like an *eternal child*,[1] who needs the admiration, approval, strength and guidance of at least one other person to be able to operate well. The auxiliary function parent and the tertiary function child are complements, not just within the psyche, where they share a common axis of personality, but between people. Within the individual psyche they operate like the arms of consciousness because they are used, more or less consciously, to support and be supported by others, and thus define the ways in which we use our consciousnesses to reach out to others. They provide a kind of balance to the spine of consciousness (superior and inferior function), which in defining our identity concerns itself more with what we can be or do in and for ourselves.

The two axes, the spine and the arms, can be considered, respectively, the axis of our relation to self, and the axis of our relations to others. Note also that the two axes are complementary in that one is always rational ('judging' in the Myers–Briggs terminology), while the other is irrational ('perceiving'). For example, we can use the arms either to calm us down and be more reasonable in our dealings with others when we are too much in our irrational spine, or to buoy us beyond the rigidity of the spine when it is rational.

When we number the auxiliary and tertiary functions, we continue the pattern of numbering the functions begun with function #1, the superior function. In the previous chapter, I associated position #1 with the hero, and that did not create any theoretical problem, because it makes intuitive sense and accords with common experience that the most differentiated of the functions would have a heroic cast, being a preference that is usually also a competence. As we move beyond the heroic first function, however, we should recognize that not all of the eight functions follow hero psychology in being measurable by their degree of strength. They do not, in actual experience, follow a descending hierarchy of differentiation from first (superior) through fourth (inferior) to eighth. Rather, the strength, and the kind of strength, a function of consciousness displays is a consequence of the archetypal role associated with it, and archetypes are differently developed in different people. The numbering of the positions is a bit of an anachronism, left over from the early days of Jungian psychology and of Isabel Briggs Myers's adaptation of that psychology to the analysis of the MBTI findings. When I use numbering today, in these post-heroic times, the numbers are meant to be read as qualitative rather than quantitative, much the way the numbers of streets can be read in a well-differentiated city that one is intimately acquainted with. Thus the 'second' and 'third' functions are identified, like avenues in New York City, by the qualities experience has taught us to recognize when we are actually in those places.

Let us look once more at a diagram representing the different functions, positions, and archetypes in someone who has the MBTI type (confirmed by a Jungian analysis and extensive self-reflection) of ENTP:

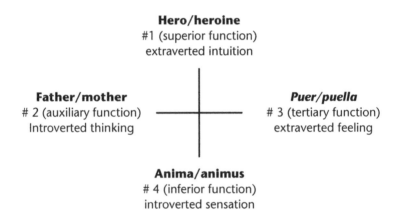

Hero/heroine
#1 (superior function)
extraverted intuition

Father/mother
2 (auxiliary function)
Introverted thinking

Puer/puella
3 (tertiary function)
extraverted feeling

Anima/animus
4 (inferior function)
introverted sensation

FIGURE 9.1 Archetypes associated with the first four functions (using ENTP as an example)

The archetypes associated with this person's superior and inferior functions, which form the 'spine' of the diagram, and with their shadows, were discussed in Chapter 8 of this book. This time, we will be concentrating on the pair of archetypes associated with the auxiliary and tertiary functions in the diagram.

I will ask the reader looking at the horizontal axis in Figure 9.2 that links the upper row of archetypes and types to regard it as shadowed by the lower row of archetypes and types. These latter appear clearly enough in the diagram, but being shadow they are much harder to see in ourselves.

The four function-attitude positions (the auxiliary and tertiary functions and their attitudinally opposed shadows) organize the way any personality reaches beyond itself to others. The archetypes in these positions structure the person's

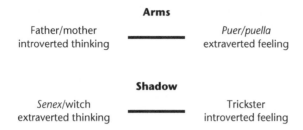

Arms

| Father/mother | | Puer/puella |
| introverted thinking | —————— | extraverted feeling |

Shadow

| Senex/witch | | Trickster |
| extraverted thinking | —————— | introverted feeling |

FIGURE 9.2 The ENTP's arms and their shadow (Note: this diagram applies also to ESTP.)

orientation to one of the most basic activities involving human consciousness, the support and care of others. Some people define their whole lives according to these parameters. They have little curiosity as to who they are, and relatively few goals for themselves, but they are greatly concerned about how they treat others and are treated by them. Such people live more on the horizontal line of Figure 9.1 than on the vertical line. Their consciousness is more organized around what their arms are doing than around what their spine is like. Working with such people, it is often easier to type the way they would ideally like to take care of another person than it is to get them to say what they want for themselves.

Others of us, even if we are fairly clear about the nature of our spines, still live a great deal out of our horizontal axis. I am like the ENTP in the diagram, and I characteristically try to take care of others by using my auxiliary introverted thinking. Much of my life as Jungian analyst, teacher, writer, editor, and friend is spent laying out for others how the situations in their lives might be better defined. Defining, clarifying, and enhancing the expression of something so that it is congruent with the thing's inner reality is a Ti (introverted thinking) function, and I am someone that people turn to when they need to avail themselves of this 'editorial' support. I am not the one usually invited to help out when the job at hand is setting up a tent on a camping trip, or making everyone feel welcome at a party, or to motivate them to follow a pre-established plan, and when I am asked to perform these functions I can feel that I am not as good at taking care of others in these ways as are people who have extraverted sensation, extraverted feeling, or extraverted thinking in a more developed place.

Like other people who use introverted thinking in a reliable way to take care of others, I am sought out by people who are looking to define something about their lives in a more introverted and also more original way, that is, when the methods of extraverted support have broken down. Although I am sometimes tempted to use my extraverted intuition to show people where I see the possibilities they haven't thought of, I have learned that people are not usually seeking that kind of help from me either. It's my parental second function I must use when taking care of others, not my heroic first function, and that means I take the best care of people not when

I heroically show them a possibility they haven't thought of, but when I help them to define more sharply what they already know. When I stay just with introverted thinking, I am rather good at helping people to define their lives in a way that speaks to the actual situation in their psyche, including the unconscious. Unfortunately, I am not always there, because the effort to help others that fills my days as a Jungian analyst also stirs my anxiety, and sets off some of my own shadow defenses, which being shadow may not always be conscious right away. I do not always understand, for instance, what I can be like when suddenly I am using thinking with the opposite attitude because then I use my thinking in an unconsciously directive, controlling, and pre-established Te (extraverted thinking) way, telling people rather grossly what their priorities ought to be in a way that can be intrusive and offensive.

This is because, in me, Te, the shadow of my Ti, carried by a helpful parent, is associated with a more sinister parental archetype – the *senex*.

The *senex* is an archetype[2] that shadows the good father that I consciously aspire to be when I try to help people. *Senex* is the Latin word for 'old man' and the root word for 'senator,' and it takes on the quality of everything that has stood the test of time and now resists change. (The mythological image is the Roman god Saturn, with his sickle, who has become less an archetypal image of the harvest and taken on a more deadly aspect as the archenemy of the processes of youth, growth and development.) Thinking is *senex* when it is dogmatic and no longer heedful of the need in life for fresh starts and new developments. Then one insists with a client on the tried and true, and argues against any move to change the status quo. This is not the way I parent, but it is the way I sometimes stultify.

This rather everyday example from the life of a working analyst shows how an auxiliary function can easily be replaced by the same function deployed with the opposite attitude. Then, the archetypal quality of the parenting has shifted. As we need to look at both the conscious and the shadow side of both the auxiliary and the tertiary functions, it may be helpful to have a diagram that lists the different possible types of auxiliary function as well as the different types of tertiary function, together with their shadows, and shows the archetypes that would be involved with the different type positions. (The archetypes for the tertiary position and its shadow will be explained later in this chapter.)

The auxiliary function can be used to encourage and enable others—to strengthen and support them in their path—but its shadow, the *senex* function, does just the opposite: it discourages and disables them; it freezes them in their tracks and makes them doubt the prudence of everything they are doing. This may sound indeed like a very unpleasant archetypal role to fall into—and it often is—but it is sometimes a necessary one. When we are confronted, for example, with a person or plan whose basic direction strikes us as fundamentally destructive and dangerous to the things we value, one effective option can be for us to pull rank and set limits, just as we might if confronted with a misbehaving child. In this sense, the *senex* archetype or role can also be thought of as the role of the negative or disapproving father, just as the female equivalent, the witch, can be envisioned as a critical mother who seems impossible to please.

TABLE 9.1 Types of auxiliary and tertiary function and their shadows

Auxiliary function	Shadow of auxiliary function	Tertiary function	Shadow of tertiary function
Father/mother	Senex/witch	Puer/puella	Trickster
Introverted thinking	Extraverted thinking	Extraverted feeling[3]	Introverted feeling
Introverted intuition	Extraverted intuition	Extraverted sensation	Introverted sensation
Introverted feeling	Extraverted feeling	Extraverted thinking	Introverted thinking
Introverted sensation	Extraverted sensation	Extraverted intuition	Introverted intuition
Extraverted thinking	Introverted thinking	Introverted feeling	Extraverted feeling
Extraverted intuition	Introverted intuition	Introverted sensation	Extraverted sensation
Extraverted feeling	Introverted feeling	Introverted thinking	Extraverted thinking
Extraverted sensation	Introverted sensation	Introverted intuition	Extraverted intuition

Where the person with auxiliary extraverted sensation carried by a mother archetype might, for example, take care of others by cooking for them, the person with extraverted sensation in the witch position might be tempted to express displeasure by banging loudly on the wall of an apartment when the neighbor's party, on the other side of the wall, is too loud, or by slapping an impudent child. Auxiliary, fatherly introverted sensation might show itself through teaching a son the series of simple steps necessary to knot a tie; *senex* introverted sensation, on the other hand, might point out the clumsiness of the son's hand movements. *Senex* or witch introverted feeling can take the form of a cold silence that implies that something someone has just said or done is in such bad taste that the person doing it deserves an unspoken excommunication.

The child who experiences the disapproving parent can remain a part of us even as we grow into adulthood, and is the common basis of a traumatic neurosis that I have come to feel we probably all carry in the area of the third function. The adult woman who sometimes acts like a frightened child in dealings with others may seem to have regressed, but she has really entered the child role in her own psyche, which may come up in situations where she must use her tertiary function. I saw this happen in a bright, articulate, well-read introverted intuitive woman with auxiliary extraverted feeling who could never think what to say to someone who wanted to take up practical business with her, such as a lawyer whom she had called to help write her will. Not only was her inferior function not much help in sorting out the sensation details of her estate, she never knew how to define what she needed from her lawyer, or what she wanted to see accomplished by her will. The lawyer's attempts to ask her questions led her to become tongue-tied, reactivating a social phobia that had always plagued her about business transactions, with the consequence that she put off writing her will as long as possible and in fact died intestate. This is an example of the paralysis that can overtake the tertiary function: in this woman's case, introverted thinking. The *puella* or *puer* archetype carries that function, and may, like a child, not be able to sustain performance. This same woman, on the other hand, when not stressed by a social demand, was able to write rather funny poetry that skillfully conveyed the states of mind she would get into—an example of the creativity of a function (again, in this case, introverted thinking) when it is carried by the archetype of the *puer aeternus* or *puella aeterna*. This ability to oscillate between states of abject empty-headedness and over-the-top inventiveness is typical of tertiary function introverted thinking, and gives a sense of the cycles of deflation and inflation all third functions go through. Sugar Cane, Marilyn Monroe's character in *Some Like It Hot* (1959), memorably says "I always get the fuzzy end of the lollipop," which conveys the cluelessness that results when someone can't define any situation adequately.

I have spoken of this inflation/deflation cycling of the third function as the 'third-function crisis,' because it surfaces in the lives of people who have begun to develop their typology to the point of trying to make the third function work for them and discovered its strange up and down quality. Often the third function operates as if in a double bind, as Monroe's telling metaphor conveys. Double binds are what people are put in by the trickster archetype so long as it remains unconscious, in which case one is vulnerable to being taken advantage of by others. It is an enormous step in type development when we are able to make the trickster conscious and put the person who is trying to take advantage of *us* in a double bind.

Alfred Hitchcock had a very developed trickster function. A shy man, whom I see as an ISTJ, he had tertiary introverted feeling and could not stand to have conflict on the set. Early in the making of *Vertigo* (1958), Kim Novak came to the director upset that the clothes he had had designed for her role did not reflect her taste. This was a challenge to Hitchcock's introverted feeling, which had taken the creative and commercial gamble of giving Novak's upper-class character an unusually conservative wardrobe (including a grey suit with black shoes) in the first part of the film—an intended effect, but not the usual presentation of an emerging Hollywood sex symbol. Giving in to Novak would have ruined the picture, but so would him insisting that he knew what he was doing, which would have sparked a resentment that might show in her face on the screen. Hitchcock drew on his trickster extraverted feeling to rescue him from the double bind. He told his star, "My dear Miss Novak, you can wear anything you want, anything—provided it's what the script calls for" (Taylor, 1980, p. 246). Somehow he succeeded in making the script (that he had in fact approved) bigger than both of them, and that put the double bind on the actress's animus: she knew how to stand up to a director, but not to a script. To do the latter would have required a level of extraverted thinking that she did not have. I am not, of course, certain of Novak's type, but I am reading her leading functions as introverted feeling and extraverted sensation, and her extraverted thinking as an inferior function, carried by an animus that Hitchcock was able to use his trickster to stymie. I do know that she and Hitchcock got on famously after, and the picture that resulted has been widely hailed as both his and her masterpiece, and a landmark of cinematic design.

An extraverted feeling parent with auxiliary introverted sensation may use trickster introverted intuition to imply damage to the archetypal order of things when an adolescent child threatens to make a choice that the parent does not approve of. In the confusion brought by this intuitive framing of the situation, the teenager may fail to notice that the same parent has never previously shown an objection to anything on such a spiritual basis. This strategy has been used to convey to a daughter who mentions the option of marrying outside the family pattern (saying she might choose a person of another race or of the same sex) that she would be destroying the very sacredness of family. It takes a very strong introverted intuition in the child to see that the direction she has considered, even if departing from a family pattern, is not necessarily a sacrilege.

A question that often arises when we discover examples of type interactions in which shadow functions are deployed is: How does the person know to use these functions? Does the situation require that we use a particular function, which we then supply even if it is normally relatively unconscious for us? Or is it a particular archetypal role that is called for, entering into which brings us to use whatever function-attitude is associated with it? The answer, I think, is both. Effective living requires, sooner or later, that we use all our function-attitudes. When it comes to responding to the needs of others and to allowing others to meet our needs, in both personal and professional situations, we need to be in touch with the parent and the child in ourselves, and with the trickster and the *senex* or witch as well. Otherwise, these same archetypes will come up, but we will be far less conscious in how we deploy them.

Notes

1 This is a translation into English of a Latin term traceable to Ovid, *puer aeternus*, which is an archetype many young men and women (the feminine form is *puella aeterna*) fall into in late adolescence and early adulthood. See von Franz, 1970 and Hillman (Ed.), 1979 for the classical descriptions of the archetype and those overidentified with it. In contradistinction to Jungian writers who have used this term as a synonym for the "Peter Pan" syndrome of the immature man or woman who can never quite settle down (see Yeoman, 1998), I regard the *puer* (or *puella*) as an aspect of all of us, associated particularly with the third function, and commonly problematic when we are trying to develop that function.
2 It was James Hillman, in his 1967 paper, "Senex and Puer: An Aspect of the Historical and Psychological Present" (Hillman, 1979, pp. 3–53), who introduced this archetype to a broader Jungian audience, and his description of the *senex* as a "hardening process of consciousness" (p. 19) has not been surpassed.

3 The type-savvy reader will note that I have shown the attitude of the third function to be the inverse of the attitude of the auxiliary and the same as that of the superior function. For what has led me to think that this is the case, see Chapter 3.

References

Hillman, J. (Ed.) (1979). *Puer papers*. Dallas, TX: Spring Publications.

Some like it hot. (1959). Wilder, B. (Producer & Director). USA: United Artists. [Motion picture].

Taylor, J. R. (1980). *Hitch*. New York: Berkeley Books.

Vertigo. (1958). Hitchcock, A. (Producer & Director). USA: Paramount Pictures. [Motion picture].

von Franz, M.-L. (1970). *Puer aeternus*. New York: Spring Publications

Yeoman, A. (1998). *Now or neverland: Peter Pan and the myth of eternal youth*. Toronto: Inner City Books.

PART III

History of type

10

PSYCHOLOGICAL TYPES

An historical overview

Introduction

It has not always been clear to students of Jung's analytical psychology what his famous 'types' are types *of*. The commonest assumption has been that they refer to types of *people*. But for Jung, they were types of *consciousness,* that is, characteristic orientations assumed by the ego in establishing and discriminating an individual's inner and outer reality. For psychotherapists, an understanding of these different natural cognitive stances can be invaluable in the daily work of supporting the basic strengths of their clients' personalities and of helping a particular consciousness to recognize its inherent limitations. The understanding of individual differences communicated on the basis of this theory can reduce a client's shame at areas of relative ego weakness and diminish the client's need to buttress the ego with strong defenses that complicate treatment.

Jung's position on psychological types

Ever since his landmark self-defining text, *Wandlungen und Symbole der Libido* (1912), it had been Jung's understanding that the movements of the psyche observable in analysis tend toward consciousness. He had already recognized that consciousness is not expressed uniformly in the same way in every person. Rather, Jung conceptualized consciousness as centered in an ego that expressed its ability to orient the psyche through different basic *attitudes* and *functions*.

Jung arrived at the germ of this point of view in the midst of his studies on word association, undertaken at the Burghölzli Mental Hospital beginning about 1902. In "The association of normal subjects," written with Franz Riklin, Jung describes how the associations produced in the subjects by calling out a series of 400 different stimulus-words can be shown to be affected by unconscious complexes. But even in this earliest research. Jung recognized that "one principal factor is the individual character." He and Riklin wrote: "From our experiments two easily recognizable types emerge: (1) A type in whose reactions subjective, often feeling-toned experiences are used. (2) A type whose reactions show an objective, impersonal tone" (Jung, 1904/1973, ¶412).

As late as September 1913, in a lecture delivered to the Psychoanalytic Congress in Munich, Jung, now turning his attention to the psychopathology observed in clinical work, still noted two basic types of "relations to the object" (and the self), that of the "hysteric," whose "centrifugal" extraversion "displays as a rule an intensity of feeling that surpasses the normal," and that of the "schizophrenic," in whom, on account of a "centripetal" introversion, "the normal level is not reached at all" (Jung, 1921/1971, ¶858).[1] This added another dimension beyond presence of complexes to the problem of analyzing the subjectivity of consciousness, a problem that other observational sciences, including experimental psychology, had already recognized as 'the personal equation,' a term Jung now adopted to describe his developing area of study (Shamdasani, 2003, pp. 30–31).

In the next seven years, in conversation with others in the newly formed Zurich School of Analytical Psychology, he began to unpack his typological theory. The correspondence with Hans Schmid-Guisan (Jung & Schmid-Guisan, 2013) was particularly helpful in getting Jung to reconsider his preliminary equation of feeling with extraversion and thinking with introversion. Another early member of the Zurich School Maria Moltzer, in a lecture to the Psychological Club in Zurich in June 1916, proposed intuition as a third type of consciousness (Shamdasani, 1999). Her suggestion as well as Jung's own increasing awareness that sensation was more than an "organ function . . . subordinate to feeling" as he had thought in 1915 (Jung & Schmid-Guisan, 2013, p. 136) made him aware that beyond extraversion–introversion and thinking–feeling, which so far organized the psyche along strictly rational grounds, there was another axis of orientation altogether that his theory would need to take into account, the "irrational" axis of sensation–intuition. (Jung himself seems to have recognized that the difference between his original thinking–feeling axis and the new sensation–intuition axis was that the first pair of functions are deployed in a rational way to interpret experience, whereas the latter merely apprehend what is already given to us by the outer or inner world, and hence do not rely on optional processes of cognition or evaluation: see Marshall, 1968.) During the years he was engaged with the active imaginations he recorded in his *Red Book*, Jung discovered how many different figures occupied his inner psychological space, each with consciousnesses distinctly their own. He came to see the types as so many standpoints, each with their own strengths and blind spots. A painting he made in 1921 (Jung 2009, plate 127 & p. 307 n240) has been interpreted by Frey (2012) to convey how the types were for Jung ways of sacrificing oneself to experience by those who submit to it consciously. That consciousness requires the experience of viewpoints that oppose and challenge one's own is also conveyed by the cruciate diagram he soon came to use (cf. Jung, 1989/2012, p. 97) to show the range of the functions and the degree of their oppositions to each other. Jung's theory had certainly undergone considerable modification after 1913 as he became more aware of the complexity of consciousness. By the time he came to write *Psychological Types* in 1919 and 1920, he had already envisioned a sophisticated system of analysis of types of consciousness as mental processes characterized by four main dichotomies: extraversion–introversion, thinking–feeling, sensation–intuition and rational–irrational. It was this system that he continued to defend for the rest of his life and that has informed all subsequent work on Jung's psychological types.

Definitions

In *Psychological Types,* Jung understands there to be four *functions of consciousness,* which he names *sensation, thinking, feeling* and *intuition.* These terms did not originate with Jung; rather, they were culled from the history of psychology, and they carry the ghost of earlier meanings placed on them by many physicians and philosophers, e.g. Hippocrates' four temperaments: Melancholic, Sanguine, Choleric and Phlegmatic. Jung's theory of psychological types resembles in some ways the eighteenth-century faculty psychology developed by theorists such as Christian Wolff (Richards, 1980), Franz Josef Gall (1835), and Thomas Reid (Brooks, 1976), according to which the mind consists of various powers or capacities, called faculties. One of these faculties had been *willing,* which became for Schopenhauer (1819/1909) the essential attribute of the *unconscious* mind. Freud (1899/2010, pp. 111–131) and Adler (1906 lecture to the Vienna Psychoanalytic Society (Nunberg & Federn, 1962, p. 42)) would develop this theme in their theories of wishing and overcompensation. Their idea of the ego was an agency that needed to defend itself against knowing too much about the willing of the unconscious mind, and whose faculties could therefore best be described as defenses, even if those defenses enabled the psyche to pursue its true aims in disguise, as it were.

Jung, consistent with his greater emphasis on the possibilities of consciousness, accepted the will as part of the ego (Jung, 1921/1971, ¶844), and concentrated on the functions the ego needs to orient itself to any reality with which it must cope. To understand reality, he reasoned, we need a function of consciousness that *registers reality as real*: this he called the *sensation* function, which delivers to us the sensation that something *is* (Jung, 1968, p. 11). Then, he said, we need a function to *define* for us what we are perceiving when we notice that something is there: this he called the *thinking* function. Next, he understood that we need a function that *assigns a value* to the thing that we have perceived and named; this is called the function of *feeling.*[2] Finally, he realized that we require a function to enable us to divine *the implications or possibilities* of the thing that has been empirically perceived, logically defined and discriminatingly evaluated: this he called the *intuitive* function.

Jung found it easier to define the first three functions than the fourth. On one occasion, he said,

> Sensation tells us that a thing *is*. Thinking tells us *what* the thing is, feeling tells us what it is *worth* to us. Now what else could there be? One would assume one has a complete picture of the world when one knows there *is* something, *what* it is, and what it is *worth* [original italics].

He added immediately:

> But there is another category, and that is time. Things have a past and they have a future. They come from somewhere, they go to somewhere, and you cannot see where they came from and you cannot know where they go to, but you get what the Americans call a hunch.
>
> *Jung, 1968, p. 13*

That ability to get, and to a certain degree to trust, the hunch is what Jung meant by *intuition*. That he understood what it means to trust this essentially irrational process of perception is part of Jung's appeal to people who are naturally disposed to use their intuition to orient themselves to reality.

Jung held that feeling and thinking are *rational* functions, and that sensation and intuition are *irrational* functions. He did not sustain the faculty psychologists' opposition between reason and passion. Jung understood 'feeling' as a rational process, that is, as neither affect (or what we sometime call 'feelings') nor the result of more unconscious emotion-based processes, even though he admitted our complexes are 'feeling-toned.' Rather, Jung made clear that he took the process of assigning feeling value to be an ego-function that was just as rational in its operation as the process of defining and creating logical links (thinking).

Jung also recognized that sensation, even though it is the evidential basis for our empirical reality testing, is as irrational a process as the intuitive one that delivers our 'hunches' to us. As a moment's reflection will demonstrate, we do not rationally choose what we manage to see, hear, smell, taste or grasp with our sense of touch. By linking feeling with thinking as rational functions, and sensation with intuition as irrational functions of consciousness, Jung broke with the nineteenth-century habit of lumping feeling with intuition as marking a 'romantic' temperament and thinking with sensation as the unmistakable signs of a 'practical' disposition. Rather, in *Psychological Types,* he convincingly makes the case that consciousness is for all of us the product of both rational and irrational processes of encountering and assessing reality.

The concept of introversion was by now fully liberated from its earlier confusion in Jung's writings with both thinking and objectivity, just as extraversion was freed from its former fixed association with feeling and subjectivity. In *Psychological Types,* Jung states that:

> The extravert is distinguished by his craving for the object, by his empathy and identification with the object, his voluntary dependence on the object. He is influenced by the object in the same degree as he strives to assimilate it.
>
> *Jung, 1921/1971, ¶535*

By contrast,

> the introvert is distinguished by his self-assertion vis à vis the object. He struggles against any dependence on the object, he repels all its influences, and even fears it. So much the more is he dependent on the idea, which shields him from external reality and gives him the feeling of inner freedom—though he pays for this with a very noticeable power psychology.
>
> *Jung, 1921/1971, ¶535*

Jung's use of personification here—his reference to the introvert and the extravert—needs some deconstruction. Read literally, as too many have read him, he seems to be saying that introversion—the "inward-turning of libido" (¶769)—and extraversion—the "outward-turning of libido" (¶710)—characterize different kinds of people. Elsewhere in the book *Psychological Types* he implies that we all use both processes, that there is an extravert and an introvert in each of us. How this can be finally becomes clear when he uses the now famous terms not as nouns but as *adjectives,* to define the way in which the various functions of consciousness happen to be deployed in a particular individual. In turn, he takes up the description of extraverted thinking, extraverted feeling, extraverted sensation, extraverted intuition, introverted thinking, introverted feeling, introverted sensation and introverted intuition, noting that these "basic psychological functions seldom or never have the same strength or degree of development in the same individual" and that as "a rule, one or the other function predominates, in both strength and development" (Jung, 1921/1971, ¶584). The implication, however, is that all eight of these distinct cognitive processes exist, at least to some degree, in every one of us. The origins of what is nowadays called "the whole-type eight-function model" of personality (Geldart, 1998; Clark, 2000; Haas, McAlpine, & Hartzler, 2001) are therefore plainly laid out in *Psychological Types.*

What Jung means by the *introverted* use of a function comes across in his personified notion of someone "dependent upon the idea." He explains that he employs the term *idea* "to express the *meaning* of a primordial image" (Jung, 1921/1971, ¶732), that is to say, an archetype. An introverted function, therefore, is one that has turned away from the object and toward the archetypal 'idea' that the object might be most closely matched to. This archetypal idea, residing in the inner world, can be understood as a profound thought, a value, a metaphorical image, or a model of reality, depending upon whether the introverted function is thinking, feeling, intuition or sensation. When an introverted function is used to orient to something external, it is in the end the comparison to the archetype, not the stimulating object or situation itself, that finally commands the attention of the function. This can seem like a withdrawal from the object.

Introverted sensation, as a process, is thus "guided by the intensity of the subjective sensation excited by the objective stimulus" (Jung, 1921/1971, ¶650). That means that the person strongly identified with the use of this function will react immediately to the internal, bodily sensations caused by, for example, the food served at a meal, so that the distension of his stomach, or the degree of pepper in the meal, even the audibility of others at his table, may turn out to be more determinative of his happiness at a dinner party than the carefully assembled company that the host or hostess has arranged for the gathering. This is because a dissonance with the archetype of the good meal has been constellated by the excessive stimulation. This process is not usually visible. When someone has been using the introverted sensation function primarily,

> seen from the outside, it looks as though the effect of the object did not penetrate into the subject at all. This impression is correct inasmuch as a subjective content does, in fact, intervene from the unconscious and intercept the effect of the object. The intervention may be so abrupt that the individual appears to be shielding himself directly from all objective influences.
>
> *Jung, 1921/1971, ¶651*

Introverted sensation, of course, can be just as guided by a visual cue: the films of Alfred Hitchcock, who used this function cinematically in a dominant way, dazzle us with the uncanny power of seemingly ordinary images to stimulate unexpected, archetypal reactions.

Those who make abundant use of an introverted function—introverted intuition, say, or introverted feeling—can nevertheless be perceived by others as depreciating the object. Jungian case studies sometimes seem, when introverted intuition is taking the lead, to leave the patient behind in a maze of mythological 'amplifications.' The poet Rilke, who seems to have known that his sensibility was masked by a strong introverted feeling, is said to have written to a new mistress, "I love you, but of course it's none of your business" (von Franz, 1971/1998, p. 49).

A particularly difficult introverted function, from the standpoint of personal relations, is introverted thinking, because, when the object of introverted thinking is a person, "this person has a distinct feeling that he matters only in a negative way." Often, "he feels himself warded off as something definitely disturbing" (Jung, 1921/1971, ¶633). The object, when this function is being used, *is* being avoided because the person using this function is "building up his world of ideas, and never shrinks from thinking a thought because it might prove to be dangerous, subversive, heretical, or wounding to other people's feelings" (Jung, 1921/1971, ¶634). The ideas introverted thinking dwells on are archetypal ideas. These are notions that may either be *sui generis* or, if once cultural, long out of circulation, which nevertheless seem entirely appropriate to the exact definition of a situation at hand, since they fit it better than the currently accepted dictates of conventional extraverted thinking. These 'new' thoughts, however, take effort to explain and the introverted thinking function frequently goes on refining its conceptions when the patience of others has been exhausted: it does not know when to stop.

Introverted intuition, as a function, is concerned with "the background processes of consciousness," and for the person using that function in a differentiated way, "unconscious images acquire the dignity of things" (Jung, 1921/1971, ¶657).

This is the one type of consciousness that naturally "apprehends the images arising from the *a priori* inherited foundations of the unconscious." That is, rather than thinking about, experientially comparing, or feeling the archetype that arises in relation to a situation, the introverted intuitive function becomes directly aware of the archetype as an image, as if 'seeing' it: introverted intuition is therefore the function responsible for visionary experience, which often seems 'mystical' to others.

Introverted feeling, by contrast, can only feel the archetypal image of a situation. It cannot see it. The hoary Indian story of the three blind men and the elephant takes on more meaning if one considers that India is a country where introverted feeling seems to predominate in collective consciousness. Thus, all of the blind men (there are as many as six in some versions, and sometimes they come from a city in which all of the inhabitants are blind) could be said to represent the introverted feeling function, literally feeling its way slowly around the archetype, the elephant in their midst. Necessarily, a thinking definition of that experience at any moment will be partial—"It's a rope," "It's a snake," "It's a great mud wall"—but the *process* never ceases until the elephant is felt entirely. It is important to realize that, when the introverted feeling function is, for example, feeling 'bad,' it is feeling the entire archetypal category of 'bad' and is not likely to quit until that archetypal badness is felt through. As Jung says,

> The depth of this feeling can only be guessed—it can never be clearly grasped. It makes people silent and difficult of access; it shrinks back like a violet from the brute nature of the object in order to fill the depths of the subject. It comes out with negative judgments or assumes an air of profound indifference as a means of defense.
>
> *Jung, 1921/1971, ¶638*

Perhaps we all get into our introverted feeling when we are depressed. The important thing to grasp, in understanding introverted feeling, is that archetypes can be *felt* every bit as much as they can be thought about, directly intuited, or experienced somatically. As Jung puts it,

> The primordial images are, of course, just as much ideas as feeling. Fundamental ideas, ideas like God, freedom, and immortality, are just as much feeling-values as they are significant ideas.
>
> *Jung, 1921/1971, ¶639*

The extraverted functions, as Jung has already been quoted as informing us, tend so completely to merge with the object as to identify with it. They often end up without adequate distance from the stimuli that are presented to them. In the case of extraverted feeling, these are the feelings—that is, the emotions and prejudices—of others, and often of society at large, so that the personality of a person strongly identified with this function "appears adjusted in relation to external conditions. Her feelings harmonize with objective situations and general values" (Jung, 1921/1971, ¶597). The woman led by extraverted feeling in her "love choice," Jung tells us, will see to it that "the 'suitable' man is loved, and no one else" (Jung, 1921/1971, ¶597). On the other hand, no type is more capable of appreciation and sympathy.

Similarly, extraverted thinking tends to become enamored of established ideas, frequently neglecting the duty to think freshly about what is being expressed and the language that is really appropriate to it. There is no brake, therefore, against insisting that these ideas should govern everyone's behavior. As Jung puts it, the person strongly identified with this function "elevates . . . an objectively oriented intellectual formula . . . into the ruling principle not only for himself but for his whole environment" (Jung, 1921/1971, ¶585). On the other hand, this most characteristic function of the Enlightenment period must have guided John Locke in establishing principles of government that many in the West still believe have universal applicability—as well as Mozart in elaborating musical ideas that everyone soon could follow.

Extraverted sensation, as a cognitive process, seeks "an accumulation of actual experiences of concrete objects" (Jung, 1921/1971, ¶606) and the function can become, in the moment, so riveted on the reality 'out there' that it cannot recognize that other things may also be happening at that same time: this is a function perfect for watching a basketball game, but it may not notice that someone is about to say or do something unexpected.

Extraverted intuition can become so engaged with the possibilities of its objects that, for the person strongly identified with this function, "it is as though his whole life vanished in the new situation" (Jung, 1921/1971, ¶613). To use a metaphor to describe what is really an unmediated, instinctive process, this function operates like a traffic signal, indicating with its green light when it is time to proceed to develop something, with its red light when it is time to stop, and with its yellow light when one must proceed with caution. A significant problem is that people without a similar degree of development of extraverted intuition may not perceive the presence of any signal at all and thus cannot understand why the person led by such intuitions is rushing ahead, stopping, or pausing when he does. And extraverted intuition's failure to heed sensation cues can undermine its claim to have 'seen' anything at all.

In *Psychological Types,* Jung offered the all-important notion of a selective *differentiation* of the various functions of consciousness as the key to the different degrees and styles of consciousness individual people display. As he puts it in his 79-page section of definitions at the end of the book,

> Differentiation means the development of differences, the separation of parts from the whole. In this work I employ the concept of differentiation chiefly with respect to the psychological *functions*. So long as a function is still so fused with one or more other functions—thinking with feeling, feeling with sensation, etc.—that it is unable to operate on its own, it is in an archaic condition, i.e., not differentiated, not separated from the whole as a special

part and existing by itself. Undifferentiated thinking is incapable of thinking apart from other functions; it is continually mixed up with sensations, feelings, intuitions, just as undifferentiated feeling is mixed up with sensations and fantasies, as for instance in the sexualization (Freud) of feeling and thinking in a neurosis.

Jung, 1921/1971, ¶705

As long as a function is undifferentiated, moreover, it cannot be deployed in the conscious manner of a directed mental process that is truly under the control of the ego, and capable of being applied to tasks and goals: "Without differentiation direction is impossible, since the direction of a function towards a goal depends on the elimination of anything irrelevant. Fusion with the irrelevant precludes direction; only a differentiated function is *capable* of being directed" (Jung, 1921/1971, ¶705).

These passages hold the key to why, in the first English translation (by H. G. Baynes) of *Pyschologische Typen,* the work bore the subtitle, "or, The Psychology of Individuation" (Jung 1921, 1923). One way to understand what Jung meant by individuation is the progressive differentiation of the various psychological functions of consciousness. For, as he puts it elsewhere in the Definitions section, "Individuation . . . is a process of *differentiation* (q.v.) having for its goal the development of the individual personality." It is "an extension of the sphere of consciousness, an enriching of conscious psychological life" (Jung, 1921/1971, ¶¶757, 762).

Since Jung also believed that individuation, i.e. the development of consciousness, is a natural process, he felt that there was a way to describe its orderly unfolding in all of us, and he used his idea of psychological types to offer certain developmental guidelines. These guidelines have been mostly ignored outside the narrow circle of those who are interested in the theory of psychological types, but they are most important, as they hold the key to much of what happens in psychotherapy when a personality starts to develop.

Jung believed that we all get a head start in individuation through a natural tendency to differentiate at least two function-attitudes out of our total potential complement of eight.[3] The two function-attitudes that most naturally tend to differentiate early in our development of ego-consciousness will not be the same for each individual. Because they develop so early they appear to be innate, although later "falsification of type" as a result of environmental influences can distort the individual's typological bent (Benziger, 1995). Sixteen psychological type profiles can be distinguished simply on the basis of which of the eight function-attitudes turns out to be the most differentiated—the dominant or 'superior' function—and which the next most differentiated—the 'auxiliary' function.

Jung found that "[f]or all the types met with in practice, the rule holds good that besides the conscious, primary function there is a relatively unconscious, auxiliary function which is in every respect different from the nature of the primary function" (Jung, 1921/1971, ¶669). Since he also believed that "naturally only these functions can appear as auxiliary whose nature is not *opposed* to the dominant function" (the emphasis is mine), feeling, for instance, "can never act as the second function alongside thinking" (¶667) nor sensation alongside intuition. Rather, if with respect to differentiation someone's first, or superior, function is on the rational axis (i.e. is either thinking or feeling) then that individual's auxiliary function will have to come from the irrational axis (be either sensation or intuition).

A superior thinking function will thus be paired with only one of two possible other functions in the course of normal type development—either an auxiliary sensation or an auxiliary intuition. Similarly, a superior sensation function, being on the irrational axis, will take as its auxiliary a function from the rational axis, meaning that it can be paired only with thinking or feeling. The following possibilities naturally emerge:

Superior/Auxiliary
Feeling/Intuition
Feeling/Sensation
Thinking/Intuition
Thinking/Sensation
Intuition/Feeling
Intuition/Thinking
Sensation/Feeling
Sensation/Thinking

This scheme is the basic model for the differentiation of the eight function-attitudes into different types of people. Given that each of the leading functions can be either extraverted or introverted (for instance, feeling/intuition could describe the typology of a person with either introverted feeling with auxiliary intuition or extraverted feeling with auxiliary intuition), it follows that, typologically speaking, there are at least sixteen kinds of people.

Even this differentiation does not, unfortunately, clarify the problem of whether there is any difference in *attitude* between the first two functions in an actual individual. The clinician should be aware that Jung's text has been interpreted in two different ways by later commentators. Apparently seizing on Jung's assertion that the secondary function is "not antagonistic to" the primary one, Jo Wheelwright (1982) concluded that the first two functions would have the same attitude with respect to extraversion and introversion. Isabel Briggs Myers, on the other hand, took Jung's subsequent statement, that the auxiliary function is "in every respect different from the nature of the primary function," to mean that the auxiliary must differ from the superior function in attitude (Myers & Myers, 1980, pp. 18–21).

It should be noted that Jung took for granted that most consciousnesses are so *un*differentiated that even the auxiliary function is rarely more than "relatively unconscious" (¶669). Too fine a distinction regarding the attitude of the auxiliary would not have made a great deal of sense to him: everything besides the superior function was still more or less unconscious anyway. He spoke of a shadowy tertiary function, and a fourth, 'inferior' function to which he gave a special status, as a source of problematic, touchy reactions because of its especial closeness to the unconscious. This inferior function (a notion that can be traced to Schiller, as Bishop (2008) has recently emphasized) is "the function that lags behind in the process of differentiation" (Jung, 1921/1971, ¶763). Often a source of shame, the inferior function is conceived of as being carried by the anima in a man, and the animus in a woman, in contrast to the superior function, which is identified with the persona.

The inferior function will always be the other pole of the typological axis (whether rational or irrational) on which the superior function falls; so a superior thinking function will be plagued by an inferior feeling function, superior sensation by inferior intuition, superior intuition by inferior sensation, and superior feeling by inferior thinking. Moreover (and here there is more agreement in the Jungian tradition) if the superior function is introverted, the inferior function will be extraverted; and if the superior is extraverted, the inferior function will be introverted. The axis between the superior and inferior functions is what I have called the 'spine' of personality (Beebe, 1992, pp. 106–107). There are eight possible spines (shown in Figure 3.4, p. 39, as vertical lines). If one imagines each of these line diagrams as a stick figure representing a person who is facing the reader, the auxiliary function appears as the figure's 'right hand,' which will be to the reader's left. The different figures that share the same superior function are shown in pairs, as two figures side by side, with identical spines but different auxiliary functions, making sixteen standpoints in all.

These are the famous sixteen 'types' of personality that most people are referring to when they use the term 'psychological types': they have been described as the 'MBTI types' by those who have learned to recognize the superior and auxiliary functions with the help of the Myers–Briggs Type Indicator. However, it might be clearer to call them 'type profiles.' Using Jung's rules for type differentiation and understanding Isabel Briggs Myers' notion of "good type development" (Myers & Kirby, 2000), it is clear that the differentiation of a strong natural superior and accompanying auxiliary function that is different in every respect is the starting point for further differentiation. The other function-attitudes operate largely out of awareness until and unless they become conscious in the course of development.

Innovations, criticisms and developments

Although types were carefully studied by other analysts who were trained by Jung, including Meier (1959, 1989), Henderson (1970) and Wheelwright (1982), the most important development of psychological types within analytical psychology came from Marie-Louise von Franz (1971/1998), who colorfully described the eight different types of the inferior function. She also clarified the relation of the inferior function to Jung's transcendent function, pointing out that if the inferior function is made conscious, then the relation to the unconscious changes and the personality is unified (von Franz, 1971/1998, pp. 67–79; see also Beebe 1992, pp. 102–109). She explained that Jung's hierarchy of first, second and third functions implies a relative order in which the functions can be differentiated in the course of a psychotherapy, although she indicated that once the superior function has been established one can choose whether to develop the second or third function next. No one, she argued (and Jung also says this), can simply take up the inferior function directly and develop it. Not only does it tend to "stay low" (E. Osterman, personal communication, 1972), it cannot even be approached effectively until the first three functions have been differentiated.

I pursued this line of thought by clarifying the archetypal constraints around the differentiation of the function-attitudes in the course of development (for a discussion of my ideas about this, see Harris, 1996, pp. 65–76). Noting that the superiority of the leading function derives from its association with the hero archetype, I went on to identify the archetypal figures that carry the other three functions in the hierarchy that Jung and von Franz established. Following the evidence of dreams and also movies in which the auxiliary and tertiary functions are often symbolized as an older and younger person of the same sex as the figure identified with the superior function, I have concluded that the auxiliary function is carried by a stable parental figure (usually a father in a man and a mother in a woman) and the tertiary function by an unstable child figure who is given to cycles of inflation and deflation (*puer aeternus* in a man, *puella aeterna* in a woman). Although von Franz spoke broadly of the fourth, inferior function as "the door through which all the figures of the unconscious come" (1971/1998, p. 67), I have identified the fourth function, since it is consciously experienced as a problematic aspect of oneself, not with the shadow, but with the anima and animus. It is the other four functions that constitute the true shadow of the first four, a shadow accentuated by the process of differentiation that allows the first four to develop and become conscious function-attitudes.[4] For example, a man with superior extraverted thinking and auxiliary introverted sensation will have introverted thinking and extraverted sensation strongly in shadow. When he develops tertiary extraverted intuition, introverted intuition will be rejected and become an aspect of his shadow. The inferior function has a shadow too. In this individual, who would have inferior introverted feeling carried by the anima, a shadow of extraverted feeling could be found as an intelligence operating outside his awareness.

In this way, I was able to conceptualize a first typology of the shadow (although Naomi Quenk (1993), not long after, produced her own typological model of the shadow in the book *Beside Ourselves*). According to the model of typology I have developed (Chapter 3), specific archetypes carry the shadows of the first four functions: the opposing personality (carrying the shadow of the hero), the *senex* or witch (shadow of the father or mother), the trickster (shadow of the *puer* or *puella*), and the demonic/daimonic personality (shadow of the anima/animus). Figure 10.1 shows how this model organizes the basic archetypal complexes as part-personalities that express themselves through their individual function-attitudes. The example depicted here is of a person with dominant extraverted thinking and auxiliary introverted sensation (ESTJ).

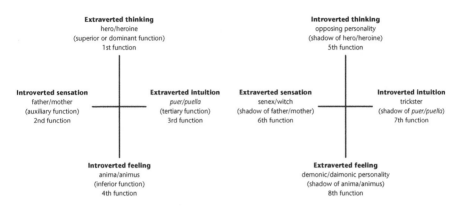

Extraverted thinking
hero/heroine
(superior or dominant function)
1st function

Introverted thinking
opposing personality
(shadow of hero/heroine)
5th function

Introverted sensation
father/mother
(auxiliary function)
2nd function

Extraverted intuition
puer/puella
(tertiary function)
3rd function

Extraverted sensation
senex/witch
(shadow of father/mother)
6th function

Introverted intuition
trickster
(shadow of *puer/puella*)
7th function

Introverted feeling
anima/animus
(inferior function)
4th function

Extraverted feeling
demonic/daimonic personality
(shadow of anima/animus)
8th function

FIGURE 10.1   Archetypal/type complexes (using ESTJ as an example)

My model implies that development of all eight function-attitudes will involve a significant engagement with each of the archetypal complexes, and a differentiation of each function out of its archetypal manifestation. In integrating one's typology, the issues associated with each archetypal complex must be faced, exactly as in classical individuation, which has been conceived as the progressive integration of the collective unconscious through engagement with a series of archetypal figures. Moreover, as Papadopoulos (1992, vol. 2, p. 6) pointed out, the model provides a rational basis for analyzing archetypal interactions between individuals on the basis of typology. Recognizing correlations between functions and complexes in an individual patient can be very helpful to the therapist, especially when encountering markedly altered states of mind in patients. At such times the therapist can often help to re-establish ego strength in the patient by speaking the language of the patient's superior function rather than mirroring the typological idiom of the possessing complex (Sandner & Beebe, 1995, pp. 317–344). An account of the way Jung worked with an analytic patient whose reality testing was overwhelmed by an eruption of intuitive religious imagery reveals how he used his understanding of typology to guide an intervention that helped her recover her natural sensation type orientation (von der Heydt, 1975). In less florid, but nevertheless demanding, borderline and narcissistic conditions, function-attitudes that are in shadow for a client can be associated with archetypal defenses of the self, and it advances therapy to understand their precise character (Beebe, 1998b).

Other noteworthy contributions to the conceptual and clinical elucidation of the theory of psychological types have been as follows:

• Meier's (1959) exposition of the transference–countertransference in terms of a 'rotation' of the analyst's typological mandala to bring his or her orientation into attunement with the analysand's;

- Mann, Siegler and Osmond's (1968) discussion of the different relations to time among the different functions (sensation, in their view, being present oriented, feeling being past oriented, intuition future oriented, and thinking having a continuous time line through past, present, and future);
- Marshall's (1968) clarification of 'rational' and 'irrational' through his conceptual analysis of the functions (sensation and intuition revealed to be 'functions of the given' and thinking and feeling as 'functions of option');
- James Hillman's (1971/1998) well-drawn distinctions between aspects of the feeling function and affect, the anima, and the persona, and his discussion of the role of inferior feeling in synchronistic phenomena;
- William Willeford's (1975, 1976, 1977) insistence on the 'primacy' of feeling in the hierarchy of functions (because it is the function that discriminates affect) and his demonstration of the importance of the mother–infant relationship in the evocation of the feeling function (1987);
- Shapiro and Alexander's (1975) phenomenological analysis of the characteristic 'moves' of extraversion (merger with the object) and introversion (matching with the archetype) in creating experience;
- Groesbeck's (1978) examination of the role of the analyst's tertiary and inferior functions in the constellation of the 'wounded healer' archetype during analysis;
- Kirsch's (1980) observation that introverted therapists tend to interpret dreams on the subject level and extraverted therapists on the object level;
- Sabini's (1988) discussion of the therapist's inferior function;
- Murphy's (1992) demonstration that the dominant function is a recognizable structure of personality that is stably present from early childhood, providing a basic orientation that persists through the various stages of a child's development in which auxiliary, tertiary, and inferior functions gradually make their additional appearances;
- Hill's (1998) discussion of the typology of the anima;
- Ulanov's (2009) analysis of the relation of the inferior function to the facing of life itself;
- Pilard's (2015) comprehensive survey of the psychological nature of intuition, including the philosophical background, its acceptance by Jung as one of the functions of consciousness, and the development of the concept by post-Jungian analysts.

All of these writers have appreciated and extended the therapeutic possibilities of Jung's typological formulations.

Another significant line of development of the theory of psychological types has been in the area of standardized type assessment instruments. Although in the 1940s Jo Wheelwright, together with his wife Jane Wheelwright plus Horace Gray and later John Buehler, produced the first paper-and-pencil type assessment, the Gray–Wheelwrights Jungian Type Survey (JTS), and did pioneering research with this instrument (Mattoon & Davis, 1995), it was really the Myers–Briggs Type

Indicator (MBTI) developed by Isabel Briggs Myers and her mother Katherine Briggs, who were not Jungian analysts, that put standardized type instruments on the map internationally. The MBTI, developed in earnest from 1942 and finally licensed in the 1960s, has become one of the most popular psychological instruments in the English-speaking world and is starting to be used in translation in other countries (see Quenk, 2000 for a description). It is regularly used by career counselors to assess the 'type' of clients looking for work that suits them, as well as in human resources and personnel departments all over the world. A Center for Applications of Psychological Type in Gainesville, Florida, maintains a large statistical database of MBTI results. In the United States, the Association for Psychological Type, which in the mid-1980s, when Jungian ideas were everywhere popular, had several thousand members, continues now, as the Association for Psychological Type International, to host conferences sharing experience and research based on not only the MBTI, but other approaches to typology (including my own). There are similar organizations in other countries. There is also a type assessment for children, the Murphy–Meisgeier Type Indicator for Children (MMTIC). All of these paper-and-pencil questionnaires involve forced choices constructed according to Jung's "bipolar assumption" that we cannot think and feel, or take in sensation and use intuition, at the same time. In 1980, Jungian analysts June Singer and Mary Loomis offered their own instrument, the Singer–Loomis Inventory of Personality (SLIP), which does not build on this assumption; instead it assesses the level of development of each of the eight function-attitudes separately (Loomis, 1982). A comparison of findings, undertaken to determine the extent of agreement between the JTS, MBTI and SLIP was published in 1994.

> Results found that the MBTI and the JTS both indicated extraversion–introversion with substantial agreement, sensing–intuition with moderate agreement, and thinking–feeling with limited agreement. Evidence was equivocal for the instruments' ability to indicate dominant function. It appears that the SLIP measures different constructs than either the MBTI or the JTS, so that little support was found for Singer and Loomis' challenge to Jung's bipolarity assumption.
>
> *Karesh, Pieper, & Holland, 1994, p. 30*

The popularity of the MBTI has resulted in a spate of publications in print and online, the *Australian Psychological Type Review,* the *Bulletin of Psychological Type,* the *Journal of Psychological Type, Personality Type in Depth,* and *TypeFace* being some of the main ones in English. Myers also is responsible for the terms 'judging' and 'perceiving' as less loaded synonyms for 'rational' and 'irrational,' although the instrument confines its J and P descriptors to the characterization of the leading extraverted function. Myers also introduced the notion of 'good type development' to suggest a progressive differentiation of the functions according to the hierarchy of superior, auxiliary, tertiary and inferior. In recent years, a controversy has developed as to whether the third and fourth functions continue the alternation of attitudes (with respect to extraversion or introversion) begun by the first two functions. The regularly alternating pattern I first proposed publically at the initial Ghost Ranch Conference of Jungian Analysts and Candidates in 1983 (Beebe, 1984) and proceeded to teach across the United States over the next five years as the key to the attitude of the third function (opposite from the auxiliary) was separately proposed with near simultaneity by Grant, Thompson, and Clarke (1983) and Brownsword (1988). At present, it is a popular view, although leading type practitioners and Jungian analysts who have devoted attention to the types have certainly dissented, Spoto (1995) in the matter of the third function-changing attitude from that of the auxiliary, and Wheelwright and Wheelwright (1987) as to the attitude of the auxiliary function being different from that of the dominant. Everyone seems to agree on one point, however: that the fourth or inferior function has the opposite attitude from the first or dominant function.

Important attempts to integrate the empirical discoveries of those who have developed the MBTI instrument into the clinical and conceptual tradition of analytical psychology have been made by Angelo Spoto (1995), John Giannini (2004) and myself (Beebe, 1984). Elizabeth Murphy (1992) has spearheaded the study of type development in children and has produced materials to help parents and teachers understand how to communicate effectively with children of different types. There have also been attempts to link the eight Jungian function-attitudes and sixteen MBTI type profiles to a new notion of temperament (Keirsey & Bates, 1984; Berens, 1998), Sheldon's body types (Arraj & Arraj, 1988), the *DSM-IV* personality disorders (Ekstrom, 1988), the Neo-PI 'Big-5' Personality Factors (McCrae & Costa, 1989; Wiggins, 1996; Scanlon, 1999), and the 'multiple intelligences' of cognitive psychology (Gardner, 1983; Thompson, 1985; Goleman, 1995). The types have been linked to religious orientation (Ross, 1992) and moral decision-making styles (Beebe, 1992, 1998a; Burleson, 2001). Within academic psychology, Kagan (1994, 1998) has recognized Jung's contributions to a theory of temperament but warned of the problems inherent in trying to understand these issues without a grasp of inherent physiology as well as psychology. Dario Nardi (2011) has pioneered research to find correlations between brain activity and Jung's eight functions of consciousness. Linda Berens (2008) has been a unifying leader in the types movement, integrating multiple approaches to analyzing psychological diversity into an intellectually consistent framework. Her recent work with Christopher Montoya on a "cognitive styles lens" (Montoya, 2014) holds promise in the way that it implicitly looks at whole axes rather than only at individual function preferences.

Current status and trends

Type is still a 'hard sell' among many analysts. A study published by Plaut (1972) revealed that less than half of Jungian analysts use type in their clinical work.[5] Those who do often rely on questionnaire results rather than clinical observation to establish the 'type diagnosis.' Many of these analysts are unaware that the Association for Psychological Type considers it unethical to type someone simply on the basis of their results on the MBTI, which is after all only an 'Indicator.' There must be at least a follow-up interview in which the results of the assessment are explained with a proviso along the lines of, 'this is the type the instrument *indicates,* and you can see if it really fits you.' Nevertheless, Annie Murphy Paul (2004) has severely criticized the way the MBTI has been used by teachers and career counselors to assign identities to individuals.

In psychotherapeutic circles, sadly, few clinicians can even recognize the eight function-attitudes, confusing introverted feeling with introverted intuition, not knowing the difference between extraverted and introverted thinking and so on. (Sharp's (1987) book is an excellent remedial primer.) Many do not really understand the difference between introversion and extraversion as processes in the self. (This is helpfully addressed in Lavin's (1995) article.)

One place type theory has taken limited, but promising, hold in clinical work is in the area of couple therapy and marriage counseling. Therapists who have explained the types to their clients have often reported that the results are very satisfying, in terms of creating appropriate expectations between the partners and helping them to adjust their communication styles.

There can be no real advance in the understanding of Jung's most subtle and far-reaching contribution to ego psychology, however, until many more analytical psychologists become much more type-literate than they are nowadays. Then we can hope for some interesting research that follows up the implications of Jung's theory of psychological types, research that can also move our understanding of the actual path of individuation forward.

Those of us who are interested in this theory need to establish its relevance to cognitive psychology in general, and to what, in a contemporary nod to faculty psychology, has been called "the modularity of mind" (Fodor, 1983). That a differentiation of functions emerges out of the complexity of consciousness itself suggests that consciousness is rooted in the very same structures, our complexes, that threaten to restrict and cloud our egos. Complexes enable new capacities to appear to the degree that we engage with them. Jung demonstrated that letting our complexes tell their different stories of how they see things is a way to experience the range of consciousness. The psychological processes that facilitate the emergence of consciousness (Cambray, 2006) Jung called archetypal, which today we recognize in their predilection for sorting themselves in a self-organizing way (Saunders & Sklar, 2001; Hogenson, 2007). That consciousness appears to the psyche as a quaternity of functions, mirrored by an equally quaternary shadow showing the same functions with the opposite attitudes, means that its structure imitates that of the Self, as became clear to the later Jung (1951/1959, ¶398). His typology has therefore turned out to be, not his ego psychology, as so many of us assumed, but his self psychology. In its patterning, typology recognizes many paths that psyche provides for consciousness to travel; in its complexity, typology demonstrates dynamic interactions between the paths that drive consciousness itself forward.

Notes

1 The terms 'extraversion' and 'introversion' were apparently adapted from Binet's terms 'externospection' and 'introspection' (Binet, 1903, cited by Oliver Brachfeld (1954) in Ellenberger (1970, pp. 702–703).
2 Carolyn Fay (1996) has suggested this be called "feeling value."
3 'Function,' strictly, refers to the four functions of consciousness—sensation, thinking, feeling and intuition—whereas 'attitude' suggests the habitual way the attention is directed —whether extraverted or introverted—when the psyche acts or reacts (Jung, 1921/1971, ¶687). In the type literature, it is common to identify the extraverted and introverted deployment of a function when specifying it; hence rather than speaking of four functions and two attitudes, people nowadays speak of eight function-attitudes (Thompson, 1996). These eight cognitive modes offer a total complement of possibilities for conscious orientation that can potentially be differentiated as we individuate.
4 Here, I have followed Myers, and not Wheelwright, in finding that the auxiliary function is different in attitude from the superior function, and have asserted that the attitudes of the functions alternate in the course of their differentiation, so that if the first, superior, function is extraverted, the auxiliary function will be introverted, the tertiary extraverted, and the inferior introverted.
5 Bradway and Detloff (1976) established the incidence of the different psychological types among Jungian analysts, and Bradway and Wheelwright (1978) studied the relation of the psychological type of the analyst to the analysts' actual analytical practices, finding, for instance, that extraverts tend to use typology more than introverts in making connections and interpretations with their patients and that typology is used more often by San Francisco than by London Jungian analysts.

References

Arraj, J. & Arraj, T. (1988). *Tracking the elusive human, vol. 1*. Chiloquin, OR: Inner Growth.
Beebe, J. (1984). Psychological types in transference, countertransference, and the therapeutic interaction. In N. Schwartz-Salant & M. Stein (Eds.), *Transference/countertransference* (pp. 147–161). Wilmette, IL: Chiron.
Beebe, J. (1992). *Integrity in depth*. College Station, TX: Texas A&M University Press.
Beebe, J. (1998a). Toward a Jungian analysis of character. In A. Casement (Ed.), *Post-Jungians today* (pp. 53–66). London: Routledge.
Beebe, J. (1998b). Review of Donald Kalsched's *The inner world of trauma: Archetypal defenses of the personal spirit*. *Quadrant, 28*(1), 92–96.
Benziger, K. (1995). *Falsification of type*. Dillon, CO: KBA.
Berens, L. (1998). *Understanding yourself and others: An introduction to temperament*. Huntington Beach, CA: Temperament Research Institute.
Berens, L. (2008). *Understanding yourself and others: An introduction to interaction styles*. Huntington Beach, CA: Telos Publications.
Binet, A. (1903). *L'Etude expérimental de l'intelligence*. Paris: Schleicher.
Bishop, P. (2008). Schiller and the problem of typology. In *Analytical psychology and German classical aesthetics: Goethe, Schiller, and Jung, vol. 1: The development of the personality* (pp. 81–125). London: Routledge.
Brachfeld, O. (1954). Gelenkte Tagträume als Hilfsmittel der Psychotherapie. *Zeitschrift für Psychotherapie, 4*, 79–93.
Bradway, K. & Detloff, W. (1976). Incidence of psychological types among Jungian analysts, classified by self and by test. *Journal of Analytical Psychology, 21*(2), 134–146.

Bradway, K. & Wheelwright, J. (1978). The psychological type of the analyst and its relation to analytical practice. *Journal of Analytical Psychology*, *23*(3), 211–225.

Brooks, G. P. (1976). The faculty psychology of Thomas Reid. *Journal of the History of the Behavioral Sciences*, *12*(1), 65–77.

Brownsword, A. (1988). *Psychological type: An introduction*. Nicasio, CA: Human Resources Management Press.

Burleson, B. (2001). *Pathways to integrity: Ethics and psychological type*. Gainesville, FL: Center for Applications of Psychological Type.

Cambray, J (2006). Towards the feeling of emergence. *Journal of Analytical Psychology*, *51*(1), 1–20.

Clark, P. (2000). Work and the eight function model. *Bulletin of Psychological Type*, *23*(7).

Ekstrom, S. (1988). Jung's typology and DSM-III personality disorders: A comparison of two systems of classification. *Journal of Analytical Psychology*, *33*(4), 329–344.

Ellenberger, H. (1970). *The discovery of the unconscious: The history and evolution of dynamic psychiatry*. New York: Basic Books.

Fay, C. (1996). *At the threshold* (video cassette). Houston, TX: C. G. Jung Educational Center.

Fodor, J. (1983). The modularity of mind. Cambridge, MA: MIT Press.

Freud, S. (1899/2010). *The interpretation of dreams,* J. M. Masson (Ed.), A. A. Brill (Trans.) New York: Sterling Publishing.

Frey, A. (2012). Jung's vision of suffering one's psychological type. *Bulletin of Psychological Type*, *35*(2), 15–17.

Gall, F. J. (1835). *On the functions of the brain and of each of its parts: With observations on the possibility of determining the instincts, propensities, and talents, or the moral and intellectual dispositions of men and animals, by the configuration of the brain and head, vol. 1*. Boston, MA: Marsh, Capen & Lyon.

Gardner, H. (1983). *Frames of mind*. New York: Basic Books.

Geldart, W. (1998). Katharine Downing Myers and whole MBTI type—an interview. *The Enneagram and the MBTI: An electronic journal* http://tap3x.net/EMBTI/journal.html (February 1998).

Giannini, J. (2004). *Compass of the soul: Archetypal guides to a fuller life*. Gainesville, FL: Center for Applications of Psychological Type.

Goleman, D. (1995). *Emotional intelligence*. New York: Bantam.

Grant, W. H., Thompson, M. M. & Clarke, T. E. (1983). *From image to likeness: A Jungian path in the gospel journey*. Ramsey, NJ: Paulist Press.

Groesbeck, C. (1978). Psychological types in the analysis of the transference. *Journal of Analytical Psychology*, *23*(1), 23–53.

Haas, L., McAlpine, R., & Hartzler, M. (2001). *Journey of understanding: MBTI® interpretation using the eight Jungian functions*. Palo Alto, CA: Consulting Psychologists Press.

Harris, A. (1996). *Living with paradox: An introduction to Jungian psychology*. Pacific Grove, CA: Brooks/Cole.

Henderson, J. (1970). Inner perception in terms of depth psychology. *Annals of the New York Academy of Sciences*, *169*, 664–672.

Hill, G. (1998). Men, the anima, and the feminine. *San Francisco Jung Institute Library Journal*, *17*(3), 49–61.

Hillman, J. (1971/1998). The feeling function. In M.-L. von Franz & J. Hillman, *Lectures on Jung's typology* (pp. 89–179). Woodstock, CT: Spring.

Hogenson, G. (2007). From moments of meeting to archetypal consciousness: Emergence and the fractal structure of analytic practice. In A. Casement (Ed.), *Who owns Jung?* (pp. 293–314). London: Karnac.

Jung, C. G. (1912). *Wandlungen und Symbole der Libido*. Leipzig: Franz Deuticke.

Jung, C. G. (1921). *Psychologische Typen*. Zurich: Rascher.

Jung, C. G. (1921/1971). Psychological types. In *Cw 6*.

Jung, C. G. (1923). *Psychological types, or, The psychology of individuation* (H. G. Baynes, Trans.) New York: Harcourt Brace.

Jung, C. G. (1951/1959). Aion: Researches into the phenomenology of the self. In *Cw 9*, ii.

Jung, C. G. (1968). *Analytical psychology: Its theory and practice*. New York: Pantheon.

Jung, C. G. (1989/2012). *Analytical psychology: Notes on the seminar given in 1925*. W. McGuire (Ed). Revised and updated by Sonu Shamdasani (Ed). Princeton, NJ: Princeton University Press.

Jung, C. G. (2009). *The red book: Liber novus*. New York: W. W. Norton.

Jung, C. G. & Riklin, F. (1904/1973). Associations of normal subjects. In Experimental Researches. In *Cw 2* (L. Stein & D. Riviere, Trans.) (pp. 3–196).

Jung, C. G. & Schmid-Guisan, H. (2013). *The question of psychological types*. J. Beebe & E. Falzeder (Eds.), E. Falzeder (Trans.) Princeton, NJ: Princeton, University Press.

Kagan, J. (1994). *Galen's prophecy: Temperament in human nature*. New York: Basic Books.

Kagan, J. (1998). *Three seductive ideas*. Cambridge, MA: Harvard University Press.

Karesh, D. M., Pieper, W. A., & Holland, C. L. (1994). Comparing the MBTI, the Jungian type survey, and the Singer–Loomis Inventory of Personality. *Journal of Psychological Type, 30*, 30–38.

Keirsey, D. & Bates, M. (1984). *Please understand me: Character and temperament types*. Del Mar, CA: Prometheus Nemesis Books.

Kirsch, T. (1980). Dreams and psychological types. In I. Baker (Ed.), *Methods of treatment in analytical psychology* (pp. 139–144). Stuttgart: Bonz Verlag.

Lavin, T. (1995). The art of practicing Jung's psychological types in analysis. In M. Stein (Ed.), *Jungian analysis, Second ed.* (pp. 260–277). La Salle, IL: Open Court.

Loomis, M. (1982). A new perspective for Jung's typology: the Singer–Loomis Inventory of Personality. *Journal of Analytical Psychology, 27*(1), 59–70.

McCrae, R. & Costa, P. (1989). Reinterpreting the Myers–Briggs Type Indicator from the perspective of the five-factor model of personality. *Journal of Personality, 57,* 17–40.

Mann, H., Siegler, M., & Osmond, H. (1968). The many worlds of time. *Journal of Analytical Psychology, 13*(1), 33–56.

Marshall, I. (1968). The four functions: A conceptual analysis. *Journal of Analytical Psychology, 13*(1), 1–32.

Mattoon, M. & Davis, M. (1995). The Gray–Wheelwrights Jungian type survey: Development and history. *Journal of Analytical Psychology, 40*(2), 205–234.

Meier, C. A. (1959). Projection, transference, and the subject-object relation. *Journal of Analytical Psychology, 4*(1), 21–34.

Meier, C. A. (1989). *Consciousness*. D. N. Roscoe (Trans.) Boston, MA: Sigo Press.

Montoya, C. L. (2014). The cognitive styles lens. *Association for Psychological Type International Bulletin,* September 2014.

Murphy, E. (1992). *The developing child: Using Jungian type to understand children*. Palo Alto, CA: Davies-Black Publishing.

Myers, I. & Myers, P. (1980). *Gifts differing: Understanding personality type*. Palo Alto, CA: Consulting Psychologists Press.

Myers, K. & Kirby, L. (2000). *Introduction to type dynamics and development*. Palo Alto, CA, Consulting Psychologists Press.

Nardi, D. (2011). *Neuroscience of personality: Brain savvy insights for all types of people*. Los Angeles, CA: Radiance House.

Nunberg, H. & Federn, E. (Eds.) (1962). *Minutes of the Vienna Psychoanalytic Society, vol. 1. 1906–1908.* Madison, CT: International Universities Press.

Papadopoulos, R. (Ed.) (1992). *Carl Gustav Jung: Critical assessments.* London: Routledge.

Paul, A. M. (2004). *The cult of personality.* New York: Free Press.

Pilard, N. (2015). *Jung and intuition: On the centrality and variety of forms of intuition in Jung and the post-Jungians.* London: Karnac.

Plaut, F. (1972). Analytical psychologists and psychological types: Comment on replies to a survey. *Journal of Analytical Psychology, 17*(2), 137–151.

Quenk, N. (1993). *Beside ourselves: Our hidden personality in everyday life.* Palo Alto, CA: Consulting Psychologists Press.

Quenk, N. (2000). *Essentials of Myers–Briggs Type Indicator assessment.* New York: John Wiley.

Richards, R. J. (1980). Christian Wolff's prolegomena to empirical and rational psychology: translation and commentary. *Proceedings of the American Philosophical Society 124*(3), 227–239. http://home.uchicago.edu/~rjr6/articles/Wolff.pdf. Consulted 8.2.15.

Ross, C. (1992). The intuitive function and religious orientation. *Journal of Analytical Psychology, 37*(1), 83–103.

Sabini, M. (1988). The therapist's inferior function. *Journal of Analytical Psychology, 3*(4), 373–394.

Sandner, D. & Beebe, J. (1995). Psychopathology and analysis. In M. Stein (Ed.) *Jungian analysis, 2nd Ed.* (pp. 294–334). La Salle, IL: Open Court.

Saunders, P. & Sklar, P. (2001). Archetypes, complexes, and self-organisation. *Journal of Analytical Psychology, 46*(2), 305–323.

Scanlon, S. (Ed.) (1999). The MBTI and other personality theories: Part 2—"The big five" and the NEO-PI. *The Type Reporter, 7.*

Schopenhauer, A. (1819/1909). *The world as will and idea. Seventh Ed., vol. 1.*, R. B. Haldane & J. Kemp (Trans.). London: Kegan Paul, Trench, Truebner & Co. Project Gutenberg (2011) Online: https://www.gutenberg.org/files/38427/38427-pdf.pdf. Consulted 8.2.2015.

Shamdasani, S. (1999). The lost contributions of Maria Moltzer to analytical psychology. *Spring 64*, 103–106.

Shamdasani, S. (2003). *Jung and the making of modern psychology: The dream of a science.* Cambridge: Cambridge University Press.

Shapiro, K. & Alexander, I. (1975). *The experience of introversion: An integration of phenomenological, empirical, and Jungian approaches.* Durham, NC: Duke University Press.

Sharp, D. (1987). *Personality types: Jung's model of typology.* Toronto: Inner City.

Singer, J. & Loomis, M. (n.d.). *The Singer–Loomis Inventory of Personality: Experimental edition* (booklet). Palo Alto, CA: Consulting Psychologists Press.

Spoto, A. (1995). *Jung's typology in perspective.* Wilmette, IL: Chiron.

Thompson, H. (1996). *Jung's function-attitudes explained.* Watkinsville, GA: Wormhole.

Thompson, K. (1985). Cognitive and analytical psychology. *San Francisco Jung Institute Library Journal, 5*(4), 40–64.

Ulanov, A. (2009). The danger and the treasure of the inferior function. *Psychological Perspectives, 52*, 9–23.

Von der Heydt, V. (1975). A session with Jung. *Harvest 21*, 108–110.

von Franz, M.-L. (1971/1998). The inferior function. In M.-L. von Franz & J. Hillman, *Lectures on Jung's typology* (pp. 3–88). Woodstock, CT: Spring.

Wheelwright, J. B. (1982). Psychological types. In J. B. Wheelwright, *Saint George and the dandelion* (pp. 53–77). San Francisco, CA: C. G. Jung Institute of San Francisco.

Wheelwright, J. H. & Wheelwright, J. B. (1987). Personal communication (at a seminar, Four concepts in greater depth: Psychological types) given with the author of this book at the C. G. Jung Institute in San Francisco, March 7, 1987 (audiocassette in the Library of the Institute).

Wiggins, J. (Ed.) (1996). *The five-factor model of personality: Theoretical perspectives*. New York: Guilford.

Willeford, W. (1975). Toward a dynamic concept of feeling. *Journal of Analytical Psychology*, *20*(1), 18–40.

Willeford, W. (1976). The primacy of feeling (Part I). *Journal of Analytical Psychology*, *21*(2), 115–133.

Willeford, W. (1977). The primacy of feeling (Part II). *Journal of Analytical Psychology*, *22*(1), 1–16.

Willeford, W. (1987). *Feeling, imagination, and the self*. Evanston, IL: Northwestern University Press.

11

THE *RED BOOK* AS A WORK OF CONSCIENCE

Introduction: finding a way in

A series of philosophical distillations about very difficult subjects, and written in very difficult times, Jung's *Red Book* sparks, for many of us, enormous resistance. When I have brought myself to read and surrender to it, however, I've been so pleased! I feel I'm having an experience. I'm relieved to notice that I'm not being told what I must think, what I must do.

In *The Red Book*, each thought is identified with a particular character—sometimes an historical person, sometimes a fantasy figure. There is no final word that is *the* word, although there are certainly philosophic crescendos when, for a moment, an igniting truth, at least for Jung, emerges. Yet there are plenty of reminders that one man's truth cannot be every person's truth. In that sense, once you surrender to the book, there is plenty of room for you to breathe in it.

Those who have already known Jung's work may experience a difficulty that newcomers to Jungian thought who start with *The Red Book* won't have: relating the narrative of this book to what is already established in our minds about Jung. Here, I will offer a few guideposts that have helped me to find my way in the book, elements that link it to Jungian concepts that I have been thinking about for a long time.

My work in recent years has been focused on three main subjects: integrity, psychological types, and film, and I have found it possible usefully to bring my knowledge of these subjects to my reading of *The Red Book*. To my amazement, for instance, Jung has a short, charming section in which he meets an unemployed fellow—the text says "a tramp"—and draws him out on the subject of cinema, an art form that Jung regards with distaste (2009, p. 265). I find this amusing, because *The Red Book* itself can be outrageously cinematic in bringing disparate reflections together in a narrative linked by images. In *The Red Book*, the unity is provided by the conscience with which Jung keeps addressing the problem of what he needs to take aboard to bring justice to his soul. We could see the tramp as an expression of a shadowy extraverted intuition. The fellow looks outside himself for images that will help him to make sense of his soul's turmoil, a strategy Jung finds lazy. Jung returns to his own active imagination, which will eventually identify the images that will be essential to his own development in a far more original, introverted intuitive way.

Disentangling from the spirit of the time

It seems improbable that there would have been a *Red Book* at all, had Jung not broken free of his prestigious role as Freud's chosen son. The key letter in this transaction—Jung's to Freud dated December 18, 1912 (McGuire, 1974, pp. 534–535)—is an example of what can be accomplished by deploying extraverted feeling in a tricksterish way. Through this letter, itself an escalation of hostility in what had already become an unhappy correspondence, Jung succeeded in getting Freud to sever their personal relations much the way that an adolescent son, about ready to face the world on his own, might provoke a parent into kicking him out of the house. A complete break in their professional relations followed sixteen months later.

In *The Red Book*, Jung reports a dream vision that occurred on the first anniversary of writing that precipitating letter—December 18, 1913 (2009, p. 241, n.112)—though nowhere does Jung draw the connection to the anniversary. In this dream, which Jung (1989) also recounted in the 1925 Seminar on Analytical Psychology (pp. 56–57) and in *Memories, Dreams, Reflections* (Jung/Jaffe, 1963, pp. 179–180) and which E. A. Bennet (1985, pp. 61–62) records in yet another version, Jung and a brown-skinned man are together in a rocky landscape. Jung hears from high up in the mountains the exultant horn of Siegfried, the hero of the *Nibelungenlied*. Jung and the brown man realize that Siegfried is the enemy they must kill. Armed with rifles, they lie in wait for him and assassinate him as he passes by, driving "boldly and magnificently over the steep rocks" in his "chariot made of the bones of the dead" (2009, p. 241).

Jung recalled that the vision left him with an almost unbearable anguish comprised of guilt, compassion for the slain hero, and stupefaction at why he should have undertaken such a surprising and underhanded crime. Gradually, he came to understand that the dream reflects a painful process of disidentifying from the archetype of the conquering hero who, however idealistic, operates in the world by imposing his will (Jung, 1989/2012, pp. 56–57; Jung/Jaffe, 1963, pp. 180–181).

The American psychiatrist Josephine Hilgard (Hilgard & Newman, 1959) pioneered the exploration of 'anniversary reactions,' demonstrating the uncanny way in which the unconscious often honors the anniversaries of traumatic events. The dating of the dream would suggest that it was such a reaction. Rosenberg (1978, pp. 28–30), who suggests a variety of interpretations of the dream, was perhaps the first to note the anniversary and to propose that Siegfried is a thinly disguised stand-in for Sigmund Freud, the heroic father Jung had once venerated but who, by the time of the dream, had become an Oedipal oppressor.[1] He notes, however, that, in the mythology, Siegfried is the son of Sigmund. I would assert, therefore, as a few others have done (for instance Walker, 2002, pp. 65–69,[2] and Kushner, 2006, pp. 90–92), that the murdered Siegfried represents not Freud or his introject but Jung's *sonship* to Freud. During the time that Jung was traveling back and forth from Zürich to Vienna to attend psychoanalytic conferences, he was sometimes called by his colleagues "the Blond Siegfried" (Ellenberger, 1970, p. 739, n. 41). Freud, who loved to speak in mythological language, admonished Jung in April 1909: "I formally adopted you as eldest son and anointed you . . . as my successor and crown prince" (McGuire, 1974, p. 218), meaning in leadership of the psychoanalytic movement. Siegfried was likewise a prince, who carried a shield with a crown on it (Mackenzie, 1912/2010, p. 363). The chariot, which Siegfried was driving in so debonair a fashion, "made of the bones of the dead" (Jung, 2009, p. 241), might represent the psychoanalytic theory that Jung had begun to feel was already dead, psychologically, in the sense of being inadequate to understanding the living complexity of psychic life. The notion that the unconscious was caused by the repression of unacceptable instincts seemed to reduce lived experience to its bare bones.[3]

In Jung's own telling, however, the impetus he felt to explore the unconscious in another way with *The Red Book* came not from his struggle with Freud but from his intuitive perception of events in the wider world. On a short train trip in October, 1913, he was suddenly seized by an image of Europe—from the North Sea to the Alps, from England to Russia—covered by a sea of blood and scattered with thousands of corpses (Jung, 2009, p. 231; Jung/Jaffe, 1963, p. 175). The vision returned a few weeks later, and he still didn't know how to interpret it.

In April, May, and June of 1914, three related dreams showed him Europe suffering cataclysmic destruction, with all life frozen out. By this time, Jung had concluded not that Europe was headed for disaster but that these dreams and visions indicated a looming psychosis in himself. As a specialist in schizophrenia, he knew that it was common for fantasies of world catastrophe to appear just prior to the onset of a psychotic break. Uneasily, he went on with his work, waiting to see what would happen. At the end of July, he was lecturing in Scotland when the news arrived that Archduke Ferdinand, Crown Prince of the Austro-Hungarian Empire, had been assassinated and war declared between Britain and Germany. Years later, Jung recalled the experience to Mircea Eliade this way:

> when I disembarked in Holland the next day, nobody was happier than I. Now I was sure that no schizophrenia was threatening me. I understood that my dreams and my visions came to me from the subsoil of the collective unconscious.[4]
>
> *McGuire & Hull, 1977, pp. 233–234*

The catastrophic events of the Great War helped Jung to understand more clearly why he had had to unmoor himself from the psychoanalytic worldview. The premonitory visions that Jung experienced and recorded in *The Red Book* showed him that the mind is an instrument which is capable of registering, in words Gregory

Bateson (1972) would later use, "news of a difference" (p. 460). If he had ever doubted it, Jung now knew in a visceral way that the psyche doesn't only process traumas, it intuitively picks up trends; its field of interest is greater than the personal. The collective forces that shook him cemented Jung's discovery of the aliveness of the unconscious and of the reach of its supra-personal aspect.

In *The Red Book* Jung makes clear that, once he learned that Crown Prince Ferdinand had been killed, the intuition that developed, informed by his own dream of killing a prince, was that in some way Europeans *needed* to kill the crown prince, but didn't know it. He writes:

> Because I carried the murder in me, I foresaw it.
>
> Because I carried the war in me, I foresaw it. . . . And thus was the fate of the people: The murder of one was the poisonous arrow that flew into the hearts of men, and kindled the fiercest war. This murder is the indignation of incapacity against will, a Judas betrayal that one would like someone else to have committed. We are still seeking the goat that should bear our sin.
>
> *2009, p. 241*

Rhetorically addressing his fellow Europeans, he tells them:

> You all have a share in the murder. . . . I would like you to see what the murdered hero means. Those nameless men who in our day have murdered a prince are blind prophets who demonstrate in events what then is valid only for the soul. Through the murder of princes we will learn that the prince in us, the hero, is threatened.
>
> *2009, pp. 239–240*

When Jung writes here of "incapacity" rising up against "will," I think he is referring to the part of each of us that does not have mastery. In his later work on typology, he emphasizes the clumsy, disappointing piece in all of us that is the inferior function as the center of the vulnerability that is the gateway to the soul.[5]

Therefore, the heroic attitude, the heroic ideal of what a man or a nation should be, was a threat to the soul, because it needed to deny incapacity with a can-do attitude. Siegfried, Jung (1989/2012) confessed to his students in 1925, was an ideal of force and efficiency he had cultivated (p. 57) in the course of making himself a world famous psychiatrist. This, he had recognized by 1915 when he started entering his visions in *The Red Book*, was too great a concession to "the spirit of this time" (2009, p. 229).

In 1915, former President Theodore Roosevelt was advising Americans:

> The indispensable thing for every free people to do in the present day is with efficiency to prepare against war by making itself able physically to defend its rights and by cultivating that stern and manly spirit without which no material preparation will avail.
>
> *Roosevelt, 1915, p. 203*

Such veneration of heroism was not a universal sentiment, however. Two months after America entered the war, voluntary enlistment failed to get the necessary numbers. There was a draft, from which as many as two-thirds of those who had to register tried to get exemption (Solomon, 2010). For a significant number, however, it was finally possible to sign up for a chance to be part of the greatest event they had ever heard of. Such young men rushed to the opportunity to do their heroic duty. This psychology is depicted in Redford's film *A River Runs through It* (1992). Some of the heroism, of course, existed only in retrospect—an example of the mythmaking that often follows seduction and trauma (Fussell, 1974, pp. 139–191).

Infinitely closer to the chaos of that time than we are now, Jung is groping in *The Red Book* to discover what it is in himself and other Europeans that is expressing itself through the war, which he senses has more to do with overthrowing the heroic attitude than with living up to it. His insight that this outer calamity reflected an inner complex is one that he codified much later as the psychological rule, "when an inner situation is not made conscious, it happens outside, as fate" (Jung, 1959, ¶126).

In *The Red Book* he analyzes the attachment to prestige and power that overtook him in the years 1902–1913, estranging him from his soul, as an identification with "the spirit of this time" (2009, pp. 229–230). As he takes up the "spirit of the depths" that he pursues in *The Red Book*, he not only resigns as President of the International Psychoanalytic Association but also gives up his post at the University of Zürich. He makes a conscious decision to move away from collective medical power.

These choices reflect the ethical instinct that marks *The Red Book* for me as a work of conscience. Jung seems to be saying: "OK, I am not crazy to have seen and felt these destructive powers in advance of the crisis, yet neither am I guiltless. I am partly responsible." And I see him taking steps to atone. On the other hand, when Jung wrote that we should sacrifice the hero in ourselves (2009, p. 239), a rare call on his part to collective action, I do not believe he meant that we should eschew the part of our personalities that is most competent, reliably rises to challenges, and masters difficult tasks. I believe he meant instead that we should sacrifice the false heroism that would impose our will on ourselves and others. In his own case; he associated the dream figure, Siegfried, with the extraverted thinking function (Jung, 1989/2012, pp. 56–57). Speaking of the Siegfried dream in 1925, he said, "I had killed my intellect. . . . I deposed my superior function." Having decided to "sacrifice" his thinking, he began to conceive of his intuition as his new "superior" function (p. 90).

"The rain that fell" at the end of the dream, he said, "is a symbol of the release of tension; that is, the forces of the unconscious are loosed." [6] Jung said, "There is a chance for other sides of the personality to be born into life" (p. 57). I would say that he needed to kill the heroic rationality that had become his ideal, and for which Freud had chosen him as his chief general to fight for the place of psychoanalysis as a basic science, in order to be able to embrace the irrationality that was needed for a more phenomenological exploration of the unconscious. What was released for Jung was a different sort of heroism, his courageous and resourceful introverted intuition, which was capable of exploring the depths where he could find his soul. This is not quite the same thing as 'deposing' his superior function. Rather, it is establishing what I call in *Integrity in Depth* the "spine of personality" (Beebe, 1992, pp. 106–107). My view is that his thinking was never his true superior function. Rather, his using it as if it were a superior function was "a falsification of type," a not uncommon consequence of "abnormal external influences" (Jung, 1921/1971, ¶560).

The spirit of the depths

When Jung began the introverted process that is recorded in *The Red Book*, he was exploring his own unconscious but not in a logical, planned way. Rather he did so through an irrational, engaged process of perception, meeting almost always as if real whatever fantastic figures he found there. This was at least as much an extraverted sensation process as it was an introverted intuitive one. It is not surprising, then, that it led him to discover an anima figure that could relate to his extraverted sensation.

She was, of all people, Salome, the same seductive Salome who is described, but not named, in the New Testament as dancing for her stepfather Herod and his guests. Offered a reward for her pleasing dance, Salome asked, at her mother's instigation, for the head of John the Baptist, because the Baptist had rebuked Herod for taking the woman who was his brother's wife for his own (Mark 6, Matthew 14). Essentially, she is asking to punish John for his rejection of the feminine and the body.

By the end of the nineteenth century, Salome had become a trope in art and literature for everything that despised Christianity. In Oscar Wilde's play, originally written and performed both in Paris and London in French (1891/1917), when John's severed head is brought to Salome she says, "Ah! thou wouldst not suffer me to kiss thy mouth, Jokanaan. Well, I will kiss it now" (Kuryluk, 1987, p. 224). This is certainly the hands-on, immediate, physical energy that I associate with extraverted sensation, but it is *inferior* extraverted sensation.[7] Jung's Salome is blind, the image of instinctive action that can no longer envision its consequences. Despite his reservations, Jung doesn't reject her, but rather, with some difficulty, humbles himself enough to listen to her.

I see a direct line from *The Red Book* to Jung's achievement in *Psychological Types*. To me the miracle of that book is not just that it recognizes both feeling and thinking as rational functions and accords them equal status, although that was quite a step. What's most remarkable to me is that Jung includes the irrational functions and makes them of equal value to the rational. That is a leap that would not easily have grown out of his enlightenment education. Through his work on *The Red Book*, Jung accepts the irrational as a source of knowledge. In doing this, I think he is moved not just by a "self that knows what's good for itself" (Beebe, 1997, p. 189) but also by an ethical instinct that to do anything less is to endorse the spirit of the times that is ruining the world.

The red one

Nurturing a strong relationship between the ego standpoint and the anima, however, is not something that usually happens all at once. There is a journey involved,
a series of adventures along the way. As we enter midlife, it often happens that the
emphasis in our type development shifts from the auxiliary function to the third
function. We get tired of always using the same two functions of consciousness
and want to see another part of our personality blossom. I think this was happening for Jung.

In teaching about typology, I call the process of discovering and engaging with
the third function, of finding its limitations and vulnerability, the *third-function crisis*.
Associated with the archetype of the *puer* or *puella*, the inner child or youth, the
third function can soar in flights of idealism only, moments later, to panic at its lack
of solid foundation and crash, Icarus-like, to earth. Just as the inferior, or fourth,
function is opposite from the superior, so the third function is opposite from the
auxiliary. So if I am correct that Jung's over-used auxiliary was extraverted thinking, his third function was introverted feeling.

Introverted feeling is always a bit reserved, concerned with what is suitable,
what's proper. As the Myers–Briggs Type Indicator people have taught us, it is a
judging function. A common symbol of introverted feeling in dreams is the judge,
because the function evaluates things, holding them to an archetypal standard of
appropriateness. It makes judgments, even if, out of courtesy, it often keeps its
findings to itself. It must be held in mind, however, that introverted feeling as a
third function is a less reliable judge than when it is one of two most preferred and
developed functions. Like a child, it may show delight or turn up its nose at certain
things, but because its experience is limited, its judgment is not necessarily mature.

We encounter this aspect of Jung's midlife personality in the very first chapter
of Liber Secundus in *The Red Book*, a very appealing part of the book. Jung has
entrusted himself to the spirit of the depths and, not knowing what to do next,
must wait. "I find that I am standing on the highest tower of a castle. . . . My gaze
wanders widely over solitary countryside, a combination of fields and forests"
(2009, p. 259). *Puer*-like, Jung is up in the air, ungrounded. Suddenly, in the
distance, he notices a red point that seems to be moving along a winding road, so
that it sometimes disappears from view, then reappears as it rounds a bend.

> it is a horseman in a red coat, the red horseman. He is coming to my castle:
> he is already riding through the gate. I hear steps on the stairway, the steps
> creak, he knocks: a strange fear comes over me: there stands the Red One,
> his long shape wholly shrouded in red, even his hair is red. I think: in the
> end he will turn out to be the devil.
>
> *p. 259*

Here is the shadow of the idealistic *puer aeternus*: the trickster. The trickster employs
the same function as the *puer* or *puella*, but with the opposite attitude. As Jung's

puer expresses itself through introverted feeling, his trickster comes, as we shall see, bearing extraverted feeling.

The red fellow tells Jung that he saw from far away that Jung was sitting high up on the tower watching for something to happen. It is this disengaged but expectant attitude that has attracted the Red One to him.

Naturally surprised and a bit suspicious at this explanation, Jung asks the Red One who he is.

> Who am I? You think I am the devil. Do not pass judgment. Perhaps you can also talk to me without knowing who I am. What sort of a superstitious fellow are you, that immediately you think of the devil?
>
> *p. 259*

Notice that the figure starts off right away commenting on what is going through Jung's mind. This is no different from the extraverted feeling door-to-door salesman of yesteryear who, as soon as you opened the door a crack, burst out cheerfully, "You're wondering who this stranger could be at your door. You're thinking you probably shouldn't trust him. But I have something in this briefcase that I'm sure you're going to like!"

The life-changing encounter between *puer* and trickster is so much a staple of the archetypal world that we can find it envisioned in many films. Consider, for example, the unsettling meeting between Elliot (introverted feeling *puer*) and E.T. (extraverted feeling trickster) in Spielberg's *E.T.* (1982), or between the introverted thinking *puer* Simon and the extraverted thinking trickster, Henry, in Hal Hartley's *Henry Fool* (1997). The same disorienting/reorienting encounter can be seen in Percy Adlon's *Bagdad Café* (1987) between extraverted intuitive *puella* Brenda and introverted intuitive trickster Jasmin. (In considering these films as psychological documents, think of the screen characters as part-personalities within the overall psyche depicted by the film.)

Jung is intrigued, yet puzzled. He notices that there is something not quite normal—uncanny even—about the Red One. As their conversation develops, it takes on the quality of verbal sparring. At a certain point, Jung seems to feel, paradoxically, that he has established enough trust with the figure to express his distrust openly: "You sound cool and sneering. Have you never broken your heart over the holiest mysteries of our Christian religion?" (2009, p. 261)

This remark exemplifies the spiritual inflation that so often overtakes the *puer aeternus*. Jung sounds so precious and appears to take his Christianity so very seriously! The trickster, having no sense of respect or propriety, is ideally suited to puncture the *puer*'s idealistic pretensions and bring him right to earth. He sees that Jung's introverted feeling is too pure, too critical of others, and too removed from the give and take of real life.

The Red One says: "Your solemnity smells of fanaticism. You have an ethical air and a simplicity that smacks of stale bread and water" (p. 261).

Of special interest in this section is an exchange in which the Red One accuses Jung of anti-Semitism and we glimpse a psychological root of Jung's tone-deafness on this subject. His exacting, ungrounded introverted feeling has detected something he can't quite endorse in the souls of Jewish people he has met, but it does not occur to him, due to his lack of extraverted feeling, that the difference he is picking up might be the result of two millennia of unremitting prejudice rather than some doctrinal deficit. It is touching and brave that Jung knows that he ought to do something about this *puer* problem—that he needs this possible devil, the trickster extraverted feeling—to stand up to him.

Throughout *The Red Book*, we find Jung working on his feeling problem—perhaps that's even the reason he chose a red leather to cover the work.[8]

Reflecting on his encounter with the Red One, Jung writes, "Taking the devil seriously does not mean going over to his side" (p. 261). This is the toughness of work on integrating the shadow. It doesn't mean capitulating; it means coming to an understanding, thereby to accept your other standpoint.

And:

> Through my coming to terms with the devil, he accepted some of my seriousness and I accepted some of his joy. . . . It is always a risky thing to accept joy, but it leads us to life and its disappointments, from which the wholeness of our life becomes.
>
> *p. 261*

The unconscious changes when we engage with it, just as we change if we accept the unconscious figure. Jung shows himself ready to give up some of that *puer* unrealness, the above-it-all-ness, the untouched-ness. I find this interesting and moving.

Philemon and the dead

The name 'Philemon' comes from the Greek word for 'kiss,' so you would expect this character to represent a feeling function capable of a tender, loving attitude toward the feminine. The myth, told by Ovid, that shows him to be happily married, late in life, to his wife Baucis, was one of the most loved myths of late antiquity. Jupiter and Mercury came to earth dressed as traveling hobos. Every household that they visited refused to invite them in, but when they knocked at the door of the poor couple, Philemon and Baucis instantly made the gods feel at home: they were welcomed and given food and shelter. As a consequence, the couple was granted a long, happy old age.

When we actually hear Philemon speak in *The Red Book* however, and look at the picture Jung made of him, it is a surprise to see that he is not a feeling type. Though he is described as a magician, he does not come across as an evolved trickster figure. He is far too sincere and somber for that. His chief skill seems to lie in delineating and setting limits, as when he preaches wisely to the dead and makes them go away (pp. 346–353). There is more than a hint of the *senex* (severe old man) archetype in Philemon, even though it is clear that he is a source of wise introverted thinking for Jung. In a letter written in 1942 to Paul Schmitt, Jung contrasts Philemon and Baucis, the "hosts of the gods in a ruthless and godforsaken age" with "Faust the superman,"[9] yet in *The Red Book* we learn that, like Faust, Philemon has been schooled in dark magic (p. 312).

To me, it's at least as remarkable that Jung, so gifted at extraverted thinking, made a space in his psyche for Philemon as that Philemon made a space in his home for the gods. Even after he stopped working on *The Red Book*, Jung continued to make a place for Philemon in his life. On the wall of his retreat at Bollingen, where Jung wrote some of his most profound later work, there was a Latin inscription that can be translated as "The Sanctuary of Philemon, Faust's Repentance"[10] (p. 212, n. 264).

The most original thing in the Philemon material in *The Red Book* is the sense Jung has of what we owe the dead, a subject that he barely treats in other writings. According to what Jung learns from Philemon, what we owe the dead is no less than to take up the problems they left unsolved when their lives ended. In *Memories, Dreams, Reflections*, Jung explained that his own soul left him to provide the dead with enough animation that he could finally hear their complaints and realize what they had left unfinished in their lives. He confided to Aniela Jaffe: "From that time on, the dead have become ever more distinct for me as the voices of the Unanswered, Unresolved and Unredeemed" (Jung/Jaffe 1963, p. 191, p. 346, n. 78). (Compare Abraham and Torok's work (1994, pp. 165–205) on transgenerational "phantomatic haunting.")

One element that astonished Jung was the fact that the dead appeared to know no more than they had when they died. One would have assumed that, if still around, they would have attained greater knowledge since death. Instead, Jung discovered that the dead are waiting for answers from the living.

The dead, who appear as an itinerant troop in *The Red Book* and to whom Philemon speaks and preaches, are specifically identified as the Anabaptists (p. 294). One night, early in 1916, they crowd up to Jung's door, saying: "We have come back from Jerusalem where we did not find what we sought" (p. 346).

The radical Protestant Anabaptist movement arose in Zürich in 1525 at a time of widespread social and religious rebellion in many parts of central Europe that had sparked what has been called the Peasants' War. It has been estimated from a variety of sources that 100,000 people died in the revolts.[11] In many places, including Zürich, the Anabaptist movement was brutally suppressed and its founders executed; the movement found more tolerance in some other areas. The Anabaptists frequently spoke of the new Christian life they were trying to build as a 'new Jerusalem'—in fact, this was a name given to the commune they established in Münster, Germany. So when the Dead, who are Anabaptists in Jung's vision, state that they are back from Jerusalem where they didn't find what they sought, I understand them to mean that they were not able to solve the problem of making Christian community a practicality on earth.[12] Perhaps their movement was too idealistic (see Rothbard, 2010 for its history and the way it continues to attract the censure of political conservatives).

The Anabaptists' dilemma is an unexpected preoccupation for Jung to have in the middle of World War I. We have to ask why the Anabaptists' unresolved problem was particularly relevant to Jung. When Ezechiel, the spokesperson for the Anabaptists in

The Red Book, first presents himself to Jung, he tells Jung that Jung cannot join the Anabaptists' pilgrimage because he has a body, unlike the Anabaptists, who are dead. He also tells Jung that the dead still have no peace "although we died in true belief" (p. 294). They are compelled to wander ceaselessly from one holy place to another. I see them as representing an ungrounded, restless introverted sensation in Jung that has yet to verify the empirical ground of his own soul.

When Jung asks why, Ezechiel says: "It always seems to me as if we had not come to a proper end with life. . . . It seems to me that we forgot something important that should also have been lived." Jung asks, "And what was that?" Unexpectedly, Ezechiel turns the question back on Jung: "Would you happen to know?" Just then, Ezechiel "reaches out greedily and uncannily toward" Jung, "his eyes shining as if from inner heat." Jung is shocked into the answer. He cries: "Let go, daimon. You did not live your animal" (p. 294).

Shamdasani's note tells us that Jung asserted in 1918 "that Christianity had suppressed the animal element. . . . In 1939, he argued that the 'psychological sin' which Christ committed was that 'he did not live the animal side of himself'" (p. 294, n. 174).

Thus one of the things Jung believes he owes the dead is to conceive of a way to live Christianity that honors the physical part of man's nature. His selection of Salome as a soul figure, then, has represented a very important move in that direction. By overcoming his disdainful, moral repugnance toward Salome and taking her seriously, he begins to meet his obligation to the Christians of the past to include the body and the feminine and perhaps even the inevitability of evil.

In this way, *The Red Book* is in the Protestant tradition, a work of conscience trying to reform and redeem Christianity with the recognition that, as Stein (1993) puts it, "Conscience demands, ultimately that all the gods be served" (p. 9).[13] Through Salome, Jung returned the pagan tradition to Christianity without losing the latter's focused, ethical standpoint. As he puts it in the draft for what ultimately was entered in *The Red Book*, "Nothing of the law of love is abrogated, but much has been added to it" (2009, p. 300, n. 205).

As if he has grasped the inner significance of Jung's acceptance of the anima, Philemon insists in the fifth Sermon that sexuality and spirituality are of equal importance as principles of integration of the sacred[14] and even speaks of the need for an earthly father who is identified with the phallus (pp. 352–353), something Jung's own father could not integrate or live (Beebe, 1989, pp. 7–17).

That this work may have had a redemptive effective on Jung's father problem, thus beginning to repay what Jung owed his dead father, is suggested at the very end of *The Red Book*. Jung meets Philemon once more in a garden. He notices:

> when I sought to approach him, a blue shade came from the other side, and when Philemon saw him, he [Philemon] said, I find you in the garden, beloved. The sins of the world have conferred beauty upon your countenance. The suffering of the world has straightened your shape. You are truly a king.
>
> *p. 359*

The shade asks Philemon: "are you in my garden or am I in yours?" Philemon replies: "You are, Oh Master, in my garden" (p. 359).

In a footnote (p. 259, n. 153), Sonu Shamdasani tells us that "in Black Book 6 the shade is identified as Christ" but this is not explicitly asserted in *The Red Book*. I can feel another possible interpretation. Jung's father, though a Christian minister, lost his faith when Jung was a little boy, just around the time that Nietzsche's Zarathustra was expressing astonishment that there could be a person in the world who did not yet know that God is dead.[15] We know something of the effect his father's loss of faith had on C. G. Jung (Jung/Jaffe, 1963, pp. 91–95).

In *The Red Book* I sense Jung asking, "If my father lost his faith, what is faith? What is Christian faith? Not just my father lost his faith; what about all the church fathers?"

Gilles Quispel, a Dutch scholar of church history and specialist in Gnosticism, got to know Jung after World War II. He told me that in his entire life in the field he had never met anyone who was better read in church history—Patristics—than Jung. We get a taste of that at the beginning of *Psychological Types* where Jung writes about Tertullian and Origen, implicitly comparing his own experience of consciousness with theirs.

I would amplify the image of the blue shade in terms of the weakening of the Christian spirit over centuries and specifically link it to the collapsed Christian thinking of Jung's father, Paul Achilles Jung, now finally welcome within a more inclusive spiritual ecology.

Notes

1 The anniversary is also mentioned in Alexander (1990, p. 269, n. 3).
2 This is the most complete discussion I have found of this "myth-laden 'big' dream" (p. 68), including Jung's varied renderings of it, its strong Wagnerian influences, the psychoanalytic context, its openness to multiple interpretations, and its ethical context.
3 cf. Jung's (1989/2012, pp. 40–41) interpretation, for a 1925 seminar given in English, of a dream he had while working on *Wandlungen und Symbole der Libido*, known to his audience as *The Psychology of the Unconscious*, (Jung, 1916) in which Freud appears as an Austrian customs officer of whom a shadow figure explains, "He has been dead for thirty years, but he can't die properly." In the 1925 seminar, Jung says that this dead but lingering figure "stood for the Freudian theory." See also Jung/Jaffe, 1963, pp. 163–165.
4 Quoted in Shamdasani's introduction to Jung, 2009, pp. 201–202. This interview of Jung by Eliade, conducted at the 1952 Eranos Conference, can be found in McGuire & Hull, 1977, pp. 225–234.
5 cf. Jung, 1921/1971, ¶306.
6 By 1925, Jung knew Richard Wilhelm and had read his translation of the *I Ching*. "Just as rain relieves atmospheric tension, making all the buds burst open, so a time of deliverance from burdensome pressure has a liberating and stimulating effect on life" (Hexagram of Deliverance, Wilhelm/Baynes translation).
7 For someone whose superior function is introverted intuition, the inferior function will be extraverted sensation (von Franz, 1971/1998, pp. 41–44) and carried by the anima (Jung, 1989, p. 27). Jung's own typological analysis of Salome, in the 1925 Seminar on Analytical Psychology, is one with which I can't quite agree. He says,

As I am an introverted intellectual my anima contains feeling [that is] quite blind. In my case the anima contains not only Salome, but some of the serpent, which is sensation as well. As you remember, the real Salome was involved in incestuous relations with Herod, her stepfather, and it was because of the latter's love for her that she was able to get the head of John the Baptist.

Jung, 1989, p. 92

These sexual and physical associations make me feel that Salome is better interpreted typologically as extraverted sensation, countering the part of Christianity that is too one-sidedly spiritual (John the Baptist).

8 Jung (1960) says "red, the 'warm' colour, is used for feelings and emotions" (¶414, n. 122).

9 January 5, 1942, in Jung, C. G., *Letters, I*. pp. 309–310, cited by Shamdasani in the Introduction to *The Red Book*, n. 264.

10 This repentance is for Faust's irreverent murder of Philemon and his wife Baucis—the old couple who had been willing to entertain the gods without suspicion—in Goethe's drama.

11 Selected death tolls for wars, massacres and atrocities before the twentieth century, European wars and massacres to 1700: Peasants' war Germany 1524–1525. http://necrometrics.com/pre1700a.htm (Consulted 8.27.2015).

12 How they conceived what they were trying to do is collected in Liechty (1994).

13 See also Stein (1985).

14 Jung's exact words are, "The world of the Gods is made manifest in spirituality and in sexuality. The celestial ones appear in spirituality, the earthly in sexuality" (2009, p. 352). Shamdasani adds (p. 352, n. 112) that in the Analytical Psychology seminar of 1925 Jung states, "Sexuality and spirituality are pairs of opposites that need each other" (Jung, 1989/2012, p. 29).

15 Nietzsche had written that God was dead as early as *The Gay Science* (published 1882). *Thus Spoke Zarathustra* was written in 1883–1885 but was not widely disseminated until 1891.

References

Abraham, N. & Torok, M. (1994). Secrets and posterity: The theory of the transgenerational phantom. In *The shell and the kernel: Renewals of psychoanalysis, vol. 1*, part V. Chicago, IL: University of Chicago Press.

Alexander, I. (1990). *Personology: Method and content in personality assessment and psychobiography*. Durham, NC: Duke University Press.

Bagdad café (1987). (also known as *Out of Rosenheim*). Adlon, P. (Producer & Director). Germany: Filmverlag der Autoren. [Motion picture].

Bateson, G. (1972). Form, substance and difference. In *Steps to an ecology of mind* (pp. 454–471). New York: Random House.

Beebe, J. (Ed.) (1989). Editor's Introduction to C. G. Jung, *Aspects of the masculine*. Princeton, NJ: Princeton University Press.

Beebe, J. (1992). *Integrity in depth*. College Station, TX: Texas A & M University Press.

Beebe, J. (1997). The case of Joan: A classical approach. In P. Young-Eisendrath & T. Dawson, (Eds.). *The Cambridge companion to Jung* (pp. 188–197). Cambridge: Cambridge University Press.

Bennet, E. A. (1985). *Meetings with Jung*. Zürich: Daimon Verlag.

Ellenberger, H. (1970). *The discovery of the unconscious*. New York: Basic Books.

E.T. The extra-terrestrial (1982). Spielberg, S. (Producer & Director). U.S.: Universal Pictures. [Motion picture].

Fussell, P. (1974). *The Great War and modern memory*. New York: Sterling.

Henry Fool (1997). Hartley, H. (Producer & Director). USA: Sony Picture Classics. [Motion picture].

Hilgard, J. & Newman, M. (1959). Anniversaries in mental illness. *Psychiatry 22,* 113–131.

I Ching or book of changes, The. (1950/1967). (3rd Ed.) R. Wilhelm & C. Baynes (Trans.) Princeton, NJ: Princeton University Press.

Jung, C. G. (1916). *The psychology of the unconscious.* Beatrice Hinkle (Trans.) New York: Dodd, Mead and Company.

Jung, C. G. (1921/1971). Psychological types. In *Cw 6.*

Jung, C. G. (1959). Aion. In *Cw 9, ii.*

Jung, C. G. (1960). On the nature of the psyche. In *Cw 8* (pp. 159–234).

Jung, C. G. (1989/2012). *Analytical psychology: Notes on the seminar given in 1925.* W. McGuire (Ed.) Revised and updated by Sonu Shamdasani (Ed.) Princeton, NJ: Princeton University Press.

Jung, C. G. (2009). *The red book: Liber novus.* S. Shamdasani (Ed.) M. Kyburz, J. Peck, & S. Shamdasani (Trans.) New York: W.W. Norton.

Jung, C. G. & Jaffe, A. (1963). *Memories, dreams, reflections.* R. and C. Winston (Trans.) New York: Pantheon.

Kuryluk, E. (1987). *Salome and Judas in the cave of sex.* Evanston, IL: Northwestern University Press.

Kushner, H. (2006). *Overcoming life's disappointments.* New York: Anchor Books.

Liechty, D. (Ed. & Trans.) (1994). *Early Anabaptist spirituality: Selected writings.* New York: Paulist Press.

Mackenzie, D. (1912/2008). *Teutonic myth and legend.* BiblioBazaar.

McGuire, W. (Ed.) (1974). *The Freud/Jung letters.* Princeton, NJ: Princeton University Press.

McGuire, W. & Hull, R. F. C. (Eds.) (1977). *C. G. Jung speaking: Interviews and encounters.* Princeton, NJ: Princeton University Press.

Nietzsche, F. (1882/2001). *The gay science.* B. Williams (Ed.) J. Nauckhoff (Trans.) Cambridge: Cambridge University Press.

Nietzsche, F. (1885/2006). *Thus spoke Zarathustra.* A. Del Caro & R. Pippin (Eds.) A. Del Caro (Trans.) Cambridge: Cambridge University Press.

River runs through it, A (1992). Redford, R. (Producer & Director). USA: Columbia Pictures. [Motion picture].

Roosevelt, T. (1915). *America and the world war.* New York: Scribners.

Rosenberg, S. (1978). *Why Freud fainted.* Indianapolis, IN: Bobbs Merrill.

Rothbard, M. N. (2010). Messianic communism in the protestant reformation. Excerpted from his (2006) *Economic thought before Adam Smith.* Auburn, AL: Ludwig von Mises Institute.

Solomon, A. (2010). America enters World War I: Chicago does not go willingly into the great conflict. http://www.chicagotribune.com/news/nationworld/politics/chi-chicago days-americaenterswwi-story-story.html (Consulted 8.27.2015).

Stein, M. (1985). *Jung's treatment of Christianity.* Wilmette, IL: Chiron Publications.

Stein, M. (1993). *Solar conscience, lunar conscience.* Wilmette, IL: Chiron Publications.

von Franz, M.-L. (1971/1998). The inferior function. In M.-L. von Franz & J. Hillman, *Lectures on Jung's typology.* Woodstock, CT: Spring Publications.

Walker, S. (2002). *Jung and the Jungians on myth.* London: Routledge.

Wilde, O. (1891/1917). Salomé (in French). London: Methuen. Online at https://www. gutenberg.org/files/1339/1339-h/1339-h.htm (Consulted 8.2.2015).

12

PSYCHOLOGICAL TYPES IN FREUD AND JUNG

The organizing notion of psychological types was in the air when Freud and Jung met in person for the last time—at the Fourth International Psychoanalytic Congress in Munich on September 7–8, 1913.[1] Jung's Congress paper, "A Contribution to the Study of Psychological Types" (Jung, 1913/1971, ¶¶858–882), a way station on the path to his landmark 1921 book, grew out of his findings from the association test (Jung & Riklin, 1906/1973).[2] The paper that Freud presented, "The Disposition to Obsessional Neurosis: A Contribution to the Problem of the Choice of Neurosis" (1913/1958), drew on a typology that Freud had begun elaborating in "Character and Anal Eroticism" (1908/1959) and "A Special Type of Choice of Object Made by Men" (1910/1957). In that same year of 1913, Sandor Ferenczi published "Stages in the Development of the Sense of Reality" (1913/1952), offering a typology of personalities according to how the ego manages fantasies of omnipotence.

Not surprisingly, Jung's and Freud's are very different kinds of typologies. Jung's began as a typology of temperament and developed over a period of years into one of *consciousness*.[3] The core idea of Jung's typology is that there are four functions of consciousness—thinking, feeling, sensation, and intuition—each of which exists in two forms—extraverted and introverted, making a total of eight kinds of awareness. Freud's psychological typology is organized around unconscious fixation in, or regression to, the first three (infantile) stages of psychosexual development (Freud, 1905/1953)—oral, anal, and phallic—a set of ideas that he developed into a typology of *character* (Freud, 1916/1957).

The problems that Freud and Jung addressed in these papers were not original to them—nor were all of the constituent elements that made up their solutions. The originality of these master theorists lay more in how they approached the psychological puzzles that many were struggling to solve, taking bits and pieces out of the intellectual environment and braiding them together in fresh, generative ways.

In this chapter, I will point out commonalities as well as differences in the ways that Freud and Jung approached psychological types. I will argue that each man brought a type of consciousness to the work that was unusual for him, and will show that their remarkable insights in this area were made possible by the respectful way that each man engaged with the most vulnerable part of the unconscious for him—the anima. This aspect of personality, first described by Jung, who tended to speak of it in personified, muse-like terms as the 'feminine' side of a man, can be the mediatrix that, through sensitive moods that provoke deep reflection, inspires psychological creativity (see Hillman, 1972 and 1985). Jung's first statement of type theory, for instance, emerged in his final year of professional association with Freud, when the original mood of best friendship that had graced their initial collaboration had turned into a charged atmosphere of mutual suspicion, characterized by angry resentment and hostile projections—exactly the kind of interpersonal field that tends to appear between professional men when the anima of one or both has been disappointed by the failure of their efforts to establish a satisfactory working relationship.

Type theory: use and resistance

Jung's presentation at the 1913 Congress focused on the conceptual opposites of introversion and extraversion and proposed to use these opposites to explain the difference between Freud's psychology and Adler's. Jung's timing and choice of venue for giving such a paper cannot be called tactful. Alfred Adler and many of his supporters had broken with the Psychoanalytic Association two years previously. Now Jung, though still the Association's president, was no longer on speaking terms with Freud. He had also lost the confidence of many of the Association's members, who considered him an apostate (Makari, 2009, pp. 284–287). By proposing a superordinate theory that would subsume Freud's and Adler's psychologies as subcategories, Jung all but guaranteed not only an even greater personal rift with Freud and his followers but also that the very useful concept that there are different types of consciousness—different but equally healthy ways of being attentive or aware—would be shunned by psychoanalytic thinkers for a very long time.

Psychoanalysis has paid a price for its alienation from this contribution of Jung's, just as analytical psychology pays a price if it fails to take into account Freud's developmental theory. In my work with patients, I have been impressed again and again with the healing power of Jung's understanding of psychological types. To take a single example, consider the patient whose dominant consciousness is introverted feeling. This is a person whose choices in life are guided primarily by consulting his or her own deeply held values and who evaluates everything he or she encounters by measuring it against an inner ideal of appropriateness. Such a patient might, even today, be perceived by clinicians trained in the Freudian tradition as pathologically narcissistic or even borderline (Kernberg, 1975). Clients of this type, however, respond well to a therapy that begins by accepting their introverted feeling stance and that helps them to become conscious of their natural process—being guided in life primarily by their values—before calling their attention to the different, yet equally valid and equally limiting, processes of orientation and decision-making that people of other types naturally prefer. To know the theory of psychological types is to be better able to meet patients where they are, to appreciate individual differences, and to recognize the different types as valid starting places for adaptation. To be unaware of the types is to risk unnecessarily pathologizing what may actually be adaptive and healthy.

Reluctance to take on the theory of psychological types is, of course, not limited to the psychoanalytic community. Many Jungians find the eight types difficult to distinguish and recognize. A survey of Jungian analysts undertaken by Alfred Plaut (1972) found that less than half of those surveyed reported applying type theory in their practices even though most felt that they had figured out their own psychological type. In some cases, antipathy to type theory may be almost aesthetic in nature. The fluidity with which consciousness can shift and change has been beautifully described by Virginia Woolf (Woolf, 1929/1989, p. 110; cited in Lehrer, 2008, p. 169); some therapists may feel that trying to classify consciousness does violence to its quicksilver nature. Even James Hillman, who authored one of the best typologically informed papers in the Jungian literature, which was published alongside von Franz's essential essay on the inferior function (von Franz, 1971/1998; Hillman, 1971/1998), went on to produce a withering critique of type theory with the publication of his Eranos lecture, *Egalitarian Typologies versus the Perception of the Unique* (Hillman, 1980), which revealed that he found psychological types more limiting than useful. Nevertheless, the concepts that make up Jung's type theory have permeated world culture. The Myers–Briggs Type Indicator, an assessment tool based largely on Jung's theory, is said to be the most widely used personality assessment instrument in the world.

As Jung's work on types has been both celebrated and shunned, so has Freud's developmental typology. Malcolm Macmillan, a revisionist Freud scholar who meticulously reviewed Freud's original formulations and the evidence supporting them, concluded that "Psychoanalysis as a theory of personality has little to recommend it" (Macmillan, 1997, pp. 542–562). As a clinician, my own willingness to embrace Freud's stages has varied over the years. In working on the ideas that led to the present chapter, I have noticed myself bringing the developmental stages and the concepts of fixation and regression into greater consciousness, both in my own self-awareness and in my work with patients. Freud's canny observation that our libidinal energies are like a migrating people, who, having once occupied a place, not only never entirely leave it but also return to that place if they find they need to, rings true (Freud, 1917/1963, p. 340). Years ago, as a psychiatric resident, anxious about the level of my own psychosexual development, I had a dream in which I was taking a happy trip to sunny Genoa. That seemed to me, upon waking, to represent the prospect of an advance toward the "utopia of genitality" that Erik Erikson had postulated as the ideal resolution for a young adult's struggle between intimacy and isolation (1963, p. 266). I think I found it reassuring that maturity could be, not the cold vicarage I feared, but a warmly welcoming place where a preponderant 'gen' could include earlier parts of my development that were still stuck on 'o' and 'a.'

Freud's developmental typology is also useful outside the consulting room. For example, in analyzing the sort of talk-radio monologue in which the broadcast host serves up an indigestible diet of biting attack on political positions he or she cannot accept, it can be orienting to recall Freud's discussion of oral sadism (1933/1964, p. 99).

Jung's approach to types

The process through which Jung developed his theory of psychological types has become much more open to us with the publication of *The Red Book* (Jung, 2009) and his 1915–1916 correspondence on psychological types with Hans Schmid-Guisan (Jung & Schmid-Guisan, 2012).

Writing in *Psychological Perspectives,* Wayne Detloff has said, "To me it has been an astounding phenomenon that a single person could develop such an important dynamic typology with such exhaustive inclusiveness between his 38th and 45th years of life" (Detloff, 1972, p. 64). The characterization "exhaustive inclusiveness" is especially apt. Detloff is referring to Jung's surprisingly complete and textured descriptions of the eight types (Jung, 1921/1971, Chapter X)—descriptions that are both psychological and practical.

Three generations later, Howard Gardner, unaware of Jung's earlier work, published a theory of "multiple intelligences" in which he described seven kinds of intelligence that match up fairly well to six or seven of Jung's eight (1985). As Kirk Thompson pointed out, the one consciousness that Gardner didn't admit into his schema was intuition (1985, pp. 58–60), especially intuition in its introverted aspect. In *Psychological Types,* Jung defines introverted intuition as a consciousness that "peers behind the scenes, quickly perceiving the inner image." It "is directed to the inner object," including "to the contents of the unconscious" (1921/1971, ¶¶655–656).

Jung tells us that introverted intuition often conceives through fresh metaphorical images: "It holds fast to the vision, observing with the liveliest interest how the picture changes, unfolds, and finally fades" (1921/1971, ¶656). The introverted intuitive is "the mystical dreamer and seer on the one hand, the artist and the crank on the other" (¶661). "Had this type not existed there would have been no prophets in Israel" (¶658).

That Gardner overlooked introverted intuition in his survey of 'intelligences' is no chance occurrence. Of all eight kinds of consciousness, introverted intuition is the one that is most consistently devalued in contemporary Western culture. Jung himself did not immediately accept intuition as one of his types of consciousness (Shamdasani, 2003, pp. 70–72), but he eventually did so. It is also the kind of consciousness that Jung applied most often and consistently in *The Red Book*, where he repeatedly discovered its value to him in probing the "spirit of the depths" (2009, pp. 229ff.).

Cultural devaluation of introverted intuition may explain why extraverted and introverted thinking, rather than introverted intuition, predominate in Jung's published work prior to the explorations of *The Red Book*. During his years of leadership in the Psychoanalytic Association, Jung seems to have felt that his role as 'crown prince' of the movement required his giving primacy to thinking. Indeed, the term 'crown prince' had originated with Freud in a letter underlining his dismay that, just when he had invested Jung with such a status within the scientific kingdom of psychoanalysis, the latter had taken the occasion to emphasize a psychologically significant coincidence that lay clearly outside the realm of scientific explanation, the splitting apart of a bookcase in Freud's home (McGuire, 1974, p. 218). Breaking with psychoanalysis and entering into the active imagination discoveries recounted in *The Red Book* led Jung in his subsequent writings to embrace more fully the reality of the irrational. In so doing, he was disavowing an adaptation that had begun to feel false to him—one that had been chosen to suit the collective, rational, scientific climate of his day rather than his own intuitive glimpses of the irrational force of the unconscious, which he knew could not be explained as just the consequence of certain logically linked emotional developments of the kind Freud's theory was designed to identify. To be true to himself, Jung had to put his commitment to this kind of thinking to one side. And, from a typological standpoint, I believe this came naturally to Jung. As adept as Jung's thinking function was, I believe it was never more than an auxiliary function for him and that his inborn dominant function was introverted intuition. The necessity to sacrifice his excessive adaptation to the collective by ceasing to give primacy to thinking and turning instead to his natural introverted intuition is symbolized in Jung's dream of the assassination of crown prince Siegfried (Jung, 2009, pp. 241–242. See also Chapter 11 in this book, pp. 168–172).

Jung's engagement with the anima

While introverted intuition forms the conscious standpoint in *The Red Book,* the key *unconscious* standpoint and the guiding spirit of Jung's inner journey is represented by Salome, Jung's surprising soul figure, who motivates the journey and to whom Jung feels he must submit if he is to truly know himself. Salome is an embodiment of extraverted sensation consciousness, of which Jung would later write, "Objects are valued in so far as they excite sensations. . . . The sole criterion of their value is the intensity of the sensation produced by their objective qualities" (1921/1971, ¶605). Of the man whose dominant consciousness is extraverted sensation, Jung writes, "What comes from inside seems to him morbid and suspect. . . . Once he can get back to tangible reality in any form he can breathe again" (¶607).

Salome's extraverted sensation is that of an *inferior* function. As a personification of Jung's anima, Salome stands for a part of the psyche that is relatively unconscious and that is more notable for what he calls "incapacity" than for feats of mastery. Thus, Jung's Salome is blind, even though this is neither a part of the biblical story told in the Gospels of Mark and Matthew nor of the several treatments of Salome that appeared toward the end of the nineteenth century such as Oscar Wilde's 1891 play, which was made into an opera by Richard Strauss, and Jules Laforgue's "Salome," which appeared as one of his *Six Moral Tales* in 1886 (Dijkstra, 1986, pp. 379–401; Kuryluk, 1987, pp. 207–258). Especially as conceived at the beginning of the twentieth century, the character of Salome was undeniably petty, hysterical, and concrete in demanding the head of John the Baptist. A more admirable and heroic woman in the same situation might have demonstrated magnanimity, self-restraint, and an ability to resolve conflict through a symbolic, rather than grossly physical, gesture. In dialogue with his more competent conscious standpoint of introverted intuition the anima can be a source of wisdom, but her place in the psyche is also one of vulnerability and shame.

To put the conscious standpoint in regular communication with the inferior function, which may be symbolized by the anima in a man or by the animus in a woman, is to establish a *spine of integrity* within the personality (Beebe, 1992, pp. 102–108). In many cultures, integrity has been conceived in terms of verti-cality, as in the image of a person 'standing tall,' or in the verbal conception of 'moral uprightness' (p. 6). Instituting mutually respectful communication between the consciousness of greatest mastery (the dominant function) and that of greatest vulnerability (the inferior function), with each aware of the other's relative posi-tion is, by definition, to know one's greatest strength and weakness. In *The Red Book,* before Jung's relationship to the anima begins to develop, it is foreshadowed in the kinship tie between Elijah, the wise, far-seeing prophet—emblem of intro-verted intuition—and the blind Salome, whom he introduces without apology as his daughter. We meet this pair in front of a house with columns. In their vertical strength, the columns again suggest integrity.

The relation of the anima and the animus to the inferior function is important because the inferior function is how we access and are accessed by the uncon-scious, being, as von Franz puts it, "the door through which all the figures of the unconscious come" (1971/1998, p. 67). The unconscious is active in us from the beginning of life, but our ability to gradually realize its existence, to explore its constituent consciousnesses and complexes, depends on having a relationship with the anima or animus. Naturally, this can occur without being in analysis or know-ing the Jungian names and categories. It is a matter of recognizing and accepting in ourselves that part that is the most vulnerable, the most likely to cause us embar-rassment. In *The Red Book,* we learn only gradually the extent to which Salome is orchestrating Jung's encounters with the various personified forms of awareness.

One such consciousness, introverted sensation, is represented in *The Red Book* by the desperate horde of Anabaptists, ghosts from the sixteenth century, who invade Jung's space like an attack of indigestion, demanding his immediate help to find the peace they seek, which, rather concretely, they imagine to be located in a specific geographical space. They are drawn to Jung, seeking illumination from his intuition. Introverted sensation is as distant from Jung's native introverted intuitive consciousness as possible, so it should be no surprise that the home invasion of the

Anabaptists comes as the most difficult and challenging moment for Jung in the entire *Red Book*. He is only just able to satisfy the shadowy crowd and then only by relying heavily on another unconscious figure, Philemon, who speaks to the ghosts in his "Seven Sermons to the Dead" (Jung, 2009, pp. 294, 346–357).

The payoff from this impressive encounter is the startling degree to which introverted sensation consciousness informed the most lasting part of Jung's next major published work, the 1921 *Psychological Types*—and especially the most influential part of that book, his description of the eight functions of consciousness in Chapter X. Certainly there is introverted intuition involved in recognizing the archetypal patterns, and thinking—in both extraverted and introverted forms—helps to lay out the theory and articulate its subtle discriminations, but the genius of the work comes from how well-drawn the descriptions are. It is clear that Jung has precisely observed people, compared his impressions to his memories of other similar people, noting likenesses and differences, until the grouping of people into types according to their dominant consciousnesses could be satisfactorily achieved and each type accurately described. This is, by definition, the work of introverted sensation, which Emma Jung, herself an introverted sensation type, explained as being "like a highly sensitized photographic plate" (von Franz, 1971/1998, p. 34). Jung has said of this type, "he very quickly gets a clear picture and then withdraws so as not to be overwhelmed by the object. He has a mimosa-like quality and is hyper-sensitive" (1935–1936, May 8, 1936, lecture). Jung's descriptions of the types of consciousness are almost as strongly informed by introverted sensation as *The Red Book* is by introverted intuition.

Freud's relation to the anima

During his own self-analysis, Freud had a moment that seems similar to Jung's surprising encounter with the blind Salome. It comes in the famous dream of his self-dissection, a metaphor for self-analysis. The year of this dream is not certain, but is thought to be 1899 (Anzieu, 1986, p. 419). Here is Freud's account in *The Interpretation of Dreams:*

> My old professor Brücke must have given me some task to do, strangely enough it has to do with dissecting my own lower torso, pelvis, and legs, which I can see in front of me as though I were in the dissecting room, but without feeling the lack of these limbs from my body, nor finding it at all gruesome. Louise N. is standing by and is helping me with the work. The pelvis has been eviscerated; one moment one has a view of it from above, the next a view from below, merging into each other. Thick, flesh-coloured tubercles are to be seen (which while I am still dreaming make me think of haemorrhoids). Also, something lying over it, looking like crumpled silver paper, had to be carefully picked out. Then I was once again in possession of my legs and made my way through the city, but (out of tiredness) I took

a cab. To my astonishment the cab drove in through the gateway of a house which opened up to it and let it pass along a passage which twisted at the end and finally led out into the open again.

Finally, I wandered through changing landscapes with an Alpine guide who was carrying my things. He carried me for a stretch out of consideration for my weary legs. The ground was swampy; we walked along the edge; people were sitting on the ground, like Red Indians or Gypsies, among them a girl. Just beforehand I had been moving on the slippery ground unaided, constantly surprised that I could manage so well after the dissection. At last we came to a little wooden house with an open window at the end. The guide set me down there and laid two wooden planks, which were standing ready, on the windowsill so as to bridge the chasm that had to be crossed from the window. This really filled me with fear for my legs. However, instead of the crossing I was expecting, I saw two grown men lying on wooden benches along the walls of the hut, and something like two children asleep next to them. As if not the planks, but the children, were to make the crossing possible. I wake with thoughts full of terror.

1899/1999, pp. 292–293

With the considerable benefit of hindsight, I find it tempting to see this as a predictive dream of the entire psychoanalytic movement. I think the Alpine guide is Jung. The two boards that will serve as bridges in the next phase could represent the parallel traditions of psychoanalysis and analytical psychology. Despite his willingness, Freud himself would not be able to see through to completion the extraordinarily ambitious work he had begun. Instead he would have to depend on the 'children'— perhaps bridging figures such as Bion and Kohut, or even other psychologists who are yet to come.

What touch me about this dream are the hints I see in it of Freud's relation to the anima. My attention is drawn especially to the figure of Louise N., to the Red Indian or gipsy girl, and to the crumpled silver paper. Concerning Louise N. who is working alongside Freud in the dream, he writes that in real life she had called on him and asked him to lend her something to read. He offered her H. Rider Haggard's novel, *She,* which Jung would later cite as an example of the anima archetype in literature (1959/1977, ¶545).

Freud describes *She* as "a *strange* book, but full of hidden meaning." He recounts his interaction with Louise N.[4] about Haggard's book:

I explain to her, "the eternal-feminine, the immortality of our emotions—" Then she interrupts me: "I've read it. Haven't you anything of your own?"— "No, my own immortal works haven't been written yet." "Well, when can we expect what you call your latest insights," she asked rather sarcastically, "the ones you promise we too will find readable?" Now, when I come to think about it, I note that someone else is speaking through her to warn me, and I am silent. I think of the effort of self-conquest it is costing me to publish just my work on dreams, in which I am obliged to surrender so much of my innermost self.

1899/1999, p. 293

This real life encounter sounds like a dream! When Freud says he felt that "someone else was admonishing" him through Louise N., I think he means that her words gave voice to his own self-doubt. In the last sentence, we see the force of Freud's native introversion. He felt keenly the invasion of privacy associated with publication.

Jung and von Franz believed that Freud was an introverted feeling type (Jung, 1957/1976, p. 347; von Franz, 1971/1998, p. 61). This seems to me to fit the available evidence. For example, introverted feeling types tend to have very strong confidence in their own judgments and are very concerned with determining whether power is being misappropriated. Both characteristics match what we know of Freud.

In an introverted feeling type man, the anima carries an extraverted thinking consciousness. Extraverted thinking can be conceived as goal-oriented thinking that is intended to be shared with others. Louise N.'s queries about when Freud is going to get his ideas into print thus clearly reflect extraverted thinking values. I would hazard that Louise N. is a symbol in the dream of Freud's personal anima. And, despite her doubts, Freud obviously did, in good time, develop his creative extraverted thinking, succeeding rather spectacularly in getting his ideas into the world. *Mourning and Melancholia* would be an example of Freud's extraverted thinking at its best (Freud, 1917/1957). The logic unfolds with the assurance of a fine legal brief!

Since the Red Indian or gipsy girl is of another culture, she is more Other. Freud tells us that she comes from H. Rider Haggard's novel *Heart of the World,* which he also identifies as the source of the dream's wooden house (Freud, 1899/1999, p. 294). Probably this girl knows her way through wild country that has not yet been civilized in a European sense. A sure-footed guide, she may represent a more natural path to exploring the unconscious, in contradistinction to the unnatural method of dissection. In this sense, she seems a more Jungian figure, an image of the anima that can be trusted to lead in the darkness.

The silver paper that Freud finds covering the exposed pelvic organs in the course of his self-dissections may symbolize the archetypal feminine because silver is associated, in alchemy, with the feminine principle, *Luna*. I find it touching that Freud has the integrity to see and note the silver foil even if, in his biological frame of mind, he set it aside, as if it were no more than a cultural overlay.

Freud's waking associations to the silver foil are very interesting, however. In German, silver foil is *Stanniol,* and Freud reports that his association to the silver paper was to Stannius, the author of a dissertation on the nervous system of fish that Freud had admired in his youth. Freud tells us: "The first scientific task my teacher

[Brücke] gave me did actually involve the nervous system of a fish" (1899/1999, p. 263). Freud goes into this more deeply in his *Introductory Lectures on Psychoanalysis, Part III,* delivered in 1917 (1917/1963). Frank Sulloway, in *Freud: Biologist of the Mind,* explains that Freud was asked to examine some nerve cells that were present in the spinal cord of a fish. He found that some of the cells were of a type associated with lower vertebrates, leading to the theory that these cells were vestigial evidence of the fish's evolution from lower life forms. Freud recalled this laboratory finding when he found himself needing to explain why certain psychosexual developmental elements linger, leading eventually to his understanding of fixation and regression (Sulloway, 1979, p. 267).

Introverted thinking as a source of Freud's developmental theory

The idea that the libido would course forward and then loop back is a dazzling insight and not one that I would expect from extraverted thinking, which tends to simple, elegant explanations and shuns complexity. How then did the inevitable advances and regressions suffered in everyone's early development become Freud's vision of how different types of character emerge? Extraverted thinking would say that we develop according to a series of phases, but only *introverted thinking* would dig deep enough to find that development can not only get arrested, but that it can sometimes also take advantage of this arrest of a certain portion of the libido available to development to regress back to an earlier phase we thought we had outgrown. Freud's initial idea of a progression from oral to anal and finally phallic in the character of libido, all during early childhood, was able, through this more nuanced kind of thinking, to give way to recognition of a more complex and inclusive psychosexual organization beyond the infantile distinguished by "genital primacy" (Freud, 1905/1953). By that term, Freud implied the possibility of engaging one's own psychosexual developmental history with that of another in a truly loving intercourse. It is perhaps significant that the cells that Freud studied in Brücke's lab were concerned in more than one way with the posterior nerve roots of the fish's spinal cord, for Freud was to discover that they had not only given origin to the nerve fibers of these roots from their perch in the posterior horn of the gray matter of the spinal cord, but that some of these cells were also present outside the gray matter, as they had migrated from the spinal cord along the roots of the nerves. In fact, as Freud commented years later, "in this small fish the whole path of their migration was demonstrated by the cells that had remained behind" as they progressed (1917/1963, p. 340). Their very progress could not have been tracked by the researcher, in other words, if he had not been allowed to witness where the cells had formerly been. By giving his student an opportunity to see the way development itself is revealed, "old Brücke," like a good father sharing his passion, had invited Freud to think outside the box.

Typology as an embrace of otherness

Introverted thinking seems to me to be precisely as distant from Freud's dominant consciousness as introverted sensation was from Jung's. Relatively unconscious functions generally cannot operate well without the anima. If I read the dream of self-dissection right, I believe that it is Freud's including, recognizing, and respecting the anima that leads to him being able to access, or be accessed by, the incisive introverted thinking that the theory of fixation and regression embodies. The difference from Jung is that Freud's introverted thinking operates as a *rational* function working to establish the root dynamics of developments in the psyche,[5] whereas Jung's introverted sensation is one that he describes in *Psychological Types* as irrational (1921/1971, ¶650). Jung's introverted sensation, however, was similarly attentive to the varieties of otherness. Introverted sensation concerns itself not with an interpretative take on the deep meaning of phenomena, but with the specifics of their reality. As previously noted, I believe it was Jung's introverted sensation— operating as an extension to his extraverted sensation notion of the reality of the psyche—that enabled him to notice and verify all eight types of consciousness with the level of specificity we find in *Psychological Types*. This conscientiousness reflects the religious attitude with which Jung approached the contents of the psyche at this stage of his work as an analyst.[6]

Comparing the evolution of their type models, we might, therefore, say that Freud was inspired to define the paradoxes of unconscious development and Jung to account for the consciousnesses at play within psychological life. Both practiced introspection to let the psyche tell them who they were and, guided by the anima, opened doors to understanding the peculiarities of others. Their typologies have remained uncannily relevant for many of us, seeming to emerge from the psyche itself.

Notes

1 I want to thank Steven Zemmelman, organizer of the San Francisco Jung Institute's Freud–Jung Conference in November 2010, for suggesting the idea of this chapter by pointing out to me that, like Jungians, Freudians also employ typology.

2 The history of Jung's interest in psychological types is traced in the Introduction to *The Question of Psychological Types: The Correspondence of C. G. Jung and Hans Schmid-Guisan 1915–1916* (2012, pp. 1–32).

3 That is, the consciousness that appears, in different forms, within the stream of mentation that courses through both our conscious and unconscious lives and can be heard and sorted out in psychotherapy. Jung makes this clearest in his Foreword to the Argentine edition of *Psychological Types* (Jung 1936/1971, pp. xiv–xv).

4 Anzieu believes that the "Louise N." who is present to assist Freud during the self-dissection may have actually been his sister-in-law (and likely secret lover) Minna Bernays, "with whom Freud increasingly discussed himself and his work" (Anzieu, 1986, p. 427). This suggestion is strengthened by the fact that, at the time to which Anzieu assigns the dream, May 1899 (on the basis of a letter written to Fliess near the end of that month),

Freud was reading *Ilios* by Heinrich Schliemann, the great archeologist's autobiographical account of his lifelong wish to discover Troy, which as a child Schliemann had confided to two little girl playmates, Minna and Louise (Lippman, 2009). Freud believed Schliemann's happiness, many years later, upon actually discovering the site of Troy, was based on the fulfillment of a childhood wish, and he was in a similar exuberant state at the time of this dream, which seemed to confirm to him that his own wish to discover the secret of the unconscious through psychoanalytic understanding could prevail, if not in his lifetime, at least eventually.

5 Understanding the *value* of such thinking was the achievement of Freud's dominant introverted feeling, and what guided him to regard what he was conceptualizing as a scientific breakthrough. The scientific attitude, according to Henderson (1984, pp. 76–77), is a subset of the philosophic attitude, which was the cultural attitude that enabled Freud to construct psychoanalytic theory with an expectation that it might speak to his culture. The philosophic attitude is formed by bringing together introverted feeling and introverted thinking (see Chapter 6).

6 In Chapter 6 of this book, I discuss how a psychologically minded person can construct a religious attitude by stretching introverted intuition to cooperate with introverted sensation, and how such an attitude became particularly evident in Jung after the experimental links he forged with inner figures such as the Anabaptists in the imaginations recorded in his Red Book.

References

Anzieu, D. (1986). *Freud's self-analysis*. Madison, CT: International Universities Press.

Beebe, J. (1992). *Integrity in depth*. College Station, TX: Texas A & M University Press.

Detloff, W. (1972). Psychological types: Fifty years after. *Psychological Perspectives* 3(1), 62–73.

Dijkstra, B. (1986). *Idols of perversity: Fantasies of feminine evil in fin-de-siècle culture*. New York: Oxford University Press.

Erikson, E. (1963). *Childhood and society*. Second ed. New York: W. W. Norton.

Ferenczi, S. (1913/1952). Stages in the development of the sense of reality. In S. Ferenczi (Ed.) E. Jones (Trans.) *First contributions to psycho-analysis* (pp. 213–239). New York: Brunner/Maxel.

Freud, S. (1899/1999). *The interpretation of dreams*. J. Crick (Trans.) Oxford: Oxford University Press.

Freud, S. (1905/1953). Three essays on the theory of sexuality. In J. Strachey (Ed. and Trans.) *The standard edition of the complete psychological works of Sigmund Freud, Vol. VII* (pp. 123–246). London: Hogarth Press.

Freud, S. (1908/1959). Character and anal eroticism. In J. Strachey (Ed. and Trans.) *The standard edition of the complete psychological works of Sigmund Freud, Vol. IX* (pp. 167–175). London: Hogarth Press.

Freud, S. (1910/1957). A special type of choice of object made by men (contributions to the psychology of love I). In J. Strachey (Ed. and Trans.) *The standard edition of the complete psychological works of Sigmund Freud, Vol. XI* (pp. 163–175). London: Hogarth Press.

Freud, S. (1913/1958). The disposition to obsessional neurosis. In J. Strachey (Ed. and Trans.) *The standard edition of the complete psychological works of Sigmund Freud, Vol. XII* (pp. 311–326). London: Hogarth Press.

Freud, S. (1916/1957). Some character types met with in psychoanalytic work. In J. Strachey (Ed. and Trans.) *The standard edition of the complete psychological works of Sigmund Freud, Vol. XIV* (pp. 309–333). London: Hogarth Press.

Freud, S. (1917/1957). Mourning and melancholia. In J. Strachey (Ed. and Trans.) *The standard edition of the complete psychological works of Sigmund Freud, Vol. XIV* (pp. 237–258). London: Hogarth Press.

Freud, S. (1917/1963). Introductory lectures on psycho-analysis (Part III). In J. Strachey (Ed. and Trans.) *The standard edition of the complete psychological works of Sigmund Freud, Vol. XVI* (pp. 241–463). London: Hogarth Press.

Freud, S. (1933/1964). New introductory lectures on psycho-analysis. In J. Strachey (Ed. and Trans.) *The standard edition of the complete psychological works of Sigmund Freud, Vol. XXII*, (pp. 1–182). London: Hogarth Press.

Gardner, H. (1985). *Frames of mind: The theory of multiple intelligences.* New York: Basic Books.

Henderson, J. L. (1984). *Cultural attitudes in psychological perspective.* Toronto: Inner City Books.

Hillman, J. (1971/1998). The feeling function. In M.-L. von Franz & J. Hillman, *Lectures on Jung's typology* (pp. 91–179). Woodstock, CT: Spring Publications.

Hillman, J. (1972). On psychological creativity. In *The myth of analysis: Three essays in archetypal psychology* (pp. 9–113). Evanston, IL: Northwestern University Press.

Hillman, J. (1980). *Egalitarian typologies versus the perception of the unique.* Dallas, TX: Spring Publications.

Hillman, J. (1985). *Anima: An anatomy of a personified notion.* Dallas, TX: Spring Publications.

Jung, C. G. (1913/1971). A contribution to the study of psychological types. In *Cw 6* (pp. 499–509).

Jung, C. G. (1921/1971). Psychological types. In *Cw 6*.

Jung, C. G. (1935–1936). *Notes of Jung's 1935/1936 ETH lectures.* Privately circulated; definitive edition in preparation.

Jung, C. G. (1936/1971). Foreword to the Argentine edition. In *Cw 6* (pp. xiv–xv).

Jung, C. G. (1957/1976). Letter to Ernst Hanhart, 18 February 1957. In G. Adler (Ed.) *C. G. Jung letters, Vol. 2* (pp. 346–348). Princeton, NJ: Princeton University Press.

Jung, C. G. (1959/1977). Foreword to Brunner: Die Anima als Schicksalsproblem des Mannes. In *Cw 18* (pp. 543–547).

Jung, C. G. (2009). *The red book: Liber novus.* S. Shamdasani (Ed.) M. Kyburz, J. Peck & S. Shamdasani (Trans.) New York: W.W. Norton.

Jung, C. G. & Riklin, F. (1906/1973). The associations of normal subjects. In *Cw 2* (pp. 3–196).

Jung C. G. & Schmid-Guisan, H. (2012). J. Beebe & E. Falzeder (Eds.) *The question of psychological types: The correspondence of C. G. Jung and Hans Schmid-Guisan 1915–1916.* Princeton, NJ: Princeton University Press.

Kernberg, O. (1975). *Borderline conditions and pathological narcissism.* New York: Jason Aronson.

Kuryluk, E. (1987). *Salome and Judas in the cave of sex.* Evanston, IL: Northwestern University Press.

Lehrer, J. (2008). *Proust was a neuroscientist.* Boston, MA: Houghton Mifflin.

Lippman, R. L. (2009). Freud, Minna, and Schliemann's Ilios. International Psychoanalysis website, posted November 18, 2009, http://internationalpsychoanalysis.net/2009/11/18/freud-minna-and-schliemanns-ilios-by-robert-l-lippman (Consulted 10.1.2011).

Macmillan, M. (1997). *Freud evaluated.* Cambridge, MA: MIT Press.

McGuire, W. (Ed.) (1974). *The Freud/Jung letters: The correspondence between Sigmund Freud and C. G. Jung* R. Mannheim & R. F. C. Hull (Trans.). Princeton, NJ: Princeton University Press.

Makari, G. (2009). *Revolution in mind: The creation of psychoanalysis.* New York: Harper Collins.

Plaut, A. (1972). Analytical psychologists and psychological types: Comments on replies to a survey. *Journal of Analytical Psychology* 17(2), 137–151.

Shamdasani, S. (2003). *Jung and the making of modern psychology: The dream of a science.* Cambridge: Cambridge University Press.

Sulloway, F. (1979). *Freud: Biologist of the mind.* New York: Basic Books.

Thompson, K. (1985). Cognitive and analytical psychology, review of Howard Gardner's *Frames of mind: The theory of multiple intelligences. The San Francisco Jung Institute Library Journal* 5(4), 40–64.

von Franz, M.-L. (1971/1998). The inferior function. In M.-L. von Franz & J. Hillman, *Lectures on Jung's typology* (pp. 3–88). Woodstock, CT: Spring Publications.

Woolf, V. (1929/1989). *A room of one's own.* New York: Harvest/HBJ.

PART IV

Applications of type

13

DIFFICULTIES IN THE RECOGNITION OF PSYCHOLOGICAL TYPE

Joseph Wheelwright

Jo Wheelwright, the analyst who in the years between 1940 and 1980 did so much to keep Jung's theory of psychological types alive as a clinically relevant modality of interpretation, liked to say that the ability to recognize psychological type is a 'knack.' Jo was, as he explained in his type-literate way, an "extraverted intuitive-feeling type" (Wheelwright, 1982, p. 56), which in his case meant an uncanny ability to enter into the minds of others and to know how they were feeling. His expressions of intuitive compassion, at a time when the term 'emotional intelligence' had not yet come into common usage, were unusual and impressive. To cite one example, Jo arranged for a woman colleague who was battling alcoholism to receive a bouquet of flowers once a week. The bouquets stopped arriving only after the woman had completed her first full year of recovery.

Jo had been analyzed by Jung. He was a founder of the Jung Institute of San Francisco, where I was trained. In the late 1970s, when I was a young, newly certified Jungian analyst, Jo was already in his seventies. He had been my teacher and was, additionally, a former President of the International Association for Analytical Psychology.

These differences in our experience did not stop me from arguing with Jo about type theory. We especially disagreed about the attitude of the auxiliary function under normal type development. From my own observation and from leaning on the research and writings of Isabel Briggs Myers, I was convinced that the auxiliary function normally takes the opposite attitude from the dominant. If the dominant is extraverted, the auxiliary is introverted and vice versa. From *his* observations, and perhaps influenced by what he had gathered of Jung's view, Jo was certain that the dominant, auxiliary, and tertiary shared the same attitude, counterbalanced only by the fourth, or inferior, function. Jo cited his own psychological type as evidence.

To arrive at his type, Jo assumed (1) that he was an extravert (no one who knew him doubted this), (2) that his leading consciousness—what Jung would have called his "superior function of consciousness"—was 'intuition,' and (3) that his auxiliary function was feeling. Jo concluded he was pairing 'extraverted intuition' with 'extraverted feeling' to achieve the extraordinary feats of empathy for which he was noted. But it seemed to me that Jo was pairing auxiliary 'introverted feeling' (which remembered how certain categories of experience tended to feel deep inside) with his dominant 'extraverted intuition' (which latched onto the new thing on which the individual with whom Jo was empathizing was staking her or his future). Jo always insisted that his feeling was extraverted, arguing against what the MBTI might have assumed about him, that there was "not a shred of evidence" that he had auxiliary introverted feeling. There is a recording of a seminar we shared with Jo's wife, Jane, in which I patiently explain the theoretical basis of my competing conclusion while Jo thunders back, until Jane finally shouts to me, "Will you stop it?!"

This argument about the typological structure of the psyche in general and about Jo Wheelwright's type in particular reflects the confusion Jungian clinicians often experience when trying to use type theory, despite the extensive groundwork laid out by Jung (1921/1971) in *Psychological Types* and by Isabel Briggs Myers (1980) in *Gifts Differing* and the later clarifications in both Jungian and MBTI circles that I have summarized in Chapter 10. To use the theory with precision, one has to be able not only to (1) recognize and accurately name the main 'functions' that a person is using to express his or her consciousness (thinking, feeling, intuition, and sensation), but also to (2) figure out which of the two functions that are likely being most often used is primary and which secondary—and beyond that to (3) make clear the 'attitude' with which each function is being deployed. (The choices Jung and Myers give us here are only two, extraverted and introverted, and it is Myers's view, and my own, that if the primary function is extraverted then the auxiliary will be introverted, and vice versa. This natural alternation of extraversion and introversion in our functions of consciousness is, by my observation, very adaptive: it keeps us from becoming too one-sided.)

Even those who recognized both Jo Wheelwright's intuition and his feeling (and there were many who could only see one or the other of these functions when engaged by him) did not always know what to call them (some thought Jo's extraverted intuition was simply intrusiveness, or narcissism), and few could figure out which of these functions was primary and which secondary (most people assumed that he had 'extraverted feeling' as his main modus operandi, not realizing, I believe, that they were conflating the extraversion of his superior function (intuition) with the availability or readiness of his auxiliary function (introverted feeling). This kind of conflation of the two leading functions into one—comprising the attitude of the dominant and the function of the auxiliary—is a very easy mistake to make in attempting type diagnosis.

John Beebe

I hasten to point out that my need to define type so sharply in the story I am telling ought not be promoted as a value without my admitting that my thinking function has a need to define type precisely, pulling away from the person and withdrawing into an ideal model in my mind of how a person's type can be parsed. This is so evident in me that it would be easy for the reader to conclude that I have introverted thinking as my leading function. But, no, I would argue, extraverted intuition is my leading function, and introverted thinking my auxiliary. Notice the strange inner confidence in my own thinking that led me to believe I had a right to type Jo Wheelwright at all. Also notice, though, the way this chapter begins, jumping right into the middle of the type muddle. That is extraverted intuition; it has a certain nervy urgency. The chapter starts to bog down, however, as soon as I move to specify Jo's type and my own precisely in my thinking way, because then I am writing as if consulting a model of the mind that is particular to me, one not easily accessible to the reader who doesn't already know this model. That means the reader has to ferret out the thinking in the background that is informing me to be able to follow my argument. Yet if the same reader consults his or her own experience of reading this chapter so far, the evidence for making a type assessment of its author is already at hand.

To check the assessment that this author is using extraverted intuition and introverted thinking, the reader may consider that the feeling aspect of the chapter is not its strong point. Have I considered how Jo Wheelwright *felt* about the conclusion he had reached about his type—*and* that, as he would have put it, "his thinkings" might "be hurt" by an analysis that contradicted his own? In MBTI certification training, practitioners are taught that it is *unethical* to assert what someone's type is in contradiction to what the person feels it is. It is a core feeling value in MBTI facilitation that each person should be the final judge of who they fundamentally are, including what their type is. The strength of this tradition in MBTI may owe something to Isabel Briggs Myers' own dominant function—introverted feeling.

In the case of my argument about type theory with Jo, he had as a teacher asserted his own type as evidence for his view, so, co-teaching in the same class, I felt logically justified in pushing back at him with my own understanding of his type. The reader may decide, however, that this could have been handled a little more gracefully had my own feeling function been better developed. The attentive reader may also have noticed that, as I have recounted the story of the argument between Jo and me, it has sometimes been hard to be sure what I as author feel about the events I'm narrating. In fact, I developed quite a headache that day, butting horns with Jo and Jane Wheelwright, who were not only formidable opponents but like parents to me.

Meanwhile, on the sensation front, the reader will notice that I have produced very few facts to support my assertion that Jo's auxiliary feeling was introverted. The overall tenor of the chapter so far, despite the personal example, is abstract rather than concrete and its ambition is more theoretical than diagnostic.

It is therefore not hard to see, if you simply consult your experience while reading this chapter, that its author does not particularly emphasize feeling, and that he exhibits even less sensation. And, if you are already fairly familiar with Jungian type theory, you may find the pattern of my consciousness that is emerging to be consistent with the view that when thinking is the second of the two leading functions, feeling (its opposite on the same axis of 'rational' functions) will be tertiary, and that, when intuition leads, sensation (intuition's opposite on the axis of 'irrational' functions) is going to be the inferior function. Knowing this enables us to map out the type of the author of this chapter—that is, my type—as Jung might have, by starting with a vertical straight line, which we can label at its top intuition and at its bottom sensation and next by crossing it with a horizontal line to define an axis at right angles to this spine. We will then label this horizontal axis's leftmost extent 'thinking' and its rightmost 'feeling.' The stick diagram that has resulted can then be labeled 'John Beebe's type profile.' It is meant to convey this author, for the purpose of typing him, visualized as if facing the reader, arms spread apart with his right hand to the viewer's left and his left hand to the viewer's right, and his head, trunk and legs all lined up to suggest an upright spine.

Value of the model

Why would anyone want to turn himself into a diagram? If such model-making is introverted thinking (a function which we might define as the need to make experience conform to a thinking model held and checked within for 'internal' consistency), possibly the answer to this question is found by saying: "This is what introverted thinking likes to do!" James Hillman has pointed out that the very word 'function' comes from a Sanskrit root *bhunj,* which means 'to enjoy,' and from which his own introverted thinking draws the conclusion that "The exercise and performance of a function is something to enjoy, as a pleasant or healthy activity, as the operation of one's powers in any sphere of action" (Hillman, 1971/1998, p. 91). In my case, it is true that I enjoy typing consciousness and fitting it into a thinking model.

But I am not performing this exercise in a vacuum, just for myself. It is my way of teaching, of conveying, even of trying to *take care of* the reader, who I imagine is reading this chapter in hopes of understanding how to use type in an analytic or type assessment practice. My auxiliary function, introverted thinking, is actually trying to take care of you as you read, by getting you to draw the stick figure of me so that you can visualize both the type theory and the man who is explaining it to you in the typological terms I have found most helpful. Whether you *feel* taken care of, and whether your unclarity about type is actually lessened by this instruction, is of course a result of how you receive me, which depends in part on your own typology. But I can count on your having at least some experience of me while reading this chapter, and it's on that that (as a theorist of how type might most profitably be assessed) I want you to build your own sense of my type, just as you would watching and listening to a patient or client presenting himself to you.

Parental energy of the auxiliary function

Elsewhere (see Chapter 3), I have argued that, regardless of an individual's psychological type, there is a presiding genius associated with each of the ranked 'positions' of our typology—superior, auxiliary, tertiary, and inferior—in Jung's original four-function model of consciousness. For each position, an archetype flavors the expression of the function in that place. (Although it is beyond the scope of this particular chapter, I have also identified archetypes associated with the four functions that are in shadow.) It was my discovery that the auxiliary function is used as if parentally—as a way of taking care of others. (Again, I am focusing on the individual's intent when using a particular type of consciousness.) It follows that, when making a type assessment, we need to take into account the archetypal stance that accompanies the deployment of a particular function. If you can experience me as at least trying to take care of you using an intricate, even private, logic, based on my love of my own particular version of type theory, then you can begin to see how my introverted thinking is auxiliary, because that's what an auxiliary function aims at, taking care of another.

We can learn a lot by observing how someone takes care of someone else. Following a professional meeting, Jo Wheelwright was once in a hotel bar leading some other colleagues in an informal sing-along when the woman playing the piano realized her menstrual period had suddenly come. She stopped playing, got up gracefully and walked to the bathroom, at which point the pool of blood that had been hidden by her skirt was evident on the piano bench. The moment was naturally uncomfortable for all present: everyone knew what had happened, but no one knew what to say or do. Wordlessly, Jo went over to the bar, picked up some paper napkins and used them to wipe off the bench. Then he sat down and began playing the piano so the sing-along could continue. When the woman reappeared ten minutes later, she was able to resume playing. I believe Jo used his introverted feeling to fully realize how humiliating such an experience might be for the woman and how helpless everyone else might feel about how to act, and he simply concentrated on quietly removing the thing that was producing the embarrassment: the blood on the bench. He himself would likely have read his action as an extraverted feeling one, and he would not have been alone in drawing that conclusion. I think it is clear that it was just as much a parental gesture, one that involved using his authority as a senior analyst to make the caretaking move of cleaning up a junior colleague's mess in his exquisitely calibrated feeling way. I cannot imagine approaching the typology of that story, whether as an example of extraverted or introverted feeling, without also looking at the fatherly way the consciousness he was using was being deployed. And I doubt that those present could have experienced the gesture, though involving the sensation function (wiping up the blood), as motivated by anything other than a profound level of feeling.

To help the reader understand why, in recounting this story, I experience Jo's fatherly, auxiliary feeling as introverted, I will begin by pointing out how few words he expressed in these feeling interactions. Jo was a man who talked a great deal, but in sending weekly bouquets to the colleague recovering from alcoholism and easing the transition for the woman at the piano, he used no words at all. Wordless expression is a common feature of introverted feeling. It is more interested in solving an underlying feeling problem than in making communications to address people's expressions of discomfort triggered by the problem. Extraverted feeling, by contrast, tends to be more communicative, even chatty, using a stream of reassuring words to put people at ease. I would say that Jo was a very fatherly man, whose caretaking took the form of a keen, authoritative empathy that didn't need to express itself in words.

Another marker of introverted feeling is that, like any introverted function, it tends to be more thoroughly original and thus to appear 'quirkier' than its extraverted sibling. Jo's feeling interventions were unusual—they were never quite what one would expect. In fact, in contrast to extraverted feeling, Jo's feeling expressions tended first to make people slightly uncomfortable before he proceeded to win them over by the bell-like purity of his caring. For example, in a building where he and several of the senior San Francisco analysts had offices, Jo would frequently alarm new patients waiting to see other analysts by ducking into the waiting room through the open window, unfolding himself, and striking up a conversation. I don't think this is a behavior that extraverted feeling, with its unyielding concern for putting people at ease, would engage in. Jo did it regularly, though, and ended by charming, with his originality, gentlemanliness, and unadorned sincerity of feeling, the surprised patients. Extraverted feeling can be charming, but not usually, I would assert, through originality and rough-edged sincerity.

Still another clue to the nature of Jo's feeling function was its readiness to appraise others. Here is an example: A young man in whom Jo had begun to take a fatherly interest confided to Jo that he had recently entered analysis with a member of our Institute. Jo asked the young man if he would mind revealing his analyst's name. Upon hearing the name, Jo burst out loudly, "Thank God!" He did not comment further and the conversation moved on to other subjects. The young man, who recently told me the anecdote, remarked that he was surprised and touched to find that Jo cared so much that he have an analyst who could help him.

Had Jo's feeling been mainly of the extraverted variety, I would assert that he probably would not have taken the risk of asking the young man the name of his analyst since this violated a cultural norm of our Institute and could have elicited an angry refusal. If Jo had been focused on extraverted feeling, I think he also would have taken more care to keep the young man from drawing the conclusion that Jo considered some Institute analysts to be unsuitable or unhelpful—a view that, if it became known, would certainly not have fostered democratic harmony within the community of analysts.

Heroic energy of the dominant function

In contrast to the auxiliary function, the dominant or 'superior' function is less involved in the care of others and more in the assertion of self. Jung's discussion of the archetypal motif of the night-sea journey of the hero in *Symbols of*

Transformation (1952/1967, ¶¶308–312) provides a beautiful model for the way a heroic introverted intuition approaches the problem of relating to the unconscious. In asserting this vision of a consciously irrational ego (i.e. an intuitive type), he sacrificed his caretaking role with regard to Freudian psychology, which was the very basis on which Freud had anointed him his 'crown prince.' He was ever after accused by Freud of abandoning the scientific study of the unconscious, which for Freud could only be accomplished rationally, that is (to use Jung's later terminology) through a dialectic of thinking and feeling.

In an essay completed shortly before his death, Jung described how the need to assert his own more intuition-and-sensation-based (and thus in his own language for these functions, "irrational") standpoint developed out of the unconscious itself. He recounts a dream that he shared with Freud when the two men were on their way to America to a conference at Clark University at which many leading psychologists, including William James, would be present. Freud expected Jung to help him sell the theory of psychoanalysis to the American psychologists. In the dream, Jung encountered for the first time his own house, which mirrored through its furnishings and contents not only his intellectual history and interests but also a multilayered model of the psyche. Discussing the dream with Freud, he tells us, he had the "sudden and most unexpected insight that my dream meant myself, *my* life and *my* world, my whole reality as against a theoretical structure erected by another. . . . It was not Freud's dream, it was mine; and suddenly I understood in a flash what my dream meant" (Jung, 1961/1980, ¶490).

One could say that in response to this dream Jung's identity emerged, and that his identity was expressed through a rather characteristic burst of introverted intuition. In contrast to the type designation of introverted thinking given Jung by many Jungians, including occasionally Jung himself, I myself read Jung as an introverted intuitive type, with extraverted thinking his auxiliary function. What is important here is to note that, in the way he approaches the dream he tried to share with Freud, Jung asserts his intuition at the moment he sees it as presenting his 'own' standpoint. There is narcissism in this as well as a certain heroic combativeness. He is emphatically *not* taking care of Freud, as he does in the more 'rational' writings he was publishing at the time of the dream, where he uses extraverted thinking to argue for the validity of psychoanalysis. Jung's dream, and the way he interprets it, is compensatory to letting himself be used in this way. The dream fosters the emergence of an extreme self-assertion carried by the intuitive function, which (at that moment of insight at least) became the superior function for Jung.

With a patient in the therapeutic situation, we often have to distinguish between the way the patient asserts self and the way the patient takes care of another. This is not so hard to do because in the analytic situation the 'other' will usually be the analyst. There is something heroic about self-assertion (it should be noted that many patients have a considerable difficulty asserting themselves with anything like the definiteness Jung describes in taking ownership of his dream), and there is something parental about taking care of the other. The analyst may want to note the ways the patient is parental in the transference, and not just the ways the patient is infantile. (Developing Winnicott's (1987) notion of the analyst's way of 'holding' the patient throughout an analysis, contemporary relational psychoanalysts have implied that the patient holds the analyst during treatment quite as much the analyst holds the patient [Samuels, 2008, personal communication] and of course there are wide variations both in patients' capacities to do this and in the ways they do this, into which both the strength and the typology of the patient's auxiliary function figures.) This distinction helps us to differentiate the patient's (heroic) dominant function from his or her (parental, caretaking) auxiliary function, and that can be an enormous help in establishing a reliable type diagnosis.

Recognizing the eight function-attitudes

Although locating the 'position' of a function of consciousness is critical in the assessment of type, it is of little help if one does not also know how to recognize and distinguish the different types of consciousness (eight in all) that can appear in particular positions such as 'superior' and 'auxiliary.' (These two do not exhaust the positions in which a type of consciousness may appear, but I am concentrating on them because they are the most frequent to manifest.) One has, in other words, to be able to recognize, and tell the difference, between introverted thinking, introverted feeling, introverted sensation, introverted intuition, and extraverted thinking, extraverted feeling, extraverted sensation, and extraverted intuition. Learning to do this requires conscious practice. It is not unlike the way one learns how to read music. Unfortunately, we don't have a mnemonic song like "Do-Re-Mi," which Mary Martin, and later Julie Andrews, sang in *The Sound of Music,* to learn type recognition the way we learn to recognize the basic tones of the Western musical scale.

There is, however, a European story, "A Dinner Party with the Types," which is included as an appendix in Daryl Sharp's book, *Personality Types: Jung's Model of Typology* (1987, pp. 113–119), that does a very good job of describing the eight different types of consciousness personified as guests at a dinner party. The hostess, appropriate to her role, embodies extraverted feeling. Her husband, a quiet, slender professor of art history, doubtless excels at noticing the minute differences between similar works of art. He represents introverted sensation. An extraverted thinking lawyer is the first guest to arrive. An industrialist, well dressed but loud, and a greedy though appreciative eater, comes later. He stands for extraverted sensation. His wife, a quiet, extremely ladylike woman with mysterious eyes, the type in whom 'still waters run deep,' is with him. She exerts a strangely magnetic effect on the other guests with her introverted feeling. An introverted thinking professor of medicine is next. He comes without his wife, and is apparently preoccupied with the disease he has been studying. He is followed by an extraverted intuitive engineer who rhapsodizes about his ambitious plans, which one suspects will come to fruition only if someone else carries them out. While speaking, he gobbles his food without noticing what he is eating. The last intended guest, a poor young poet, forgets to come to the party but, when he realizes his mistake, plans by way of apology to send his hostess the poem he was working on while the party was taking place. (Sharp's own descriptions of these eight types of consciousness follow Jung and are presented at more length in the main section of his book.)

Beyond dominant and auxiliary

The functions are not as easily recognized in therapy. A real-life person, unlike a stereotyped character identified with a single function, has access to all eight functions of consciousness, even if some are in shadow, and will deploy one or another depending on the context and the type of consciousness called for by that context. Also, the patient in analysis is often in the grip of complexes, which notoriously produce what Jung, quoting Janet, called an *abaissment du niveau mentale,* a reduction of the mental level, such that the energy that normally attaches itself to the superior and auxiliary function, allowing them to surface, is absent. When these functions are not active, the tertiary and inferior functions emerge. 'Tertiary' and 'inferior' are terms that imply that there is a gradient of differentiation in the four types of consciousness that normally describe some-one's 'ego,' at least as that sometimes inexactly defined term is understood by analytical psychology. (I prefer to think of them as less conscious parts of a 'little-s' self.) As the least differentiated of the functions consciously available to the patient, the tertiary and inferior functions tend to be less adapted to real-ity and more influenced by unconscious complexes, which are in fact usually dominating the psyche when the third and fourth functions emerge in recogniz-able form. Their presentation is thus often floridly neurotic, easily characterized as obsessive, cyclothymic, hysterical, or paranoid, creating an obvious link to psychopathology. When it is easy to diagnose neurotic traits or character pathol-ogy in an analytic patient, it is a tip-off that one is looking not at the patient's natural (superior and auxiliary function) typology but at "a falsification of the original personality" (Jung 1950/1959, ¶214). Naturally, a person can also fal-sify his or her original personality in a more adaptive way by conforming to the expectations of a family, school, occupation, or culture.

We should be cautious, therefore, in making any type diagnosis. It is best not to try to type someone who has not yet made a connection to the self that would be natural to him or her, because all you may be doing is noting the "negative personality" (Jung, 1950/1959, ¶214) that has swallowed up the patient's true self (Beebe, 1988). Sometimes, however, knowing that the inferior and tertiary func-tions reflect what someone 'is least good at' can be a clue to the actual type. The person who constantly obsesses about small feeling matters, finding other people's feelings an endless burden, may be not an extraverted feeling type, for whom other people's feelings naturally matter and are thus relatively easy to deal with, but someone with inferior extraverted feeling, that is, an introverted thinking type, who is in constant danger of ignoring the feelings of others. Marie-Louise von

Franz (1971/1998) has written the definitive text on the inferior function, and in many ways her monograph is also the best book on type for clinicians because it portrays the way many kinds of patients present themselves in the office when in the grip of the inferior function. It should be required reading in all Jungian training programs. A companion essay by James Hillman on the feeling function shows the number of other psychological entities that can confuse the identification of a function of consciousness and the need for clinicians to differentiate all of these. To cite just one example:

> Extraverted feeling ought not to be confused with the persona. Although in Jung both refer to the process of adaptation, extraverted feeling is a function of personality. It is a manner of performing and can be an expression of an individual style. By means of it a person gives values and adapts to values in ways which can be highly differentiated, uncollective and original. The persona, on the other hand, is a fundamental archetype of the psyche referring to the manner in which consciousness reflects with society. The persona in Jung's stricter usage of the term, therefore, . . . would mean a developed reflection of the collective consensus. If one is a prisoner, or an addict, or a hermit, or a general, one can have a developed persona by behaving in the styles and forms collectively belonging to these patterns of existence. They are archetypal patterns. Feeling may have little or nothing to do with this adaptation, for one can be connected very well to the collective through thinking, intuition and sensation. In a nutshell: classically the persona is a collective way of playing a role in the world; the feeling function is an individual instrument of self-affirmation.
>
> *Hillman, 1971/1998, pp. 123–124*

Connection to the Self

To discover a patient's typology, it is better to wait until the patient shows an original gift for accurately construing or managing some aspect of what comes up in therapy, rather than attempt to 'type' the person when he or she is manifesting a collective persona that could belong to anybody in the patient's situation, or when the patient is so evidently suffering from psychopathology that a syndrome has all but replaced the person.

The typology of the true self (defined as the personal, 'little-s' self in touch with the transpersonal 'big-S' Self (Gordon, 1985; Beebe, 1988)) is rarely so stereotyped; rather it opens up the use of the most differentiated parts of the personality in an individual way that is a revelation and a pleasure to experience. It's when the patient is exhibiting his or her strengths as an authentic person that we can begin to appreciate the skill with which feeling, thinking, sensation and intuition are being used. At such moments, we can also see what effective extraversion and introversion are like when they are used as conscious attitudes.

Extraversion and introversion

When the patient is using a well-differentiated extraverted function, the function will seek to merge with some aspect of the analyst in a way that the analyst does not find particularly uncomfortable. When extraverted feeling is differentiated, the analyst feels appreciated and respected, and there is a sense of one's good will being seen and met. When extraverted thinking is highly differentiated, the analyst will find that it is safe to let the patient set the agenda, like a general directing the campaign of the therapy. When the patient's extraverted sensation is well developed, the analyst has the experience of a ready participation in what is happening in the moment and an accompanying impatience with abstractions, as if what is already there is sufficient without much interpretation. Extraverted intuition can feel intrusive, but it is also entertaining and astonishing in the way it can pick up on fresh possibilities for developing the objectives of the therapy in the world.

Introversion, when used consciously, is not as easy to discriminate, and indeed the functions of introverted feeling, introverted sensation, and introverted intuition are easily confused with each other. Introverted thinking can usually be distinguished by the fact that it tends not to know when to stop, and needs to define everything freshly, to the point that it becomes exhausting and hard to follow. It, like the other introverted functions, seeks to match its experience of an object with an a priori, archetypal understanding of that category of object *already present in the unconscious.* The introverted move away from the outer object is therefore the first step in a process that takes the introverted function's libido deep into the unconscious of the introverted subject, to see if the object really matches up. (That it often doesn't live up to the archetype helps to explain the frequent disappointment that introverted functions register in analysis, a disappointment that must not be confused with a condition to be treated, even if it is dysphoric to the subject. People with superior introverted functions must register this disappointment when the object simply doesn't match up. It's their normal way of reacting.) Introverted intuition seeks to match up the experience with an image of an archetype, something like a visual metaphor. Introverted sensation likes to establish whether the experience of the object checks out with an inner sense of what has already been established through long human experience as 'real.' And introverted feeling wants to know if the object as experienced is conducting itself in accord with what is fitting for such an object, that is, if a bride is acting like a bride, if a home feels like a home, if the boss is behaving as she should in her role.

The practitioner should grow accustomed to the way introverted functions are constantly sizing up what happens in a therapeutic or in a type assessment encounter, to see if it checks out with the rich inner world of already-known, archetypal experience, against which an introverted function measures everything. Recognizing the introverted types in their normal functioning is one way to realize Jung's enormous contribution to opening up the introverted world as a part of healthy functioning. Simply not pathologizing introversion is perhaps the most healing thing a therapist or type counselor can do in our pathologically extraverted, world-despoiling times. And it is a sign that the practitioner is well along in the knack of type recognition.

References

Beebe, J. (1988). Primary ambivalence toward the Self: Its nature and treatment. In N. Schwartz-Salant & M. Stein (Eds.) *The borderline personality in analysis* (pp. 97–127). Wilmette, IL: Chiron Publications.

Gordon, R. (1985). Big Self and little self: Some reflections. *Journal of Analytical Psychology* 30(3), 261–271.

Hillman, J. (1971/1998). The feeling function. In M.-L. von Franz & J. Hillman, *Lectures on Jung's typology* (pp. 89–179). Woodstock, CT: Spring Publications.

Jung, C. G. (1921/1971). Psychological types. In *Cw 6*.

Jung, C. G. (1950/1959). Concerning rebirth. In *Cw 9, I* (pp. 113–147).

Jung, C. G. (1952/1967). Symbols of transformation, 2nd ed. In *Cw 5*.

Jung, C. G. (1961/1980). Symbols and the interpretation of dreams. In *Cw 18* (pp. 185–264).

Myers, I. (with Myers, P. B.). (1980). *Gifts differing*. Palo Alto, CA: Davies-Black Publishing.

Sharp, D. (1987). *Personality types: Jung's model of typology*. Toronto: Inner City Books.

von Franz, M.-L. (1971/1998). The inferior function. In M.-L. von Franz & J. Hillman, *Lectures on Jung's typology* (pp. 3–88). Woodstock, CT: Spring Publications.

Wheelwright, J. (1982). Psychological types. *In Saint George and the dandelion: 40 years of practice as a Jungian analyst* (pp. 53–77). San Francisco: C.G. Jung Institute of San Francisco.

Winnicott, D. (1987). *Holding and interpretation: Fragment of an analysis*. New York: Grove Press.

14

AN ARCHETYPAL MODEL OF THE SELF IN DIALOGUE

The idea that the psyche consists of different centers of agency and identity capable of entering into meaningful relations with each other is central to the notion of the dialogical self. Noting that "conceptions of multiple centers of awareness (sometimes equivalent to 'souls') within one individual are widespread in the early stages of many cultures," Parkes traces Western consciousness of this "psychical polycentricity" to the archaic age in Greece. Homer recognized "a plurality of centers of psychic awareness" as "responsible for waking consciousness in the living human being" and gave them discrete names "to connote distinct . . . manifestations of the 'life-force'" (Parkes, 1994, p. 252). The Homeric division of psychic consciousness into meaningfully interrelated "'organs' of experience," such as *thumos* (life force), *noos* (thought), and *kradie* (heart), already implies what Norman Austin has called "an interior society" whose relations suggest "a community of internal agents" (Austin, 1975, pp. 111–112, cited in Parkes, 1994, p. 253). Further, each of these "internal agents," to which (as E. R. Dodds [1951] had pointed out earlier) the Homeric *daimones,* as embodied tutelary spirits, gave a degree of personification (Hillman, 1972, pp. 71–72), had its own distinct image. Accepting Jung's notion that "[e]very psychic process is an image and an 'imagining,' otherwise no consciousness could exist" (Jung, 1939/1969, ¶889), Hillman (1983) follows Dodds in interpreting archaic Greek myth psychologically, seeing the gods themselves as primary images or 'ideas,' according to "the original meaning of idea (from Greek *eidos* and *ediolon)*: not only that which one sees but also that by means of which one sees" (1983, p. 21). Elsewhere, Hillman (1977) notes that "any image," that is, any depiction of an internal perspective, "can be considered archetypal" (p. 82). As he puts it, "the word 'archetypal' . . . rather than point at something archetypal points to something, and this is value . . . by archetypal psychology we mean a psychology of value" (pp. 82–83; also Hillman, 1983, pp. 21–22). The word 'archetypal' is a way of stressing the inherent value of each of the distinct valuations by which the psyche proceeds in its construction of consciousness. Homer's polytheism is thus in the background of psychical polycentricity, or what Hermans, following the literary critic Bakhtin, has called the "polyphony" of the dialogical self. Bakhtin credited Dostoevsky with creating "the polyphonic novel," in which each character gives voice to a different point of view within the total mind of the work (Honeycutt, 1994). (That this technique is not confined to the novel is obvious to anyone who has seen Pirandello's well-known play *Six Characters in Search of an Author*.) An extreme present-day example of the polyphonic novel is the *Requiem* (1985), arranged by its author, Peer Hultberg, for "a choir of 537 mixed voices"— each of the novel's 537 chapters expresses the consciousness of a separate character and, consistent with the author's aim of expressing the fragmentation as well as the commonality of modern experience, consists of "one long sentence, one breath, one voice, one story with no connection to the others" (Ravn, 1998).

This, as Parkes recognizes, was also the way Nietzsche chose to write his philosophy, as a set of paragraphic reflections each with its own point of view, to emphasize in the very style of his argument his notion that the soul is multiple. Parkes links Nietzsche's perspectivism to Emerson's essay on "Experience" (1844, p. 235), in which the American philosopher writes, "I accept the clangor and jangle of contrary tendencies.... The middle region of our being is the temperate zone" (cited in Parkes, 1994, p. 106).

Following not only Nietzsche but also his psychological mentors William James, who had spoken of "alternating selves" (1890, pp. xi, 379), and Théodore Flournoy (1899/1994), who studied "multiple personality" as a paradigm for the structure of the mind, Jung made the idea of a multiplicity of souls a cornerstone of his analytical psychology. Bringing also the French Dissociationist insights of Pierre Janet into line with the German-language research Jung had already encountered at Bleuler's Burghölzli psychiatric hospital in Zürich (Shamdasani, 1998), Jung postulated that the psyche is actually composed of the "feeling-toned complexes" that Ziehen's researches on the association of ideas had identified (Ziehen, 1899; see also Kerr, 1993, p. 45). Jung (1934/1960) found that each complex is capable not only of being represented, but actually as functioning as a "splinter psyche" (¶203) having its own measure of consciousness. Complexes, as Jung was among the first to recognize, are represented with particular clarity in dreams, where they are shown as part-persons of our psyche in interaction with each other. Jung accepted the manifest content of dreams as prima facie evidence that each subpersonality has its own unique emotional stance. By studying the valuations expressed by the figures in our dreams, he felt we could recognize the standpoints of our complexes (Jung, 1906/1973).

Jung's work on complexes and typology has provided a bridge within the discipline of psychology between the perspective of William James (1890), who had spoken of the "rivalry and conflict of the different selves" (p. 309), and that of Henry Murray, whose method of Personology, inaugurated in 1938, seeks to establish a narrative line linking the person's different temporary identities into the pattern we recognize as a personality. They create dynamics in the 'little-s' self.

This rich intellectual tradition lies in the background of H. J. M. Hermans's use of valuation theory to explicate the dynamics of the dialogical self (Hermans & Kempen, 1993). In terms of Jung's theory of complexes, the different valuations that an individual may express across the course of a life represent the feeling-toned standpoints that dominate that person's consciousness in the passing parade of complex-driven states of mind that constitute the 'little-s' self. But, unlike Jung, Hermans does not postulate a supraordinate, unified Self as the driving force of individuation. As Hermans (1993) has emphasized, the effect of these standpoints is not necessarily to provide unitary states of mind: even at a given moment of consciousness, they often take the form of a pair of opposites coexisting in the Heraclitean sense and therefore generating conflict. The tension we feel when two complexes are expressing opposite valuations is quite often resolved not by a decision between the two, or even by a transcendent synthesis that expresses the best of both, but by moving to a new pair of opposite positions. This movement into a dialogue between different complexes is experienced by the subject of the original conflict as intensely meaningful, even though it introduces a new order of conflict.

In the light of the Heraclitean flux that is produced by the way the complexes of the psyche continually replace each other in an endless round, the task of the scientific or therapeutic investigator seeking an orderly structure to personality is, to say the least, daunting. Much of Jung's later work on the archetypal cores of the complexes can be understood as his attempt to find structures that locate the dialogue of complexes within meaningful narratives. Yet many have thought that the essential narratives Jung claimed to have glimpsed read like metanarratives of his own construction of a 'big-S' Self that is no longer a person.

Can we then find any structure within the dialogical self? My work as a Jungian analyst can be described as on ongoing attempt to answer this question. To find a pattern within the interaction of complexes that accounts for (1) their tendency to take up opposed positions, (2) the archetypal qualities of the positions they take, and (3) their capacity, as movement takes place between these archetypal positions of conflict, to generate meaningful narratives, I have been led to draw upon another of Jung's theoretical contributions. I have found that his theory of psychological types, to which I have made "additions and extensions" (Henderson, 1991), is a theoretical tool well suited to addressing these problems, which are so relevant to the understanding of the dialogical self in clinical work.

Jung's theory, unfortunately, is often misunderstood to be only a way of typing people, whether as extraverts and introverts, or as feeling, thinking, sensation or intuitive types, and thus of limited value in understanding intrapsychic dynamics, such as the dialogues between complexes representing opposite points of view within the psyche. It was nevertheless Jung's intention in offering his theory of types of psychological consciousness to introduce "some kind of order among the chaotic multiplicity of points of view," to offer it as a "critical psychology" to "sort out and organize the welter of empirical material" of "psychic processes that can be shown to be typical" (Jung, 1921/1971, pp. xiv–xv). In this spirit of identifying typical processes rather than typical people, I use type theory to differentiate the dialogic positions of the complexes that can be observed within the course of a therapeutic analysis of a single individual. I take seriously Jung's idea that complexes are *characteristic expressions of the psyche* (Jung, 1934/1960, p. 101) and assume (against his relative uncertainty on this point) that "such small psychic fragments as complexes are . . . capable of consciousness" (Jung, 1934/1960, p. 97). As expressions of the psyche with a certain consciousness, complexes can most certainly be 'typed' according to Jung's system of classification of the various kinds of consciousness psychological systems are capable of manifesting. It then can be demonstrated that our complexes display the same kind of order that can be readily observed in the system of psychological types.

According to this system, the 'rationally' evaluative cognitive processes Jung called "feeling" and "thinking" are naturally opposed, as are the 'irrationally' perceptive processes that he named "sensation" and "intuition".[1] Metaphorically, our innate capacity for conscious orientation operates like an inner compass, in which the thinking–feeling dimension operates like a North/South rational axis to the irrational East/West of the intuitive–sensation dimension (Figure 14.1).

In terms of valuation theory, each of these four types of cognitive functioning puts a premium on one set of considerations. "Feeling," for instance, is often spoken of by Jung and by Jungians as if it were a synonym for valuing, but it is not the only function associated with making a valuation; it is merely the function that places the highest premium on the psychological act of assigning value. The other functions are just as emphatic in their own kinds of valuation. "Thinking" places the highest value on the logical processes of defining, conceptually discriminating and reasonably deploying ideas. "Intuition" places the highest value on establishing the potential connections between things, even when such connections seem to fly in the face of reason. "Sensation" puts the highest value on the efficient management and sensuous appreciation of things in time and space.

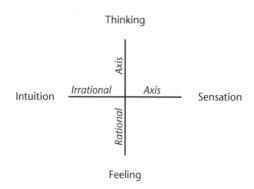

FIGURE 14.1 Jung's four types of cognitive functioning

Each of these four "functions of consciousness" can be deployed in either an extraverted or an introverted way: that is, by assigning the highest valuation to the objective experience of the 'other' or to the subjective experience of the 'self'. The options that result consist of eight possible valuation orientations that Jung has named extraverted thinking, introverted thinking, extraverted sensation, introverted sensation, extraverted intuition, introverted intuition, extraverted feeling and introverted feeling.

For example, the valuation "I enjoy elder-blossoms, the smell of hay, and the silence," which appears in *Self-Narratives* (Hermans & Hermans-Jansen, 1995, p. 84), implies an extraverted sensation orientation to experience, involving a passionate contact with the environment as a significant other. By contrast, the valuation "I feel like a complete woman if I can determine when a man has his orgasm" (p. 85) reflects a more introverted sensation orientation, because the empirical observation of the other is used to enhance the experience of self. Note that in this second example, when the subject herself was asked to measure her own valuation according to Hermans's instructions, the sum of the scores for the affect terms expressing self-enhancement (strength, self-esteem, self-confidence and pride) was greater than the scores for the affect terms expressing contact and union with the other (love, tenderness, intimacy and caring). In the earlier, extraverted sensation example, the opposite was true.

These functions are not arranged randomly in the psyche but rather appear as specific pairs of opposites within the rational or irrational dimensions of consciousness, which can be described as four discrete axes, as in Figure 14.2.

This theory, from the standpoint of the dialogical self, provides a way to understand the opposites that participate in conflictual dialogues, both conscious and unconscious. In the dreams of clients in analytic treatment, for instance, figures in conflict often represent the different valuations of opposed 'types' of psychological consciousness. As I recount in Chapter 3 of this book, I dreamed in the course of the analysis that accompanied my Jungian training that an older man—a 'father'—was chasing his 'son' around the dining-room table with a butcher's knife. This rather grisly scene drew upon an actual event that had been related to me by my paternal grandmother, a college teacher who often mentored young people from difficult psychological backgrounds. From a psychoanalytic

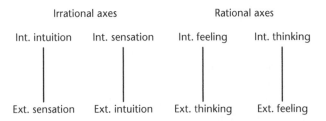

FIGURE 14.2 Axes of typological opposites

perspective, the dream suggests castration anxiety associated with a severe father complex, although the association to the helpful grandmother suggests a potential, within the inner world of positive and negative objects, to draw upon a more caring, maternal perspective to resolve this problem. Jung's theory of psychological types enabled me to link the butcher's knife to my tendency to use my medically trained extraverted thinking to dissect my own analytic material. This came at the expense of my much less well-developed feeling function that, in the language of the dream, was terrified of this aggressively objective way of taking apart emotions. My thinking function, in other words, had become a brutal 'father' bullying my feeling function, which, now, in the analytic enterprise, was like a frightened boy. This dream had the effect of enlisting my support for my analyst's efforts to get me to use feeling to discriminate and relate to my psychic material in lieu of the competitive sort of thinking I had brought to analysis from my medical psychiatric training.

The idea that my own more developed thinking function could be symbolized by a 'father' and my less developed feeling function by a 'boy' led me to begin to conceptualize the relations between the types as relations between members of an internal family. The relative positions of power within the family of 'father' and 'son,' so starkly evident in the dream, in which the father has the initiative to which the son must respond, seemed to me a matter of greater development of the thinking function relative to the feeling function. In the literature stemming from the theory of the dialogical self, such differences are discussed in terms of dominance relations between positions in the dialogical self, and these include a number of dimensions, including asymmetry in terms of initiative/response, the ability of one position to control the content or topic of the dialogue, and the quantity and strategic character of the moves of the dominant partner within a dialogic relationship (Hermans & Kempen, 1993, pp. 75–76). A similar understanding of what might be called the politics of dialogue informs my view of the interaction between complexes. Over years of mapping out the typology of my own and my clients' complexes and seeing how they arrange themselves into archetypal pairs of opposites, I have concluded that the eight psychological 'types' that Jung identified appear only in association with part-personality complexes that have arranged themselves into some sort of hierarchy. The types, that is, occupy various archetypal positions holding relative degrees of dominance out of which the various functions of consciousness will express themselves in symmetrical and asymmetrical ways.

Hermans and Kempen (1993) have noted, "Parents are in a position to use extensively the dominance aspects of the dialogue so that children do not have much opportunity to express their views themselves" (p. 76). Similarly, the developmental status of a psychological type, readily observable in a dream by its personification as a person of certain age, affects its dominance position within the total system of valuations that make up the political economy of the dialogical self. The type will manifest itself in ways characteristic not only of the kind of cognitive process it wants to emphasize but also of its developmental level.

In my own example, we should note that not only is the thinking function symbolized by a parent, who therefore has control of the dialogue with feeling, but that the dialogue has become non-verbal. The parent, moreover, is not disposed to take care of the child. Possibly the child, though a seeming victim, may in some way have provoked the parent, which suggests a shadowy interaction between something masochistic in the child and something sadistic in the parent.

But parent and child are not the only possible 'positions' available to the actors expressing the various typical consciousnesses within the dialogical self. These are in fact, only two of the archetypal roles the types can play. Figure 14.3 illustrates how I have arranged the archetypal figures that structure the appearance of typed complexes (and therefore the positions of valuation) in any given individual.

The relation of this scheme to Jung's system of psychological types is as follows. Jung speaks of the most differentiated function of consciousness as the "superior function"; this, in a man, is associated with the image of the hero (in a woman, the heroine). Jung calls the second most differentiated function the "auxiliary function," and this I have found to be personified by a positive parent figure (father in a man, mother in a woman). The third most differentiated function is personified by a child figure (son in a man, daughter in a woman), archetypally called a *puer* or *puella*. The fourth function is usually far less differentiated than the other three. Jung calls this the "inferior function," and it is found in association with the unconscious contrasexual 'authorities' (the anima in a man and the animus in a woman) that also personify otherness. The individual will normally identify either the superior or auxiliary function with the 'self,' and will assign the valuation position of 'other' to the figure on the other end of the axis shown in Figure 14.3. Otherness may be experienced in an inner way, but it is more likely to be projected onto another individual in the person's outer world—one's spouse or lover, child or student. The other four function complexes, which are normally in shadow, are experienced most often as negative positions of self and otherness. The typology of the shadow is the same, except that functions that are extraverted in the positive (ego-syntonic) positions are introverted in the corresponding shadow positions, and vice versa.

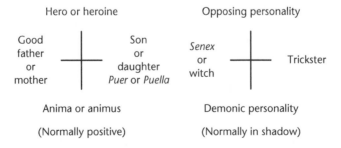

FIGURE 14.3 Eight archetypal positions for the eight typological functions

Valuation positions come to belong either to the system of 'self' or the system of 'other' partly from a hard-wired typological hierarchy (one's innate 'type') and partly as a consequence of one's developmental history of reward and trauma in family and culture, through which certain of the archetypal complexes become ego-aligned while others are dissociated from the ego and projected onto other objects (Sandner & Beebe, 1995. In Chapter 3 in this book (also see Harris, 1996, chapters 4 and 5), I offer a fuller explication of the eight basic archetypal positions and how I have seen them organizing Jung's system of eight psychological types without being equivalent to them).

An important therapeutic implication of the theory of the dialogical self is that, because it privileges the dialogue as a whole, valuations taken by less privileged positions within the self are allowed a fairer hearing. The theory of psychological types enables the clinician to identify these less privileged positions and to promote healing 'power shifts' within the psyche.

Studying the internal dialogues of clients in analytical psychotherapy, working with their dreams and using the theory of psychological types to identify the naturally occurring pairs of opposed valuation positions, I have concluded that the following pairs of archetypal complexes pattern the dialogues of the dialogical self:

1. Hero/anima (the counterpart positions in a woman's psyche are heroine/animus).
2. Good father/*puer aeternus* (the counterpart positions are good mother/*puella aeterna*).
3. *Senex*/trickster (*senex* is the Latin word for 'old man,' and it is used here, as in archetypal psychology, to connote a particular aspect of the shadow, a saturnine or punitive Old Man who can often be found in opposition to the more juvenile trickster another archetypal position of shadow). The version of this pair of opposites, when gendered female in the imagery and phenomenology of the psyche, is witch/trickster. (Particularly in the shadow positions, the gender roles are not invariable. For example, clinically, it is not uncommon to observe *senex* vs trickster in a woman's psyche, and witch vs trickster in a man's.)
4. Hero or heroine pitted against an opposing personality (often, though not invariably, of the other gender).
5. Anima or animus forced to cope with a demonic personality (frequently of the other gender, as in the fairy tale "Beauty and the Beast").
6. Divine son or daughter (*puer* or *puella*) in conflict with the trickster (whether as *enfant terrible* or perennial fool).
7. Good mother against the 'bad' witch (or sometimes *senex* [punitive old man]). In a man, good father against the *senex* or witch.
8. Opposing personality taking up a standpoint contrary or complementary to that of the demonic personality.

To test this model outside the clinical situation, I have applied it to the analysis of film, an art form that seems to me naturally polyphonic, in the sense that

Bakhtin applied this term to the Dostoyevskian novel (Honeycutt, 1994). The films of *auteur* directors (those who carefully control the system of valuations in their own films) seem to me to represent the dialogical self in particularly pure form. Each of the characters in such a film represents not a whole person but a different state of mind within the scheme of consciousness the director creates. The moviegoer witnesses the dialogue of these various voices, which the director presents to us in the guise of a drama about persons working out their relations to each other. On the screen, each character usually exemplifies one of the eight functions of consciousness in an archetypal way, consonant with the position the director assigns to the character within the drama as a whole.

Woody Allen's 1992 *Husbands and Wives* is such a polyphonic film, and can illustrate the method of typological analysis in the explication of a creative depiction of the dialogical self. In my reading, Allen's film, despite its provocative title, uses marriage as his metaphor for the dialogue between complexes representing different positions of valuation. As we shall see, these are easily recognized by the different 'types' that the characters seem to exemplify.

Husbands and Wives belongs, from the standpoint of film studies, to the genre Stanley Cavell (1981) has identified as the "Hollywood comedy of remarriage" and concerns two married couples who are best friends. One couple is separating at the outset of the movie (but eventually reunites), the other breaks up permanently. The various players in the drama are their ex- and future spouses, as well as the temporary partners the principals take up with. At times, the characters are interviewed by an unseen investigator who seems to be researching marriage: this interviewer, not unlike the psychologists trained by Hermans, pushes the characters to present their processes of valuation. The film as a whole extends the investigation, until the final frame, when Gabe, the character played by Woody Allen himself, looks toward the interrogating camera and asks, "Can I go? Is this over?" It is as if he is speaking, as *auteur*, for the dialogical self as a whole, as if to indicate that his entire scenario has been a prolonged exercise in exposing the valuations of his own subpersonalities and he is exhausted.

From this standpoint, Allen's character Gabe, who teaches creative writing at Columbia, is the hero of the film. On the basis of his imagistic philosophizing (the highpoint is a zany commentary on the differences between men and women on the basis of the manyness of sperms and the oneness of the egg to be fertilized), I would classify Gabe, typologically, as an introverted intuitive. His heroism lies in his ability to master predicaments with an original wit that penetrates to the unconscious meaning of the situation. The auxiliary, 'fatherly' function in the film is carried by his best friend Jack, who is compulsively reassuring in a typically extraverted feeling way.

The script makes clear that Gabe's wife, Judy, is not his anima. That role is carried instead by one of Gabe's students, twenty-year-old Rain, who brings a fresh sensuality to her every screen moment. In her immediacy, she personifies extraverted sensation, which is the type of anima appropriate to an introverted intuitive hero. Gabe's wife is more strongly introverted in her feeling reactions, starting with her profound upset at the news that their friends Jack and Sally are splitting up. According to the typological scheme, she represents a shadow side to the parental control exerted by Jack, who assures Gabe and Judy that the dissolution of his marriage will be no problem. Where he comforts and enables, she probes and disrupts, in the manner of an archetypal witch.

Gradually it emerges that Judy and Gabe are badly matched. In the model I have presented above (Figure 14.2), their types are not on the same axis nor do they complement each other in the way of a superior and an auxiliary function, as Gabe and Jack do. One notes that Gabe and Judy's valuations invariably reflect competing standpoints, with her introverted feeling rationally directed toward understanding the inner situation of their marriage and his introverted intuitions proceeding irrationally, via a series of epiphanies. It is not surprising that this couple finds it difficult to obtain more than pseudo-mutuality.

Jack and Sally are similarly mismatched. Jack, as we have seen, displays extraverted feeling in his valuations, which aim for a fair-minded, rationalizing assessment of any situation in which he finds himself, whereas Sally, an extraverted intuitive, draws unexpected conclusions through an irrational process of rapidly shifting standpoints. She continually leaps ahead of her body and her feeling in trying to connect with the possibilities she sees ahead. Sally is so intensely oppositional to what everyone around her is expecting as to become a figure of fun, and therefore a character in shadow, whose valuations are suspect.

After their separation, Jack and Sally experiment with developing relationships with partners on their own typological axes—an introverted thinking type for extraverted feeling Jack, and an introverted sensation type for extraverted intuitive Sally. But Sally is too ironic about the body and too much of an opposing personality to warm up to the quiet sensuality of her new lover. His easy openness to lovemaking undermines her neurotic need to stay in control. The fatherly Jack is similarly out of his element with a *puella* figure, whose incessant but undeveloped, adolescent thinking drives him crazy. After a period of tolerant appreciation for the health benefits of the New Age ideologies she espouses, he eventually discards her as a social embarrassment.

In this comedy of mismatches, neither the irrational nor the rational types end up with partners who naturally complement them by being on the same typological axis (again, see Figure 14.2). The closest we come to this is Gabe's long, emotionally satisfying kiss with his extraverted sensation student Rain which is nevertheless followed, to our relief, by his rejection of the relationship as inappropriate because of their age difference and the serious boundary problem inherent in his role as her teacher and mentor. Even the names of the characters seem to suggest a mismatch. For example, in a violation of an unwritten Hollywood convention, the film features a well-known actress named Judy Davis but gives the character named 'Judy' to another actress, Mia Farrow, who was Allen's real-life partner at the time. The effect is to privilege mismatch, bringing into relation with each other positions in the dialogical self (Figure 14.3) that normally would not get along, such as hero (Gabe) and witch (Judy), father (Jack) and opposing personality (Sally).

This may be Allen's way of depicting the neurotic personality of our time. From a psychoanalytic perspective, internal discord reigns under the Oedipal conditions that hamstring patriarchal marriage via the incest taboo. In typological terms, this means that partners who might be compatible, because their superior functions share the same axis (Figure 14.2), can't get together. Yet the farce of frustrated object relations enables interesting movements within the dialogical self. Because Judy is able to connect eventually with the most desirable man in the film and Gabe, Woody Allen's character, is left alone, having sacrificed the object of his desire, it is hard not to interpret *Husbands and Wives*, psychosexually, as the depiction of a successful castration, in which the witch makes off with the hero's desire. But the unconscious structure of the film parts company with Allen's psychoanalytic pessimism. Gabe succeeds in moving away from his unsatisfying competitive dialogue with his witch–wife, and is able to take up a dialogue that is finally characterized by integrity with his anima–student. This is a positive illustration of what Hermans (1993) means by "moving opposites" within the dialogical self.

What the film conceives as the story of Gabe's divorce is also a depiction of his individuation. If we take *Husbands and Wives* as a paradigm for how we might read the stories of our clients and our own lives when dialogue is opening up within the self, we have to consider that the dialogues that currently engage us also inhibit us from the possibility of entering others. In such a situation, as Jung (1912/1916) long ago saw, a symbolic incest—breaking the taboo against connecting with one's most closely related 'other'—is frequently the healer. It is the natural affinity between poles of our typologies that lie on the same axis (Figure 14.2) that encourages us to take up the problem of opposites. The resulting experience of opposition is the psychic price we pay for the opportunity of freedom of movement within the mind.

We end up not by marrying different positions within the dialogic self to each other, but by respecting their autonomy, and especially their right to stand up to each other by making separating distinctions. As I have found myself, connecting deeply to the typological opposites within us is a necessary step to opening the dialogical self to the full creative range of its positions.

Note

1 For a complete explanation of Jung's theory of typology, see Jung (1921/1971, ch. X).

References

Austin, N. (1975). *Archery at the dark of the moon: Poetic problems in Homer's Odyssey*. Berkeley, CA: University of California Press.

Cavell, S. (1981). *Pursuits of happiness: The Hollywood comedy of remarriage*. Cambridge, MA: Harvard University Press.

Dodds, E. R. (1951). *The Greeks and the irrational*. Berkeley, CA: University of California Press.

Emerson, R. W. (1844/2012). Experience. In D. Mikics (Ed.). *The annotated Emerson* (pp. 223–247). Cambridge, MA: Belknap Press.

Flournoy, T. (1899/1994). *From India to the planet Mars: A case of multiple personality with imaginary languages.* S. Shamdasani (Ed.). D. B. Vermilye (Trans.) Princeton, NJ: Princeton University Press.

Harris, A. S. (1996). *Living with paradox: An introduction to Jungian psychology.* Pacific Grove, CA: Brooks/Cole.

Henderson, J. L. (1991). C.G. Jung's psychology: Additions and extensions. *Journal of Analytical Psychology, 36*(4), 429–442.

Hermans, H. J. M. (1993). Moving opposites in the self: A Heraclitean approach. *Journal of Analytical Psychology, 38*(4), 437–462.

Hermans, H. J. M., & Hermans-Jansen, E. (1995). *Self-narratives.* New York: Guilford.

Hermans, H. J. M., & Kempen, H. J. G. (1993). *The dialogical self: Meaning as movement.* San Diego, CA: Academic Press.

Hillman, J. (1972). *The myth of analysis.* Evanston, IL: Northwestern University Press.

Hillman, J. (1977). An inquiry into image. *Spring,* pp. 62–88.

Hillman, J. (1983). *Archetypal psychology: A brief account.* Woodstock, CT: Spring.

Honeycutt, L. (1994). *What hath Bakhtin wrought? Toward a unified theory of literature and composition.* Master's thesis, University of North Carolina, Charlotte.

Hultberg, P. (1985). *Requiem.* Copenhagen: Gyldendal.

Husbands and wives. (1992). Allen, W. (Producer & Director). USA: Tri-Star Pictures. [Motion picture].

James, W. (1890). *The principles of psychology, vol. 1.* New York: Holt.

Jung, C. G. (1906/1973). Association, dream, and hysterical symptom. In *Cw 2* (pp. 353–407).

Jung, C. G. (1912/1916). *Psychology of the unconscious* B. M. Hinkle (Trans.) New York: Dodd, Mead.

Jung, C. G. (1921/1971). Psychological types. In *Cw 6.*

Jung, C. G. (1934/1960). A review of the complex theory. In *Cw 8* (pp. 92–104).

Jung, C. G. (1939/1969). Foreword to Suzuki's *Introduction to Zen Buddhism.* In *Cw 11* (pp. 538–557).

Kerr, J. (1993). *A most dangerous method.* New York: Knopf.

Murray, H. (1938). *Explorations in personality.* Oxford: Oxford University Press.

Parkes, G. (1994). *Composing the soul.* Chicago, IL: University of Chicago Press.

Pirandello, L. (1998). *Six characters in search of an author.* E. Bentley (Trans.) New York: Penguin Signet.

Ravn, L. (1998). Peer Hultberg. *Litteratur Net—Forfatterprofiler* [Online], 1–2.

Sandner, D. F. & Beebe, J. (1995). Psychopathology and analysis. In M. Stein (Ed.) *Jungian analysis* (2nd Ed., pp. 297–348). Chicago/La Salle, IL: Open Court.

Shamdasani, S. (1998). From Geneva to Zürich: Jung and French Switzerland. *Journal of Analytical Psychology, 43*(1), 115–126.

Ziehen, T. (1899). *Introduction to physiological psychology.* New York: Macmillan.

15

IDENTIFYING THE AMERICAN SHADOW

Typological reflections on the 1992 Los Angeles riots

It was not hard to see the image of America that triggered the conflagration sweeping over Los Angeles after the acquittal of police charged with using excessive force during their arrest of Rodney King. Anyone with a television set had access to the sequence of events. A black man was supposed to lie face down, his entire body flat against the ground. Should he attempt in any way to rise, peace officers with clubs would beat him until he was again knocked flat, and when he later complained about such treatment, the law would side with the police, not him. This was a trial for all Americans, and it seems faintly obscene to draw understanding from typology in the face of such pain, but psychological questions come at such collective moments, along with the nerve to answer them.

What part of us responds to such an image? At one level it depends upon with whom we identify and what our racial and personal experiences with authority have been. As an analytical psychologist, a specialist in the part-functions of mental and emotional consciousness in their relation to deep unconscious realities, I believe that the peculiar force of Rodney King's beating sent its alarming message to blacks and whites alike, not so much through the empathetic sympathy it evoked as through its deeper shock to introverted feeling. Introverted feeling, as Jung was the first to get us to see, is a valuation function that works at the archetypal (not the personal) level, taking the deepest possible sounding of a situation. It not only enables but compels us to feel the rightness and wrongness of images, arrogating from its very closeness to the archetypal a bench of judgment that grants it the power to decide what is appropriate and what is not.

One of the first African Americans to have her own business as an MBTI consultant and type practitioner, Pat Clark Battle (1991, pp. 6–9) has offered observations which suggest that introverted feeling, though traditionally prevalent in American black culture, is sometimes suppressed in favor of extraverted thinking by African Americans who want to adapt to the prevailing values of economically empowered whites. It is not hard to imagine that there may be also a contrary emphasis on introverted feeling in African Americans who have not succeeded when attempting an adaptation to extraverted thinking. When a strongly emphasized introverted feeling is paired with the mode of response Jung called extraverted sensation, what appears is a style of emotional realism that prefers action to reflection and can produce an explosive rather than thought-out reaction when confronted with a deeply felt injustice. Spike Lee beautifully detailed this sort of reaction in white and black characters in his 1989 film, *Do the Right Thing* (see Beebe, 1989). In the case of an event like the Rodney King verdict, in contradistinction to the Rodney King beating, the injustice is done not only to a man, but to the principle of what a man can legitimately aspire to. I believe it is this latter injustice to which introverted feeling responds so deeply and so violently when, monitoring power, it identifies abuse.

INTROVERTED FEELING

The introverted feeling function concerns itself with the values expressed in the archetypal aspect of situations, often relating to the actual situation by measuring it against an ideal. When the actual is found wanting, introverted feeling can become intensely disappointed. Although it often finds it hard to articulate its judgments, or simply prefers to keep them to itself, introverted feeling also tends to ignore social limits regarding the communication of critical responses, to the point of appearing to depreciate others. It may withhold positive feeling as insincere and fail to offer healing gestures to smooth over difficult situations. In its shadow aspect, introverted feeling becomes rageful, anxious, and sullen. It may withdraw all support for attitudes it has decided are simply wrong, even at the risk of rupturing relationship and agreed-upon standards of fellow-feeling.

Others who watched their television sets at a safe distance from all that was going on saw another image, perhaps easier for them to witness, and certainly more compelling for middle-class whites. This was the image of the white man being pulled from his truck and beaten senseless by a group of rageful blacks. Psychologically, this image pulled for the other sort of feeling: empathic, righteous, and subtly snobbish in the name of the human compact—a shadow aspect of the extraverted feeling that is so prevalent in the white collective. Viewers with that perspective simply put themselves in the young truck driver's place and withheld any sympathy from those who beat him, especially resenting their many black apologists. Pictures of the truck driver released by the papers showed a sweet, engaging open-hearted face—the kind that typically graces a California campground on summer weekends. In sharp contrast, the men who beat him were Boys 'N the Hood, fatally without charm.

And so, the opposites of feeling were joined along racial lines: From the standpoint of introverted feeling, the verdict was shockingly unjust, but from the standpoint of extraverted feeling, the reaction to the verdict was stupid and unfair—even, as one white drugstore clerk airily declared to me in the first hours of the riot, before it was clear that this was the worst civil disturbance in America in over a hundred years, "silly."

EXTRAVERTED FEELING

The extraverted feeling function concerns itself with other people's emotions—especially those that lie on or near the surface and are easy to sympathize with. Placing a value on people's feelings, extraverted feeling relates to them with discrimination, empathy, and tact. At its best, it tends to appreciate the strengths of people, but it also seeks concrete gratitude and validation. In its shadow aspect, extraverted feeling tends to discriminate against feelings that are less easy to identify with, and therefore less socially acceptable. The result is that extraverted feeling tends to ignore or harshly judge emotional needs that do not validate collective norms. This kind of response can lead to forms of bullying and prejudice, as majority values are emphasized at the expense of other, more individual values.

Then Rodney King unexpectedly spoke, reversing and perhaps atoning for the unwise decision of the prosecution to keep him off the stand, and also relieving us of the anxiety that he was too brain-damaged to speak. When he spoke, the two feeling reactions, introverted and extraverted, suddenly came together in one of those triumphs of being human that seem peculiarly American. His words, which had the poetic appropriateness of speeches that find their way into grammar school texts of composition, seemed to erase our knowledge of his criminal record, exonerating him almost as fully in the popular imagination as those inspired sentences Bartolomeo Vanzetti spoke before his execution in 1927. It became obvious that it was still possible in this country to bring not only the races together, but also the two kinds of feeling that blacks and whites had come to personify through the demeaning oversimplification that is a race riot.

The next day, people of all ethnic groups were joining in the cleanup. There was recognition that the big losers, at least where everyone's feeling was concerned, might after all be Asians, the people who had trusted this country to be better than the lands they had left. Some looters even returned what they had stolen, and many individuals acted with courage and generosity, human integrity triumphing over psychological part-functioning.

I was paying a house call to an AIDS patient when I watched Rodney King speak: swallowed in the collective, my patient and I were finding it hard to summon the energy to meet. We seemed to merge in a sort of shared fantasy, a television set dreaming that it could be a human perspective. From that unreally heightened perspective, it felt easy to see the larger drama playing behind the scenes of the riots and to know what one thought about it. One could imagine one knew the fault line in the American character that the earthquake had revealed.

I think about typology often and have often relied on the ruthless simplicity of Jung's model of types to unmask the strengths and weaknesses of any personality. Revived by the image and words of Rodney King on my patient's television, I commenced again to think, and a mini-lecture began to form in my mind, with America, this time, as the personality to be typed. America, I told myself, with the breathtaking oversimplification that characterizes such moments, is an extraverted thinking type. Our collective inferior function, as a country, is introverted feeling, and we (even when we are black) let blacks carry this, keeping 'them' wherever possible, in an 'inferior' position where 'their' feeling can be despised or at least selectively honored. Yet this, I reasoned, is not our darkest shadow: that shadow is carried by the smiling, sinister white man at the base of the American character, the man with demonic extraverted feeling.

This demonic extraverted feeling function is what some blacks call 'the man.' It was not hard to see 'the man' in the series of undermining moves that finally provoked the conflagration: in Police Chief Gates's denial that anything was amiss in his leadership and his refusal, on the grounds of morale, to step down; in the change of venue of the police officers' trial to overwhelmingly white Simi Valley for a 'fairer' hearing by peers; and, finally, in the under-reaction of Gates (still, incredibly, in charge) to the early rioting, now out of a belated gratuitous empathy for the feelings of those who might not take well to more police intervention. This chain of perverse reactions in the name of feeling for others had, in fact, been a chain of evil, and it was clear the Chief had been making mischief all along. In his stubborn wronghearted-ness as the tragic drama unfolded, Gates was the true opposite of Rodney King.

Just as television sets are not people, psychology turns demagogic when it pretends it can use its tools with any accuracy or competence to analyze what are, after all, only televised images. I did not know Rodney King or Daryl Gates, and I am not competent to evaluate their worth as persons. But as an American analytical psychologist, I can see that the fate of the happiness of our country, the way we feel about ourselves, probably still depends upon a collective judgment, a projected moral decision. The question that all Americans must answer, with whatever feeling for such things is honestly at their disposal, is this one: Which of these two unfortunate men represented the part of the American shadow of which we are most unconscious?

References

Battle, P. C. (1991). *Two warring ideals in one dark body: A phenomenological journey toward appreciating the lifeworld of the African American experience.* Master's Dissertation, University of Maryland. Ann Arbor, MI: UMI.

Beebe, J. (1989). Review. "Do the right thing." *The San Francisco Jung Institute Library Journal*, 8(4), 85–87.

Do the right thing. (1989). Lee, S. (Producer & Director). USA: Universal Pictures. [Motion picture].

NAMES INDEX

SUBJECT INDEX